APICS
Dictionary
Eighth Edition

Editors
James F. Cox III, Ph.D., CFPIM
John H. Blackstone Jr., Ph.D., CFPIM
Michael S. Spencer, Ph.D., CFPIM

APICS Dictionary

Eighth Edition – 1995
Seventh Edition – 1992
Sixth Edition – 1987
Fifth Edition – 1982
Fourth Edition – 1980
Third Edition – 1970
Second Edition – 1966
First Edition – 1963

Stock No. 01102, 9/95
Copyright 1995 by the American Production and Inventory Control Society, Inc.
International Standard Book Number: 1-55822-123-9
Library of Congress Catalog Card Number 95-79477

American Production and Inventory Control Society, Inc.
500 West Annandale Road
Falls Church, VA 22046-4274
(703) 237-8344   (800) 444-2742

Table of Contents

Preface

Since the seventh edition of the *APICS Dictionary* was produced, many critical events have occurred. Today, business is not as usual. Business is fiercely competitive. Global competition is a reality. Only the strong survive. More important, only the smart prosper. We have seen our best companies dramatically downsize, eliminating hundreds of thousands of jobs of blue-collar and white-collar employees. Whole layers of staff and managers have been deleted from the organization chart in an effort to reduce costs. Months later, the same downsizing process is conducted again to streamline operations and reduce overhead. No industry segment is immune.

This is not the story of manufacturing alone. Large retailers have eliminated hundreds of stores and tens of thousands of jobs. Retail managers have focused on reducing investment, inventory, and personnel costs. They have squeezed suppliers in an attempt to reduce item prices through volume discounts. Storage racks reach toward the sky to stock more of the same items on the lower positions. Suppliers and retailers face unrelenting pressure to reduce prices. For customers, however, service is getting poorer—stockouts of popular items and long lines at the checkout.

We have seen the peace dividend from the fall of communism begin to materialize. Two waves of military base closings have resulted in tens of thousands of unemployed military and civilian personnel. In addition, the aerospace and defense industries have laid off hundreds of thousands in an effort to gain competitiveness in the private sector.

Since the deregulation of the airline industry, several carriers have gone bankrupt or been forced to downsize and consolidate. Yet, aircraft are still flying at a 60 percent load factor. Management keeps cutting flights and personnel costs. Service continues to deteriorate.

Medical and hospital costs are skyrocketing, well above the rate of inflation. The federal government has set up numerous task forces to study the healthcare issues, with the cost of health care for the elderly a primary concern. While there is a tremendous need for health care, hospital occupancy rates are at an all-time low. New technology to identify and treat medical problems is abundant. The use of many of these technological breakthroughs by providers is quite low. Equipment sits idle while patients go without because of costs.

We've painted a dismal picture of today's reality. Yet, master of business administration (MBA) graduates keep pouring out of our finest schools. How can this be? We have more MBAs today than ever before—almost every manager has a certificate hanging on the wall. We have taught them the "best" techniques available—Just-in-Time, time-based competition, total quality management, theory of constraints, business process reengineering, vendor-managed inventory, and activity-based cost accounting. We have provided continuing education texts and articles on these topics. Dozens of new techniques and technologies are developed each year for each phase and activity of a business.

In each of the companies and industries described above, bright young and older experienced managers studied their companies' problems and made the hard decisions using the tools of the trade. Laying off company employees is not an easy task. In many instances, layoffs resulted in hiring temporary employees at a reduced cost in benefits. In others, business process reengineering was used to inject technology into the organization to replace employees. In retailing, electronic data interchange was used to speed the ordering process and link suppliers to retail sales. In many instances, whole market segments and product lines were discontinued because they were thought unprofitable.

Why do managers and workers try so hard but fail so miserably? Maybe it is because the tools we have used for almost a century (without major modification) are no longer useful in today's competitive environment. Cost and managerial accounting were developed in the early 1900s, and there was little change until activity-based cost accounting appeared in the 1990s. Even enthusiastic activity-based accountants are saying that the name should be activity-based management and not activity-based cost accounting. Time-based competition has replaced the concept of Just-in-Time. We have found that reducing the longest setup, total productive maintenance everywhere, supplier certification, etc., does not necessarily reduce cost and in most cases has no positive impact on profit. Employee empowerment and self-managed work teams fail miserably when the reward for improvement is unemployment.

As early as 1954, Peter Drucker wrote that management should reexamine its cost accounting systems as they might be causing poor decisions. A few years ago, he also wrote that we should reexamine our total business philosophy, as it is obsolete today. We agree with Drucker; something is fundamentally wrong with the way we conduct business today. In almost every instance listed above, the companies and industries made decisions based on local cost savings. Local cost savings seldom convert to increased organization profit. The organizational goal is not to save money but to make money. Decisions based on cost seldom translate into a more competitive stance.

What is blocking the business from making more money? The blockage should be the focus of improvement efforts. For example, business process reengineering (BPR) has been used in almost every organization environment. BPR is the injection of computer technology to radically change how a series of activities has been traditionally managed. Processes are examined to determine how many employees can be terminated with the successful implementation of the improved process. What if the focus was to determine the business processes that were inhibiting quality, time-to-market, etc.? What if we could identify places for local improvement to increase organizational profit? How do we link purchasing decisions, production decisions, engineering product and process design decisions, marketing decisions, and sales commission decisions—all of them local decisions—to organizational profit? We use traditional tools of accounting and management that focus on cost—cost is not the same as organizational profit. We identify projects, TQM, JIT, etc., by conducting a cost analysis. Most of our techniques are cost-driven—for example, EOQ, make-versus-buy, line balancing, methods improvement, setup reduction, scrap projects. The real focus of those tools, however, should be to satisfy customers by providing a higher quality and time-competitive product. If that is the case, why do we justify these projects using a cost-oriented methodology instead of having marketing and sales identify what the customers really want and how much customers are willing to pay for a product that meets their needs? We call those factors intangible because we don't have a method within our cost accounting systems to provide estimates of revenues. Maybe we need new accounting methods that link customer needs to the resources required to provide these needs. That is basic economic analysis—nothing new.

It is certainly time to reexamine the body of knowledge as we move into resource management as a profession. Let's question our long-standing practices and traditional management concepts to see if they fit in a world that competes on product distinctiveness, price, quality, time, and due date performance. We must eliminate the silo- or function-oriented decision-making tools that drive us to eliminate people for the sake of saving money. We must find ways to expand markets to make money. Organizational improvement should translate into improvement for the customer, the owners, the employees, and society in general.

On another topic, we would be remiss if we did not support the movement to remove gender-biased terms from our business vocabulary. Terms such as man-hour have traditionally been accepted in our field as correct. However, with the shifting mix in the work force, they are no longer accurate. We will still define them in the dictionary because they have historical significance, but, like many other terms in the dictionary, they only have a place in business history.

The future is ahead of us. We must recognize that the very way we think about our problems needs to be reexamined. We must not be afraid to question many of the traditional ways of conducting business and the traditional concepts of management. Certainly, the environment has changed. Questioning the fundamental assumptions of our body of knowledge can lead to a new understanding of organizations and methods of managing them more effectively. The integrated resource management philosophy needs to embrace new tools, new measures, and a systems perspective that recognizes that the actions in one function affect other business functions and the external environment.

We have greatly expanded this edition of the dictionary and worked with the Curricula and Certification Council to improve many of the basic definitions in our body of knowledge. We have defined numerous new terms from the rapidly emerging business areas in an attempt to represent the cutting edge of practice. Some of these new and emerging terms will drop by the wayside, but many will become standard in our field.

We hope that over the next few years, business practitioners and academicians will develop a body of knowledge capable of addressing today's new problems. We hope we can discuss the win-win solutions in the next edition's preface. For that to happen, our current business policies and practices must be reexamined with respect to the organizational goal.

James F. Cox III, Ph.D., CFPIM
John H. Blackstone Jr., Ph.D., CFPIM
Management Department
Terry College of Business
University of Georgia

Michael S. Spencer, Ph.D., CFPIM
Management Department
College of Business
University of Northern Iowa

Acknowledgments

Since the printing of the seventh edition of the *APICS Dictionary,* many people have written with corrections, additions, deletions, and ideas for improvement. We have incorporated several suggestions in this edition. The number of contributors prohibits listing all of them, but we would be remiss if we didn't recognize the significant contributions of the following individuals and organizations.

Curricula and Certification Council (1994 and 1995)

J. Thomas Brown, CFPIM
Wayne L. Douchkoff, CFPIM
John Fairbairn, CFPIM
James D. Furrow, CFPIM
Eileen Game, CFPIM, CIRM
William Giauque, CFPIM, CIRM
Thomas Hoffmann, CFPIM, CIRM
Mike Hunter, CFPIM
W. Bergen Junge, CFPIM, CIRM
Trevor Kaye, CFPIM

Keith Launchbury, CFPIM, CIRM
David Lehmann, CIRM
Ann E. Marucheck, CPIM
Ash Rao, CFPIM
John J. Revere, CFPIM
Paul J. Rosa Jr. CFPIM
William Wassweiler, CFPIM
Sarah Wenzel Kluck, CFPIM, CIRM
Roly White Jr., CFPIM

Curricula and Certification Dictionary Committee

Lloyd Andreas, CFPIM
John Collins, CPIM
John Dougherty, CFPIM
Merle Ehlers, CFPIM
Archie Lockamy III, CFPIM
R. (Nat) Natarajan, CPIM

Kathleen Oestreich, CPIM
William Robinson, CFPIM, CIRM
Patricia L. Rogus, CFPIM, CIRM
Gerald Sanderson, CFPIM, CIRM
Ben Schlussel, CPIM

Special Contributors

Michel Gavaud, CFPIM
Robert Johnson, CFPIM, CIRM
Henry J. Jordan Sr., CFPIM
Peter Langford, CFPIM, CIRM

Tom McMullen
Charles E. Miller Jr., CFPIM, CIRM
Ronald C. Parker, CFPIM
Carl Stein, CPIM

University of Georgia P/OM Ph.D. Students (past and present)

Lynn Boyd, CPIM, CPA
Linda Deane, CPIM

Edwin Wray, CPIM

MBA Graduate Assistants

Beth Buyert
Thomas Gattiker

Moira Halligan
Diego J. Todeschini

University of Georgia Staff

Robert D. Gatewood, Ph.D.
Melanie Blakeman

Karen Turner
Jenny Yearwood

APICS Staff

Ray Ayoub
Nancy Green

Herry Hernandez
Mary King

In addition to these individuals, the Institute of Industrial Engineers allowed us to include several definitions that we have reprinted from their text, *Industrial Engineering Terminology*, Revised Edition. Copyright 1991, Institute of Industrial Engineers, 25 Technology Park/Atlanta, Norcross, Georgia 30092.

The American Society for Quality Control allowed us to include several terms from Karen Bemowski's "The Quality Glossary," published in the February 1992 issue of *Quality Progress.*

The continuing support of the APICS Educational and Research Foundation and the Department of Management of the Terry College of Business, University of Georgia, was outstanding. With this edition, we also initiated the use of corporate sponsors. We appreciate their support. We would also like to thank our wives and families for having patience with us throughout the revision process.

James F. Cox III, Ph.D., CFPIM
John H. Blackstone Jr., Ph.D., CFPIM
Michael S. Spencer, Ph.D., CFPIM

A

ABC–Abbreviation for *activity-based costing*.

ABC analysis–Syn: ABC classification.

ABC classification–Classification of a group of items in decreasing order of annual dollar volume (price multiplied by projected volume) or other criteria. This array is then split into three classes, called A, B, and C. The A group usually represents 10% to 20% by number of items and 50% to 70% by projected dollar volume. The next grouping, B, usually represents about 20% of the items and about 20% of the dollar volume. The C class contains 60% to 70% of the items and represents about 10% to 30% of the dollar volume. The ABC principle states that effort and money can be saved through applying looser controls to the low-dollar-volume class items than will be applied to high-dollar-volume class items. The ABC principle is applicable to inventories, purchasing, sales, etc. Syn: ABC analysis, distribution by value, Pareto analysis. See: 80-20, Pareto's law.

ABC inventory control–An inventory control approach based on the ABC classification.

ABM–Abbreviation for *activity-based management*.

abnormal demand–An unanticipated customer order. This order may not be in the sales plan or may come from an unanticipated source. It can also be an unusually large order that consumes available-to-promise at the expense of satisfying other customer orders. See: outlier.

absenteeism–Failure of workers to report to work when scheduled. Often applied to unjustified failure to report to work.

absentee rate–A ratio comparing the number of employee-days or employee-hours lost with the total number of available employee-days of employment during some base period, usually one month.

absorption costing–An approach to inventory valuation in which variable costs and a portion of fixed costs are assigned to each unit of production. The fixed costs are usually allocated to units of output on the basis of direct labor hours, machine hours, or material costs. Syn: allocation costing. See: activity-based costing.

acceptable quality level (AQL)–When a continuing series of lots is considered, a quality level that, for the purposes of sampling inspection, is the limit of a satisfactory process average.

acceptable sampling plan–A specific plan that indicates the sampling sizes and the associated acceptance or nonacceptance criteria to be used. In attributes sampling, for example, there are single, double, multiple, sequential, chain, and skip-lot sampling plans. In variables sampling, there are single, double, and sequential sampling plans.

acceptance number–1) A number used in acceptance sampling as a cutoff at which the lot will be accepted or rejected. For example, if X or more units are bad within the sample, the lot will be rejected. 2) The value of the test statistic that divides all possible values into acceptance and rejection regions.

acceptance sampling–1) The process of sampling a portion of goods for inspection rather than examining the entire lot. The entire lot may be accepted or rejected based on the sample even though the specific units in the lot are better or worse than the sample. There are two types: attributes sampling and variables sampling. In attributes sampling, the presence or absence of a characteristic is noted in each of the units inspected. In variables sampling, the numerical magnitude of a characteristic is measured and recorded for each inspected unit; this type of sampling involves reference to a continuous scale of some kind. 2) A method of measuring random samples of lots or batches of products against predetermined standards.

accessory–A choice or feature added to the product or service offered to the customer for customizing the end product. An accessory enhances the capabilities of the product but is not necessary for the basic function of the product. In many companies, an accessory means that the choice does not have to be specified before shipment but can be added at a later date. In other companies, this choice must be made before shipment. See: feature.

accident prevention–The application of basic scientific and technical principles including education and training for the detection, analysis, and minimization of hazards, with the objective of avoiding accidents.

acclimatization–Physiological, emotional, and behavioral adjustment to changes in the environment. Proper performance depends on adequate acclimatization to the workplace, including significant mechanical features such as seat height and lighting. Heat, cold, humidity, and light are important physiologically.

accountability–Answerable, but not necessarily personally charged with doing the work. Accountability cannot be delegated, but it can be shared.

account manager–A manager who has direct responsibility for a customer's interest.

accounts payable–The value of goods and services acquired for which payment has not yet been made.

accounts receivable–The value of goods shipped or services rendered to a customer on which payment has not yet been received. Usually includes an allowance for bad debts.

accreditation–Certification by a recognized body of the facilities, capability, objectivity, competence, and integrity of an agency, service, operational group, or individual to provide the specific service or operation needed. For example, the Registrar Accreditation

Board accredits those organizations that register companies to the ISO 9000 series standards.

accumulating–The activity of combining homogeneous stocks of products or materials into larger quantities. See: staging.

accumulation bin–A place, usually a physical location, used to accumulate all components that go into an assembly before the assembly is sent out to the assembly floor. Syn: assembly bin.

accuracy–The degree of freedom from error or the degree of conformity to a standard. Accuracy is different from precision. For example, four-significant-digit numbers are less precise than six-significant-digit numbers; however, a properly computed four-significant-digit number might be more accurate than an improperly computed six-significant-digit number.

acknowledgment–A communication by a supplier to advise a purchaser that a purchase order has been received. It usually implies acceptance of the order by the supplier.

acquisition cost–Syn: ordering cost.

action message–An output of a system that identifies the need for and the type of action to be taken to correct a current or potential problem. Examples of action messages in an MRP system are "release order," "reschedule in," "reschedule out," and "cancel." Syn: exception message.

activation–The employment of a nonconstraint resource for the sake of keeping busy unrelated to whether it is useful in supporting system throughput.

active inventory–The raw materials, work in process, and finished products that will be used or sold within a given period.

active load–Work scheduled that may not be on hand.

activity–1) In ABC accounting, the tasks required in producing the organization's output of goods and services. The accumulation of tasks completed into types of activities within an organization for the purpose of activity-based costing. 2) In project management, a well-defined task or work to be completed by a resource.

activity analysis–The identification and description of activities within an organization for the purpose of activity-based costing.

activity-based costing (**ABC**)–A cost accounting system that accumulates costs based on activities performed and then uses cost drivers to allocate these costs to products or other bases, such as customers, markets, or projects. It is an attempt to allocate overhead costs on a more realistic basis than direct labor or machine hours. See: absorption costing.

activity-based management (**ABM**)–The use of activity-based costing information about cost pools and drivers, activity analysis, and business processes to identify business strategies; improve product design, manufacturing, and distribution; and remove waste from operations.

actual cost of work performed–The direct cost actually incurred and the indirect costs applied in accomplishing the work performed within a given time period. These costs should reconcile with the contractor's incurred-cost ledgers, which are regularly audited by the client.

actual costs–The labor, material, and associated overhead costs that are charged against a job as it moves through the production process.

actual cost system–A cost system that collects costs historically as they are applied to production and allocates indirect costs to products based on the specific costs and achieved volume of the products.

actual demand–Customer orders (and often allocations of items, ingredients, or raw materials to production or distribution). Actual demand nets against or "consumes" the forecast, depending on the rules chosen over a time horizon. For example, actual demand will totally replace forecast inside the sold-out customer order backlog horizon (often called the *demand time fence)* but will net against the forecast outside this horizon, based on the chosen forecast consumption rule.

actual volume–Actual output expressed as a volume of capacity. It is used in the calculation of variances when compared with demonstrated capacity (practical capacity) or budgeted capacity.

adaptive control–1) The ability of a control system to change its own parameters in response to a measured change in operating conditions. 2) Machine control units in which feeds and/or speeds are not fixed. The control unit, working from feedback sensors, is able to optimize favorable situations by automatically increasing or decreasing the machining parameters. This process ensures optimum tool life or surface finish and/or machining costs or production rates.

adaptive smoothing–A form of exponential smoothing in which the smoothing constant is automatically adjusted as a function of forecast error measurement.

additives–Special class of ingredients characterized either by being used in minimal quantities or by being introduced into the processing cycle after the initial stage.

administrative contracting officer–A government employee who ensures compliance with the terms and conditions of contracts.

advance material request–Ordering materials before the release of the formal product design. This early release is required because of long lead times.

affinity diagram–A total quality management tool whereby employees working in silence generate ideas and later categorize these ideas.

affirmative action–A hiring policy that requires employers to analyze the work force for underrepresentation of protected classes. It involves recruiting minorities and members of protected classes, changing management attitudes or prejudices toward them, removing discriminatory employment practices, and giving preferential treatment to protected classes.

aggregate forecast–An estimate of sales, often time phased, for a grouping of products or product families produced by a manufacturing facility or firm. Stated in terms of units, dollars, or both, the aggregate forecast is used for sales and production planning purposes.

aggregate inventory–The inventory for any grouping of items or products involving multiple stockkeeping units. See: base inventory level.

aggregate inventory management–Establishing the overall level (dollar value) of inventory desired and implementing controls to achieve this goal.

aggregate lead time–Syn: cumulative lead time.

aggregate plan–A plan that includes budgeted levels of finished products, inventory, production backlogs, and plans and changes in the work force to support the production strategy. Aggregated information (e.g., product line, family) rather than product information is used, hence the name *aggregate plan*.

aggregate planning–The process of developing, reviewing, analyzing, and maintaining aggregate plans. Aggregate planning usually includes total sales, total production, targeted inventory, and targeted customer backlog on families of products. The production plan is the result of the aggregate planning process. See: production planning, sales and operations planning, sales plan.

aggregate reporting–1) Reporting of process hours in general, allowing the system to assign the actual hours to specific products run during the period based on standards. 2) Also known as *gang reporting*, the reporting of total labor hours.

AGVS–Abbreviation for *automated guided vehicle system*.

AI–Abbreviation for *artificial intelligence*.

AIS–Abbreviation for *automated information system*.

aisle–The space used to accommodate the movement of people, material, firefighting apparatus, and equipment.

algorithm–A prescribed set of well-defined rules or processes for solving a problem in a finite number of steps, e.g., the full statement of the arithmetic procedure for calculating the reorder point.

allocated item–In an MRP system, an item for which a picking order has been released to the stockroom but not yet sent from the stockroom.

allocated material–Syn: reserved material.

allocation–1) The classification of quantities of items that have been assigned to specific orders but have not yet been released from the stockroom to production. It is an "uncashed" stockroom requisition. 2) A process used to distribute material in short supply. Syn: assignment. See: reservation.

allocation costing–Syn: absorption costing.

allowable cost–A reasonable cost specifically permitted under the Federal Acquisition Regulations (FAR).

allowance–1) In work measurement, a time value or percentage of time by which the normal time is increased, or the amount of nonproductive time applied, to compensate for justifiable causes or policy requirements that necessitate performance time not directly measured for each element or task. Usually includes irregular elements, incentive opportunity on machine-controlled time, minor unavoidable delays, rest time to overcome fatigue, and time for personal needs. 2) In assembly, the minimum clearance or maximum interference distance between two adjacent objects.

allowed time–A normal time value increased by appropriate allowances.

alpha factor–Syn: smoothing constant.

alteration planning–Syn: requirements alteration.

alternate feedstock–A backup supply of an item that either acts as a substitute or is used with alternate equipment.

alternate operation–Replacement for a normal step in the manufacturing process. Ant: primary operation.

alternate routing–A routing, usually less preferred than the primary routing, but resulting in an identical item. Alternate routings may be maintained in the computer or off-line via manual methods, but the computer software must be able to accept alternate routings for specific jobs.

alternate work center–The work center where an operation is not normally performed but can be performed. Ant: primary work center.

American National Standards Institute (ANSI)–Parent organization of the interindustry electronic interchange of the business transaction standard. This group is the clearinghouse on U.S. electronic data interchange standards.

American Standard Code for Information Interchange (ASCII)–A standard seven-bit character code used by computer manufacturers to represent 128 characters for information interchange among data processing systems, communications systems, and other information system equipment. An eighth bit is added as a parity bit to check a string of ASCII characters for correct transmission.

amortization–The process of recovering (via expensing) a capital investment over a period of time. See: capital recovery.

analog–As applied to an electrical or computer system, the capability of representing data in continuously varying physical phenomena (as in a voltmeter) and converting them into numbers.

analysis of variance (ANOVA)–A basic statistical technique for analyzing experimental data. It subdivides the total variation of a data set into meaningful component parts associated with specific sources of variation in order to test a hypothesis on the parameters of the model or to estimate variance components. There are three models: fixed, random, and mixed.

analytic workplace design—Design based on established biomechanical and behavioral concepts, including the known operating characteristics of people. Produces a workplace situation well within the range of human capacity and does not generally require modification, improvement, or preliminary experimental "mock-up."

andon—1) An electronic board that provides visibility of floor status and provides information to help coordinate the efforts to linked work centers. Signal lights are green (running), red (stop), and yellow (needs attention). 2) A visual signaling system.

annual inventory count—Syn: physical inventory.

annualized contract—A negotiated agreement with a supplier for one year that sets pricing, helps ensure a continuous supply of material, and provides the supplier with estimated future requirements.

ANOVA—Acronym for *analysis of variance.*

ANSI—Acronym for *American National Standards Institute.*

anticipated delay report—A report, normally issued by both manufacturing and purchasing to the material planning function, regarding jobs or purchase orders that will not be completed on time and explaining why the jobs or purchases are delayed and when they will be completed. This report is an essential ingredient of the closed-loop MRP system. It is normally a handwritten report. Syn: delay report.

anticipation inventories—Additional inventory above basic pipeline stock to cover projected trends of increasing sales, planned sales promotion programs, seasonal fluctuations, plant shutdowns, and vacations.

AOQ—Abbreviation for *average outgoing quality.*

AOQL—Abbreviation for *average outgoing quality limit.*

APICS—Acronym for *The American Production and Inventory Control Society, Inc.* A nonprofit educational organization consisting of 70,000 members in the production/operations, materials, and, more recently, integrated resource management areas.

application package—A computer program or set of programs designed for a specific application; e.g., inventory control, MRP.

application system—A set of programs of specific instructions for processing activities needed to compute specific tasks for computer users, as opposed to operating systems that control the computer's internal operations. Examples are payroll, spreadsheets, and word processing programs.

appraisal—1) A method of measurement and evaluation, done as fairly as possible, of the variable results brought about by the employee's individual behavior in the workplace. 2) In TQM, the formal evaluation and audit of quality.

appraisal costs—Those costs associated with the formal evaluation and audit of quality in the firm. Typical costs include inspection, quality audits, testing, calibration, and checking time.

AQL—Abbreviation for *acceptable quality level.*

arbitration—The process by which an independent third party is brought in to settle a dispute or to preserve the interest of two conflicting parties.

arithmetic mean—Syn: mean.

arrival date—The date purchased material is due to arrive at the receiving site. The arrival date can be input, it can be equal to the current due date, or it can be calculated from the ship date plus transit time. Syn: expected receipt date. See: due date.

arrow—The graphic presentation of an activity. The tail of the arrow represents the start of the activity. The head of the arrow represents the finish. Unless a time scale is used, the length of the arrow stem has no relation to the duration of the activity. Length and direction of the arrow are usually a matter of convenience and clarity.

arrow diagram—A technique to determine the relationships and precedence of different activities and the time estimate for project completion. The technique is useful in identifying potential problems and improvement opportunities.

artificial intelligence (AI)—1) Computer programs that can learn and reason in a manner similar to humans. The problem is defined in terms of states and operators to generate a search space that is examined for the best solution. In contrast, conventional programming collects and processes data by algorithm or fixed step-by-step procedures. 2) An area in computer science that attempts to develop AI computer programs.

ASCII—Acronym for *American Standard Code for Information Interchange.*

ASQC—Abbreviation for *American Society for Quality Control.*

AS/RS—Abbreviation for *automated storage/retrieval system.*

assays—Tests of the physical and chemical properties of a sample.

assemble-to-order—An environment where a product or service can be assembled after receipt of a customer's order. The key components (bulk, semifinished, intermediate, subassembly, fabricated, purchased, packaging, etc.) used in the assembly or finishing process are planned and possibly stocked in anticipation of a customer order. Receipt of an order initiates assembly of the customized product. This strategy is useful where a large number of end products (based on the selection of options and accessories) can be assembled from common components. Syn: finish-to-order. See: make-to-order, make-to-stock.

assembly—A group of subassemblies and/or parts that are put together and that constitute a major subdivision for the final product. An assembly may be an end item or a component of a higher level assembly.

assembly bin–Syn: accumulation bin.

assembly lead time–The time that normally elapses between the issuance of a work order to the assembly floor and work completion.

assembly order–A manufacturing order to an assembly department authorizing it to put components together into an assembly. See: blend order.

assembly parts list–As used in the manufacturing process, a list of all parts (and subassemblies) that make up a particular assembly. See: batch card, manufacturing order.

asset value–The adjusted purchase price of the asset plus any costs necessary to prepare the asset for use.

assignable cause–A source of variation in a process that can be isolated, especially when its significantly larger magnitude or different origin readily distinguishes it from random causes of variation. Syn: special cause. See: common causes.

assigned material–Syn: reserved material.

assignment–Syn: allocation.

assorting–The activity of mixing items into the assortments that are needed by customers and end users. This activity is usually performed at a market-oriented distribution facility.

ATP–Abbreviation for *available-to-promise.*

attachment–An accessory that has to be physically attached to the product. See: feature.

attribute data–Go/no-go information. The control charts based on attribute data include percent chart, number of affected units chart, count chart, count-per-unit chart, quality score chart, and demerit chart.

attrition factor–The budget fraction apportioned for replacement personnel training because of projected personnel losses (retirements, promotions, and terminations).

audit–An objective comparison of actions to policies and plans.

authorized deviation–Permission for a supplier or the plant to manufacture an item that is not in conformance with the applicable drawings or specifications.

automated guided vehicle system (**AGVS**)–A transportation network that automatically routes one or more material handling devices, such as carts or pallet trucks, and positions them at predetermined destinations without operator intervention.

automated information system (**AIS**)–Computer hardware and software configured to automate the calculating, computing, sequencing, storing, retrieving, displaying, communicating, or otherwise manipulating data and textual material to provide information.

automated storage/retrieval system (**AS/RS**)–A high-density rack inventory storage system with vehicles automatically loading and unloading the racks.

automatic relief–A set of inventory bookkeeping methods that automatically adjusts computerized inventory records based on a production transaction. Examples of automatic relief methods are backflushing, direct-deduct, pre-deduct, and post-deduct processing.

automatic rescheduling–Rescheduling done by the computer to automatically change due dates on scheduled receipts when it detects that due dates and need dates are out of phase. Ant: manual rescheduling.

automation–The substitution of machine work for human physical and mental work, or the use of machines for work not otherwise able to be accomplished, entailing a less continuous interaction with humans than previous equipment used for similar tasks.

autonomation–Automated shutdown of a line, process, or machine upon detection of an abnormality or defect.

autonomous work group–A production team that operates a highly focused segment of the production process to an externally imposed schedule but with little external reporting, supervision, interference, or help.

auxiliary item–An item required to support the operation of another item.

availability–The percentage of time that a worker or machine is capable of working. The formula, where S is the scheduled time and B is the downtime, is

$$\text{Availability} = \frac{(S-B)}{S} \times 100\%$$

available inventory–The on-hand inventory balance minus allocations, reservations, backorders, and (usually) quantities held for quality problems. Often called beginning available balance. Syn: beginning available balance, net inventory.

available-to-promise (**ATP**)–The uncommitted portion of a company's inventory and planned production, maintained in the master schedule to support customer order promising. The ATP quantity is the uncommitted inventory balance in the first period and is normally calculated for each period in which an MPS receipt is scheduled. In the first period, ATP includes on-hand inventory less customer orders that are due and overdue. See: order promising.

available work–Work that is actually in a department ready to be worked on as opposed to scheduled work that may not yet be physically on hand. Syn: live load.

average chart–A control chart in which the subgroup average, X-bar, is used to evaluate the stability of the process level. Syn: X-bar chart.

average cost per unit–The estimated total cost, including allocated overhead, to produce a batch of goods divided by the total number of units produced.

average forecast error–1) The arithmetic mean of the forecast errors. 2) The exponentially smoothed forecast error. See: bias.

average inventory–One-half the average lot size plus the safety stock, when demand and lot sizes are expected to be relatively uniform over time. The average can be calculated as an average of several inventory observations taken over several historical time periods; e.g., 12-month ending inventories may be averaged. When demand and lot sizes are not uniform, the stock level versus time can be graphed to determine the average.

average outgoing quality (AOQ)–The expected average quality level of outgoing product for a given value of incoming product quality.

average outgoing quality limit (AOQL)–The maximum average outgoing quality over all possible levels of incoming quality for a given acceptance sampling plan and disposal specification.

avoidable cost–A cost associated with an activity that would not be incurred if the activity was not performed (e.g., telephone cost associated with vendor support).

avoidable delay–Delay controllable by a worker and therefore not allowed in the job standard.

B

backflush–The deduction from inventory records of the component parts used in an assembly or subassembly by exploding the bill of materials by the production count of assemblies produced. See: post-deduct inventory transaction processing.

backflush costing–The application of costs based on the output of a process. Backflush costing is usually associated with repetitive manufacturing environments.

backhauling–The process of a transportation vehicle returning from the original destination point to the point of origin. The 1980 Motor Carrier Act deregulated interstate commercial trucking and thereby allowed carriers to contract for the return trip. The backhaul can be with a full, partial, or empty load. An empty backhaul is called *deadheading*. See: deadhead.

backlog–All the customer orders received but not yet shipped. Sometimes referred to as *open orders* or the *order board*. Syn: order backlog. See: past due order.

backorder–An unfilled customer order or commitment. A backorder is an immediate (or past due) demand against an item whose inventory is insufficient to satisfy the demand. See: stockout.

back scheduling–A technique for calculating operation start dates and due dates. The schedule is computed starting with the due date for the order and working backward to determine the required start date and/or due dates for each operation. Syn: backward scheduling. Ant: forward scheduling.

backup/restore–The procedure of making backup copies of computer files or disks and, in case of loss of or damage to the original, using the backups to restore the files or disks. In such a case, the only work lost is that done since the backup was made.

backup support–An alternate location or maintainer that can provide the same service response or support as the primary location or maintainer.

backward integration–Process of buying or owning elements of the production cycle and channel of distribution back toward raw material suppliers. See: vertical integration.

backward pass–Calculation of late finish times (dates) for all uncompleted network activities. Determined by working from the final activity and subtracting durations from uncompleted activities. Ant: forward pass.

backward scheduling–Syn: back scheduling.

balance–1) The act of evenly distributing the work elements between the two hands performing an operation. 2) The state of having approximately equal working times among the various operations in a process, or the stations on an assembly line. See: balance delay.

balance delay–1) The idle time of one hand in an operation caused by imperfect workload balancing. 2) The idle time of one or more operations in a series caused by imperfect workload balancing. See: balance.

balance-of-stores record–A double-entry record system that shows the balance of inventory items on hand and the balances of material on order and available for future orders. Where a reserve system of materials control is used, the balance of material on reserve is also shown.

balancing operations–In repetitive Just-in-Time production, matching actual output cycle times of all operations to the demand of use for parts as required by final assembly and, eventually, as required by the market.

bank–Syn: buffer.

bar–The darker, nonreflective element of a bar code.

bar code–A series of alternating bars and spaces printed or stamped on parts, containers, labels, or other media, representing encoded information that can be read by electronic readers. A bar code is used to facilitate timely and accurate input of data to a computer system.

bar coding–A method of encoding data using bar code for fast and accurate readability.

base index–Syn: base series.

base inventory level–The inventory level made up of aggregate lot-size inventory plus the aggregate safety stock inventory. It does not take into account the anticipation inventory that will result from the production plan. The base inventory level should be known before the production plan is made. Syn: basic stock. See: aggregate inventory.

baseline measures–A set of measurements (or metrics) that seeks to establish the current or starting level of performance of a process, function, product, firm, etc. Baseline measures are usually established before implementing improvement activities and programs.

base point pricing–A type of geographic pricing policy where customers order from designated shipping points without freight charges if they are located within a specified distance from the base point. Customers outside area boundaries pay base price plus transportation costs from the nearest base point.

base series–A standard succession of values of demand-over-time data used in forecasting seasonal items. This series of factors is usually based on the relative level of demand during the corresponding period of previous years. The average value of the base series over a seasonal cycle will be 1.0. A figure higher than 1.0 indicates that the demand for that period is more than the average; a figure less than 1.0 indicates less than the average. For forecasting purposes, the base series is superimposed upon the average demand and trend in demand for the item in question. Syn: base index. See: seasonal index, seasonality.

base stock system–A method of inventory control that includes as special cases most of the systems in practice. In this system, when an order is received for any item, it is used as a picking ticket, and duplicate copies, called *replenishment orders,* are sent back to all stages of production to initiate replenishment of stocks. Positive or negative orders, called *base stock orders,* are also used from time to time to adjust the level of the base stock of each item. In actual practice, replenishment orders are usually accumulated when they are issued and are released at regular intervals.

basic producer–A manufacturer that uses natural resources to produce materials for other manufacturing. A typical example is a steel company that processes iron ore and produces steel ingots; others are those making wood pulp, glass, and rubber.

basic stock–Syn: base inventory level.

batch–1) A quantity scheduled to be produced or in production. See: process batch, transfer batch. 2) For discrete products, the batch is planned to be the standard batch quantity, but during production, the standard batch quantity may be broken into smaller lots. See: lot. 3) In nondiscrete products, the batch is a quantity that is planned to be produced in a given time period based on a formula or recipe, which often is developed to produce a given number of end items.

batch bill of materials–A recipe or formula in which the statement of quantity per is based on the standard batch quantity of the parent. Syn: batch formula.

batch card–A document used in the process industries to authorize and control the production of a quantity of material. Batch cards usually contain quantities and lot numbers of ingredients to be used, processing variables, pack-out instructions, and product disposition. See: assembly parts list, batch sheet, blend formula, fabrication order, manufacturing order, mix ticket.

batch formula–Syn: batch bill of materials.

batch number–Syn: lot number.

batch processing–1) A manufacturing technique in which parts are accumulated and processed together in a lot. 2) A computer technique in which transactions are accumulated and processed together or in a lot.

batch sensitivity factor–A multiplier that is used for the rounding rules in determining the number of batches required to produce a given amount of product.

batch sheet–In many process industries, a document that combines product and process definition. See: batch card.

Bayesian analysis–Statistical analysis where uncertainty is incorporated, using all available information to choose among a number of alternative decisions.

BCP–Abbreviation for *business continuation plan.*

beginning available balance–Syn: available inventory.

beginning inventory–A statement of the inventory count at the end of last period, usually from a perpetual inventory record.

benchmarking–The continuous process of measuring the company's products, services, costs, and practices against those of competitors or firms that display the "best in class" achievements.

benchmark measures–A set of measurements (or metrics) that is used to establish goals for improvements in processes, functions, products, etc. Benchmark measures are often derived from other firms that display "best in class" achievement.

beta test–A term used to describe the pilot evaluation of a product or service, i.e., "the second evaluation."

bias–A consistent deviation from the mean in one direction (high or low). A normal property of a good forecast is that it is not biased. See: average forecast error.

bid–A quotation specifically given to a prospective purchaser upon request, usually in competition with other vendors.

bid pricing–Offering a specific price for each job rather than setting a standard price that applies for all customers.

bid proposal–The response to the written request from a potential customer asking for the submission of a quotation or proposal to provide products or services. The bid proposal is in response to an RFP or RFQ.

big Q, little q–A term used to contrast the difference between managing for quality in all business processes and products (big Q) and managing for quality in a limited capacity–traditionally in only factory products and processes (little q).

bill of batches–A method of tracking the specific multi-level batch composition of a manufactured item. The bill of batches provides the necessary where-used and where-from relationships required for lot traceability.

bill of capacity–Syn: bill of resources.

bill of distribution–Syn: distribution network structure.

bill of labor–A structured listing of all labor requirements for the fabrication, assembly, and testing of a parent item. See: bill of resources, routing.

bill of lading (uniform)–A carrier's contract and receipt for goods the carrier agrees to transport from one place to another and to deliver to a designated person. In case of loss, damage, or delay, the bill of lading is the basis for filing freight claims.

bill of material (BOM)–A listing of all the subassemblies, intermediates, parts, and raw materials that go into a parent assembly showing the quantity of each required to make an assembly. It is used in conjunction with the master production schedule to determine the items for which purchase requisitions and production orders must be released. A variety of display formats exists for bills of material, including the single-level bill of material, indented bill of material, modular (planning) bill of material, transient bill of material, matrix bill of material, and costed bill of material. The bill of material may also be called the *formula, recipe,* or *ingredients list* in certain process industries.

bill-of-material explosion–The process of determining component identities, quantities per assembly, and other parent/component relationship data for a parent item. Explosion may be single level, indented, or summarized.

bill-of-material processor–A computer program for maintaining and retrieving bill-of-material information.

bill-of-material structuring–The process of organizing bills of material to perform specific functions.

bill of operations–Syn: routing.

bill of resources–A listing of the required capacity and key resources needed to manufacture one unit of a selected item or family. Rough-cut capacity planning uses these bills to calculate the approximate capacity requirements of the master production schedule. Resource planning may use a form of this bill. Syn: bill of capacity. See: bill of labor, capacity planning using overall factors, product load profile, resource profile, rough-cut capacity planning, routing.

bin–1) A storage device designed to hold small discrete parts. 2) A shelving unit with physical dividers separating the storage locations.

bin location file–A file that specifically identifies the location where each item in inventory is stored.

bin reserve system–Syn: two-bin system.

bin tag–1) A type of perpetual inventory record, designed for storekeeping purposes, maintained at the storage area for each inventory item. 2) An identifying marking on a storage location.

bin transfer–An inventory transaction to move a quantity from one valid location (bin) to another valid location (bin).

bin trips–Usually, the number of transactions per stockkeeping unit per unit of time.

blanket order–Syn: blanket purchase order.

blanket purchase order–A long-term commitment to a supplier for material against which short-term releases will be generated to satisfy requirements. Often blanket orders cover only one item with predetermined delivery dates. Syn: blanket order, standing order.

blanket release–Authorization to ship and/or produce against a blanket agreement or contract.

blanket routing–A routing that lists groups of operations needed to produce a family of items. The items may have small differences in size, but they use the same sequence of operations. Specific times or tools for each individual item can be included.

blemish–An imperfection that is severe enough to be noticed but should not cause any real impairment with respect to intended normal or reasonably foreseeable use. See: defect, imperfection, nonconformity.

blend formula–An ingredient list for a product in process industries. See: batch card, manufacturing order, mix ticket.

blending–The process of physically mixing two or more lots or types of material to produce a homogeneous lot. Blends normally receive new identification and require testing.

blending department–In process industries, the name of the department where the ingredients are mixed. See: final assembly department.

blend off–In process industries, the rework of material by introducing a small percentage into another run of the same product.

blend order–A manufacturing order to a blending department authorizing it to mix the ingredients of a product. See: assembly order.

block control–Control of the production process in groups, or "blocks," of shop orders for products undergoing the same basic processes.

block diagram–A diagram that shows the operations, interrelationships, and interdependencies of components in a system. Boxes, or blocks (hence the name), represent the components; connecting lines between the blocks represent interfaces. There are two types of block diagrams: functional block diagrams, which show a system's subsystems and lower level products, their interrelationships, and interfaces with other systems; and reliability block diagrams, which are similar to the functional block diagram except that they are modified to emphasize those aspects influencing reliability. See: flowchart.

blocked operation–An upstream work center that is not permitted to produce because of a full queue at a downstream work center or because no kanban authorizes production.

blocked operations–A group of operations identified separately for instructions and documentation but reported as one.

blocking–The condition requiring a work center that has parts to process to remain idle as long as the queue to which the parts would be sent is full or kanbans authorizing production are not present.

block scheduling–An operation scheduling technique where each operation is allowed a "block" of time, such as a day or a week.

block system–A system for selecting items to be cycle counted by a group or block of numbers.

blowthrough–Syn: phantom bill of material.

blueprint–In engineering, a line drawing showing the physical characteristics of a part.

boilerplate–The standard terms and conditions on a purchase order or other document.

BOM–Abbreviation for *bill of material*.

bond (performance)–A guarantee of satisfactory work completion that is executed in connection with a contract and that secures the performance and fulfillment of all the undertakings, covenants, terms, conditions, and agreements contained in the contract.

bonded warehouse–Buildings or parts of buildings designated by the U.S. Secretary of the Treasury for storing imported merchandise, operated under customs supervision.

book inventory–An accounting definition of inventory units or value obtained from perpetual inventory records rather than by actual count.

Boolean algebra–A form of algebra that, like ordinary algebra, represents relationships and properties with symbols. However, Boolean algebra also has classes, propositions, on-off circuit elements, and operators *(and, or, not, except, if, then)*. Boolean algebra is useful in defining the logic of a complex system.

bottleneck–A facility, function, department, or resource whose capacity is less than the demand placed upon it. For example, a bottleneck machine or work center exists where jobs are processed at a slower rate than they are demanded.

bottom-up replanning–In MRP, the process of using pegging data to solve material availability or other problems. This process is accomplished by the planner (not the computer system), who evaluates the effects of possible solutions. Potential solutions include compressing lead time, cutting order quantity, substituting material, and changing the master schedule.

bounded–The adjustment of a shop order quantity of a parent to use the remaining units of a component, raw material, or lot.

Box-Jenkins model–A forecasting approach based on regression and moving average models. The model is based not on regression of independent variables, but on past observations of the item to be forecast at varying time lags and on previous error values from forecasting.

BPR–Abbreviation for *business process reengineering*.

bracketed recall–Recall from customers of suspect lot numbers plus a specified number of lots produced before and after the suspect ones.

brainstorming–A technique that teams use to generate ideas on a particular subject. Each person on the team is asked to think creatively and write down as many ideas as possible. The ideas are not discussed or reviewed until after the brainstorming session.

branch and bound–Operations research models for determining optimal solutions based on the enumeration of subsets of possible solutions, which implicitly enumerate all possible solutions.

branch warehouse–A distribution center.

branch warehouse demand–Syn: warehouse demand.

branding–The use of a name, term, symbol, or design, or a combination of these, to identify a product.

brand name–A word or combination of words used to identify a product and differentiate it from other products; the verbal part of a trademark, in contrast to the pictorial mark; a trademark word.

brand recognition–The degree to which customers recognize a particular brand identity and associate it with a particular product line relative to other available brands.

break-bulk–Dividing truckloads of homogeneous items into smaller, more appropriate quantities for use.

breakdown maintenance–Remedial maintenance that occurs when equipment fails and must be repaired on an emergency or priority basis.

break-even chart–A graphical tool showing the total variable cost and fixed cost curve along with the total revenue (gross income) curve. The point of intersection is defined as the *break-even point*, i.e., the point at which total revenues exactly equal total costs.

break-even point–The level of production or the volume of sales at which operations are neither profitable nor unprofitable. The break-even point is the intersection of the total revenue and total cost curves.

break-even time–The total elapsed time of a technology transfer beginning with a scientific investigation and ending when the profits from a new product offset the cost of its development.

breeder bill of material–A bill of material that recognizes and plans for the availability and usage of by-products in the manufacturing process. The breeder bill allows for complete by-product MRP and product/by-product costing.

broadcast system–A sequence of specific units to be assembled and completed at a given rate. This sequence is communicated to supply and assembly activities to perform operations and position material so that it merges with the correct assembled unit.

bubble chart–A diagram that attempts to display the interrelationships of systems, functions, or data in a sequential flow. It derives its name from the circular symbols used to enclose the statements on the chart.

bucket–A time period, usually a week.

bucketed system–An MRP, DRP, or other time-phased system in which all time-phased data are accumulated into time periods, or buckets. If the period of accumulation is one week, then the system is said to have weekly buckets.

bucketless system–An MRP, DRP, or other time-phased system in which all time-phased data are processed, stored, and usually displayed using dated records rather than defined time periods, or buckets.

budget–A plan that includes an estimate of future costs and revenues related to expected activities. The budget serves as a pattern for and a control over future operations.

budget cost of work performed–The sum of the budgets for completed portions of in-process work plus the appropriate portion of the budgets for level of effort and apportioned effort for the relevant time period. Syn: earned value.

budget cost of work scheduled–The sum of the budgets for work scheduled to be accomplished (including in-process work) plus the appropriate portion of the budgets for level of effort and apportioned effort for the relevant time period.

budgeted capacity–The volume/mix of throughput on which financial budgets were set and overhead/burden absorption rates established.

buffer–1) A quantity of materials awaiting further processing. It can refer to raw materials, semifinished stores or hold points, or a work backlog that is purposely maintained behind a work center. Syn: bank. 2) In theory of constraints, buffers can be time or material and support throughput and/or date due performance. Buffers can be maintained at the constraint, convergent points (with a constraint part), divergent points, and shipping points.

buffer management–In the theory of constraints, a process in which all expediting in a shop is driven by what is scheduled to be in the buffers (constraint, shipping, and assembly buffers). By expediting this material into the buffers, the system helps avoid idleness at the constraint and missed customer due dates. In additional, the causes of items missing from the buffer are identified, and the frequency of occurrences is used to prioritize improvement activities.

buffer stock–Syn: safety stock.

build cycle–The time period between a major setup and a cleanup. It recognizes cyclical scheduling of simi-

lar products with minor changes from one product/ model to another.

bulk issue–Parts issued from stores to work-in-process inventory, but not based on a job order. They are issued in quantities estimated to cover requirements of individual work centers and production lines. The issue may be used to cover a period of time or to fill a fixed-size container.

bulk storage–Large-scale storage for raw materials, intermediates, or finished products. Each vessel normally contains a mixture of lots and materials that may be replenished and withdrawn for use or pack-out simultaneously.

burden rate–A cost, usually in dollars per hour, that is normally added to the cost of every standard production hour to cover overhead expenses.

business continuation plan (BCP)–A contingency plan for sustained operations during periods of high risk, such as during labor unrest.

business cycle–The recurring long-term periods of recession and prosperity.

business plan–1) A statement of long-range strategy and revenue, cost, and profit objectives usually accompanied by budgets, a projected balance sheet, and a cash flow (source and application of funds) statement. A business plan is usually stated in terms of dollars and grouped by product family. The business plan, the sales and operations plan, and the production plan, although frequently stated in different terms, should agree with each other. See: long-term planning, strategic plan. 2) A document consisting of the business details (organization, strategy, financing tactics) prepared by an entrepreneur to plan for a new business.

business process–A set of logically related tasks or activities performed to achieve a defined business outcome.

business process reengineering (BPR)–A procedure that involves the fundamental rethinking and radical redesign of business processes to achieve dramatic organizational improvements in such critical measures of performance as cost, quality, service, and speed. Any BPR activity is distinguished by its emphasis on (1) process rather than functions and products and (2) the customers for the processes.

business unit–A division or segment of an organization generally treated as a separate profit-and-loss center.

buyer–An individual whose functions may include supplier selection, negotiation, order placement, supplier follow-up, measurement and control of supplier performance, value analysis, and evaluation of new materials and processes. In some companies, the functions of order placement and supplier follow-up are handled by the supplier scheduler.

buyer behavior–The way individuals or organizations behave in a purchasing situation. The customer-oriented concept finds out the wants, needs, and desires of customers and adapts resources of the organization to deliver need-satisfying products and services.

buyer code–A code used to identify the purchasing person responsible for a given item or purchase order.

buyer cycle–The purchasing sequence that generally follows the buyer's product and budget cycles.

buyer/planner–A buyer who also does material planning. This term should not be confused with planner/buyer.

buyer's market–A market in which goods can easily be secured and in which the economic forces of business tend to cause goods to be priced at the purchaser's estimate of value.

buying capacity–Syn: capacity buying.

by-product–A material of value produced as a residual of or incidental to the production process. The ratio of by-product to primary product is usually predictable. By-products may be recycled, sold as is, or used for other purposes. See: co-product.

C

CAD–Acronym for *computer-aided design*.

CAD/CAM–The integration of computer-aided design and computer-aided manufacturing to achieve automation from design through manufacturing.

CAE–Abbreviation for *computer-aided engineering*.

CAIT–Abbreviation for *computer-aided inspection and test*.

calculated capacity–Syn: rated capacity.

calculated usage–The determination of usage of components or ingredients in a manufacturing process by multiplying the receipt quantity of a parent by the quantity per of each component or ingredient in the bill or recipe, accommodating standard yields.

calendar time–The passage of days or weeks as in the definition of lead time or scheduling rules, in contrast with running time.

calibration–The comparison of a measurement instrument or system of unverified accuracy with a measurement instrument or system of a known accuracy to detect any variation from the required performance specification.

calibration frequency–Interval in days between tooling calibrations.

CAM–Acronym for *computer-aided manufacturing*.

cancellation charge–A fee charged by a seller to cover its costs associated with a customer's cancellation of an order. If the seller has started engineering work, purchased raw materials, or started manufacturing operations, these charges could also be included in the cancellation charge.

capability study–Syn: process capability analysis.

capacity–1) The capability of a system to perform its expected function. 2) The capability of a worker, machine, work center, plant, or organization to produce output per time period. Capacity required represents the system capability needed to make a given product mix (assuming technology, product specification, etc.). As a planning function, both capacity available and capacity required can be measured in the short term (capacity requirements plan), intermediate term (rough-cut capacity plan), and long term (resource requirements plan). Capacity control is the execution through the I/O control report of the short-term plan. Capacity can be classified as budgeted, dedicated, demonstrated, productive, protective, rated, safety, standing, or theoretical.

capacity available–The capability of a system or resource to produce a quantity of output in a particular time period.

capacity buying–A purchasing practice whereby a company commits to a supplier for a given amount of its capacity per unit of time. Subsequently, schedules for individual items are given to the supplier in quantities to match the committed level of capacity. Syn: buying capacity.

capacity control–The process of measuring production output and comparing it with the capacity requirements plan, determining if the variance exceeds pre-established limits, and taking corrective action to get back on plan if the limits are exceeded. See: input/output control.

capacity management–The function of establishing, measuring, monitoring, and adjusting limits or levels of capacity in order to execute all manufacturing schedules; i.e., the production plan, master production schedule, material requirements plan, and dispatch list. Capacity management is executed at four levels: resource planning, rough-cut capacity planning, capacity requirements planning, and input/output control.

capacity pegging–Displaying the specific sources of capacity requirements. This is analogous to pegging in MRP, which displays the source of material requirements.

capacity planning–The process of determining the amount of capacity required to produce in the future. This process may be performed at an aggregate or product-line level (resource planning), at the master-scheduling level (rough-cut capacity planning), and at the detailed or work-center level (capacity requirements planning). See: capacity requirements planning, resource planning, rough-cut capacity planning.

capacity planning using overall factors (CPOF)–A rough-cut capacity planning technique. The master schedule items and quantities are multiplied by the total time required to build each item to provide the total number of hours to produce the schedule. Historical work center percentages are then applied to the total number of hours to provide an estimate of the hours per work center to support the master schedule. This technique eliminates the need for engineered time standards. Syn: overall factors. See: bill of resources, capacity planning, rough-cut capacity planning.

capacity required–The capacity of a system or resource needed to produce a desired output in a particular time period.

capacity requirements–The resources needed to produce the projected level of work required from a facility over a time horizon. Capacity requirements are usually expressed in terms of hours of work or, when units consume similar resources at the same rate, units of production.

capacity requirements plan–A time-phased display of present and future load (capacity required) on all resources based on the planned and released supply authorizations (i.e., orders) and the planned capacity (capacity available) of these resources over a span of time. See: load profile.

capacity requirements planning (CRP)–The function of establishing, measuring, and adjusting limits or levels of capacity. The term *capacity requirements planning* in this context refers to the process of determining in detail the amount of labor and machine resources required to accomplish the tasks of production. Open shop orders and planned orders in the MRP system are input to CRP, which through the use of parts routings and time standards translates these orders into hours of work by work center by time period. Even though rough-cut capacity planning may indicate that sufficient capacity exists to execute the MPS, CRP may show that capacity is insufficient during specific time periods. See: capacity planning.

capacity simulation–The ability to do rough-cut capacity planning using a simulated master production schedule or material plan rather than live data.

capacity smoothing–Syn: load leveling.

capacity strategy–One of the strategic choices that a firm must make as part of its manufacturing strategy. There are three commonly recognized capacity strategies: lead, lag, and tracking. A lead capacity strategy adds capacity in anticipation of increasing demand. A lag strategy does not add capacity until the firm is operating at or beyond full capacity. These two strategies may be combined and called a *chase strategy*. A tracking strategy adds capacity in small amounts or takes capacity away in small amounts to attempt to respond to changing demand in the marketplace. This strategy is also called a *level production strategy*.

capital asset–A physical object that is held by an organization for its production potential and that costs more than some threshold value.

capital budgeting–Actions relating to the planning and financing of capital outlays for such purposes as the purchase of new equipment, the introduction of new product lines, and the modernization of plant facilities.

capital recovery–1) Charging periodically to operations amounts that will ultimately equal the amount of capital expenditure (See: amortization, depletion, depreciation). 2) The replacement of the original cost of an asset plus interest. 3) The process of regaining the net investment in a project by means of revenue in excess of the cost from the project. (Usually implies amortization of principal plus interest on the diminishing unrecovered balance.)

CAPP–Acronym for *computer-aided process planning*.

cargo–A product shipped in an aircraft, railroad car, ship, or truck.

cargo container capacity–The inside usable cubic volume of a container.

carload lot–A shipment that qualifies for a reduced freight rate because it is greater than a specified minimum weight. Since carload rates usually include minimum rates per unit of volume, the higher LCL (less than carload) rate may be less expensive for a heavy but relatively small shipment.

carrying cost–Cost of carrying inventory, usually defined as a percentage of the dollar value of inventory per unit of time (generally one year). Carrying cost depends mainly on the cost of capital invested as well as such costs of maintaining the inventory as taxes and insurance, obsolescence, spoilage, and space occupied. Such costs vary from 10% to 35% annually, depending on type of industry. Carrying cost is ultimately a policy variable reflecting the opportunity cost of alternative uses for funds invested in inventory.

cascaded systems–Multistorage operations. The input to each stage is the output of a preceding stage, thereby causing interdependencies among the stages.

cascading yield loss–The condition where yield loss happens in multiple operations or tasks, resulting in a compounded yield loss. Syn: composite yield, cumulative yield.

CASE–Acronym for *computer-assisted software engineering*.

cash flow–The net flow of dollars into or out of the proposed project. The algebraic sum, in any time period, of all cash receipts, expenses, and investments. Also called *cash proceeds* or *cash generated*.

categorical plan–A method of selecting and evaluating suppliers that considers input from many departments and functions within the buyer's organization and systematically categorizes that input. Engineering, production, quality assurance, and other functional areas evaluate all suppliers for critical factors within their scope of responsibility. For example, engineering would develop a category evaluating suppliers' design flexibility. Rankings are developed across categories, and performance ratings are obtained and supplier selections are made.

cathode ray tube (CRT)–A device for displaying pictures and information. A television set has a CRT (pictures), as does a video display unit (information). Syn: video display terminal, video display unit.

cause-and-effect diagram–A tool for analyzing process dispersion. It is also referred to as the Ishikawa diagram (because Kaoru Ishikawa developed it) and the fishbone diagram (because the complete diagram resembles a fish skeleton). The diagram illustrates the main causes and subcauses leading to an effect (symptom). The cause-and-effect diagram is one of the seven tools of quality. Syn: fishbone chart, Ishikawa diagram.

caveat emptor–A Latin phrase meaning "Let the buyer beware," i.e., the purchase is at the buyer's risk.

C chart–A control chart for evaluating the stability of a process in terms of the count of events of a given classification occurring in a sample. Syn: count chart.

cell–Manufacturing unit consisting of a number of workstations and the materials transport mechanisms and storage buffers that interconnect them.

cellular layout–An equipment configuration to support cellular manufacturing.

cellular manufacturing–A manufacturing process that produces families of parts within a single line or cell of machines operated by machinists who work only within the line or cell.

centralized dispatching–Organization of the dispatching function into one central location. This structure often involves the use of data collection devices for communication between the centralized dispatching function, which usually reports to the production control department, and the shop manufacturing departments.

centralized inventory control–Inventory decision making exercised from one office or department for an entire company (all SKUs).

central processing unit (CPU)–The electronic processing unit of a computer, where mathematical calculations are performed.

certificate of compliance–A supplier's certification that the supplies or services in question meet specified requirements.

certified fixtures–Inspection models that conform to known specifications.

certified supplier–A status awarded to a supplier who consistently meets predetermined quality, cost, delivery, financial, and count objectives. Incoming inspection may not be required.

CFPIM–Abbreviation for *Certified Fellow in Production and Inventory Management.* This APICS certification recognizes superior knowledge and performance in contributing to the profession.

chance–Something that happens as a result of random, unknown, or unconsidered influences.

change order–A formal notification that a purchase order or shop order must be modified in some way. This change can result from a revised quantity, date, or specification by the customer; an engineering change; a change in inventory requirement date; etc.

changeover–Syn: setup.

changeover costs–Syn: setup costs.

channels of distribution–Any series of firms or individuals that participates in the flow of goods and services from the raw material supplier or producer to the final user or consumer.

charge–The initial loading of ingredients or raw materials into a processor, such as a reactor, to begin the manufacturing process.

charge ticket–A document used for receiving goods and charging those goods to an operating cost center.

chase method–A production planning method that maintains a stable inventory level while varying production to meet demand. Companies may combine chase and level production schedule methods.

check digit–A digit added to each number in a coding system that allows for detection of errors in the recording of the code numbers. Through the use of the check digit and a predetermined mathematical formula, recording errors such as digit reversal or omission can be discovered.

checking–Verifying and documenting the order selection in terms of both product number and quantity.

checklist–A tool used to ensure that important steps or actions in an operation have been taken. Checklists contain items that are important or relevant to an issue or situation.

check sheet–A simple data-recording device. The check sheet is designed by the user, which facilitates the user's interpretation of the results. The check sheet is one of the seven tools of quality. Check sheets are often confused with data sheets and checklists.

CIF–Abbreviation for *cost, insurance, freight.*

CIM–Acronym for *computer-integrated manufacturing.*

CIRM–Acronym for *Certified in Integrated Resource Management.* This APICS certification is a recognition of a high level of professional knowledge in enterprisewide processes and activities.

clean technology–A technical measure taken to reduce or eliminate at the source the production of any nuisance, pollution, or waste and to help save raw materials, natural resources, and energy.

cleanup–The neutralizing of the effects of production just completed. It may involve cleaning residues, sanitation, equipment refixturing, etc.

clerical/administration–Several related activities necessary for the organization's operation, generally including but not limited to the following: updating records and files based on receipts, shipments, and adjustments; maintaining labor and equipment records; and performing locating, order consolidation, correspondence preparation, and similar activities.

clock card–Syn: time card.

closed-loop MRP–A system built around material requirements planning that includes the additional planning functions of sales and operations planning (production planning), master production scheduling, and capacity requirements planning. Once this planning phase is complete and the plans have been accepted as realistic and attainable, the execution functions come into play. These functions include the manufacturing control functions of input-output (capacity) measurement, detailed scheduling and dispatching, as well as anticipated delay reports from both the plant and suppliers, supplier scheduling, etc. The term *closed loop* implies not only that each of these elements is included in the overall system, but also that feedback is provided by the execution functions so that the planning can be kept valid at all times.

closed period–Accounting time period for which the adjusting and closing entries have been posted. Ant: Open period.

CNC–Abbreviation for *computer numerical control.*

co-design–Syn: participative design/engineering.

COFC–Abbreviation for *container on a railroad flatcar.*

collective bargaining–A highly regulated system established to control conflict between labor and management. It defines and specifies the rules and procedures of initiating, negotiating, maintaining, changing, and terminating the labor-management relationship.

combined lead time–Syn: cumulative lead time.

commodity buying–Grouping like parts or materials under one buyer's control for the procurement of all requirements to support production.

commonality–A condition where given raw materials or ingredients are used in multiple parents.

common carrier–Transportation available to the public that does not provide special treatment to any one party and is regulated as to the rates charged, the liability assumed, and the service provided. A common carrier must obtain a certificate of public convenience and necessity from the Federal Trade Commission for interstate traffic.

common causes–Causes of variation that are inherent in a process over time. They affect every outcome of the process and everyone working in the process. See: assignable cause.

common material–Readily available items used in industry that require no special handling.

common parts bill of material–A type of planning bill that groups common components for a product or family of products into one bill of material, structured to a pseudo parent item number.

COMMS–Acronym for *customer-oriented manufacturing management system.*

company culture–A system of values, beliefs, and behaviors inherent in a company. To optimize business performance, top management must define and create the necessary culture.

compensation–Pay and benefits given for services rendered to an organization.

competitive advantage–An edge; e.g., a process, patent, management philosophy, or distribution system, that a seller has that enables the seller to control a larger market share or profit than the seller would otherwise have. Syn: competitive edge.

competitive analysis–An analysis of a competitor that includes its strategies, capabilities, prices, and costs.

competitive edge–Syn: competitive advantage.

competitive intelligence–Information required to conduct a competitive analysis.

component–Raw material, part, or subassembly that goes into a higher level assembly, compound, or other item. This term may also include packaging materials for finished items. See: ingredient, intermediate part.

component availability–The availability of component inventory for the manufacture of a specific parent order or group of orders or schedules.

component lead-time offset–Syn: lead-time offset.

composite lead time–Syn: cumulative lead time.

composite manufacturing lead time–Syn: cumulative manufacturing lead time.

composite part–A part that represents operations common to a family or group of parts controlled by group technology. Tools, jigs, and dies are used for the composite part; therefore, any parts of that family can be processed with the same operations and tooling. The goal here is to reduce setup costs.

composite yield–Syn: cascading yield loss.

composition–The makeup of an item, typically expressing chemical properties rather than physical properties.

compound interest–1) The type of interest that is periodically added to the amount of investment (or loan) so that subsequent interest is based on the cumulative amount. 2) The interest charges under the condition that interest is charged on any previous interest earned in any time period, as well as on the principal.

compound yield–The cumulative effect of yield loss at multiple operations within the manufacturing cycle.

computer-aided design (CAD)–The use of computers in interactive engineering drawing and storage of designs. Programs complete the layout, geometric transformations, projections, rotations, magnifications, and interval (cross-section) views of a part and its relationship with other parts.

computer-aided engineering (CAE)–The process of generating and testing engineering specifications on a computer workstation.

computer-aided inspection and test (CAIT)–The use of computer technology in the inspection and testing of manufactured products.

computer-aided manufacturing (CAM)–Use of computers to program, direct, and control production equipment in the fabrication of manufactured items.

computer-aided process planning (CAPP)–A method of process planning in which a computer system assists in the development of manufacturing process plans (defining operation sequences, machine and tooling requirements, cut parameters, part tolerances, inspection criteria, and other items). Artificial intelligence and classification and coding systems may be used in the generation of the process plan.

computer-assisted software engineering (CASE)–The use of computerized tools to assist in the process of designing, developing, and maintaining software products and systems.

computer-integrated manufacturing (CIM)–The integration of the total manufacturing organization through the use of computer systems and managerial philosophies that improve the organization's effectiveness; the application of a computer to bridge various computerized systems and connect them into a coherent, integrated whole. For example, budgets, CAD/CAM, process controls, group technology systems, MRP II, financial reporting systems, etc., are linked and interfaced.

computer numerical control (CNC)–A technique in which a machine tool control uses a minicomputer to store numerical instructions.

concentration–The percentage of an active ingredient within the whole, as a 40% solution of hydrochloric acid (HCl).

concurrent design–Syn: participative design/engineering.

concurrent engineering–Syn: participative design/ engineering.

confidence interval–The range on either side of an estimated value from a sample that is likely to contain the true value for the whole population.

confidence level–Probability that a particular value lies between an upper and a lower bound, the confidence limits.

confidence limit–The bounds of an interval. A probability can be given for the likelihood that the true value will lie between the confidence limits.

configuration–The arrangement of components as specified to produce an assembly.

configuration audit–A review of the product against the engineering specifications to determine whether the engineering documentation is accurate, up-to-date, and representative of the components, subsystems, or systems being produced.

configuration control–The function of ensuring that the product being built and shipped corresponds to the product that was designed and ordered. This means that the correct features, customer options, and engineering changes have been incorporated and documented.

configuration system–Syn: customer order servicing system.

confirming order–A purchase order issued to a supplier, listing the goods or services and terms of an order placed orally or otherwise before the usual purchase document.

conflict of interest–Any business activity, personal or company-related, that interferes with a company's goals or that entails unethical or illegal actions.

conformance–An affirmative indication or judgment that a product or service has met the requirements of a relevant specification, contract, or regulation.

consigned stocks–Inventories, generally of finished products, that are in the possession of customers, dealers, agents, etc., but remain the property of the manufacturer by agreement with those in possession.

consignment–1) A shipment that is handled by a common carrier. 2) The process of a supplier placing goods at a customer location without receiving payment until after the goods are used or sold.

consolidation–Packages and lots that move from suppliers to a carrier terminal and are sorted and then combined with similar shipments from other suppliers for travel to their final destination. See: milk run.

constant–A quantity that has a fixed value. Ant: variable.

constrained optimization–Achieving the best possible solution to a problem in terms of a specified objective function and a given set of constraints.

constraint–Any element or factor that prevents a system from achieving a higher level of performance with respect to its goal. Constraints can be physical, such as a machine center or lack of material, but they can also be managerial, such as a policy or procedure.

constraint management–The practice of managing resources and organizations in accordance with theory of constraints (TOC) principles. See: theory of constraints.

constraint theory–Syn: theory of constraints.

consumables–Supplies or materials (such as paint, cleaning materials, or fuel) that are consumed or exhausted in the production or sale of a product or service. Syn: consumable tooling, supplies; expendables.

consumable tooling, supplies–Syn: consumables.

consumer's risk (β)–For a given sampling plan, the probability of acceptance of a lot, the quality of which has designated numerical value representing a level that is worse than some threshold value. See: type II error.

consuming the forecast–The process of reducing the forecast by customer orders or other types of actual demands as they are received. The adjustments yield the value of the remaining forecast for each period. Syn: forecast consumption.

consumption–The amount of each bill-of-material component used in the production process to make the parent.

container–A large box in which commodities to be shipped are placed.

containerization–A shipment method in which commodities are placed in containers, and after initial loading, the commodities per se are not rehandled in shipment until they are unloaded at the destination.

container on a railroad flatcar (COFC)–A specialized form of containerization in which rail and motor transport coordinate.

continuous flow (production)–Lotless production in which products flow continuously rather than being divided.

continuous process control–The use of transducers (sensors) to monitor a process and make automatic changes in operations through the design of appropriate feedback control loops. Although such devices have historically been mechanical or electromechanical, there is now widespread use of microcomputers and centralized control.

continuous process improvement (CPI)–A never-ending effort to expose and eliminate root causes of problems; small-step improvement as opposed to big-step improvement. See: kaizen.

continuous production–A production system in which the productive equipment is organized and sequenced according to the steps involved to produce the product. This term denotes that material flow is continuous during the production process. The routing of the jobs is fixed, and setups are seldom changed. See: mass production.

contract–An agreement between two or more competent persons or companies to perform or not to perform specific acts or services or to deliver merchandise. A contract may be oral or written. A purchase order, when accepted by a supplier, becomes a contract. Acceptance may be in writing or by performance, unless the purchase order requires acceptance in writing.

contract accounting–The function of collecting costs incurred on a given job or contract, usually in a progress payment situation. Certain U.S. government contracting procedures require contract accounting.

contract carrier–A carrier that does not serve the general public, but provides transportation for hire for one or a limited number of shippers under a specific contract.

contract date–The date when a contract is accepted by all parties.

contract labor–Self-employed individuals or firms contracted by an organization to perform specific services on an intermittent or short-term basis.

contract pegging–Syn: full pegging.

contract reporting–Reporting of and the accumulation of finished production against commitments to a customer.

contract target cost–The estimated cost negotiated in a contract.

contribution–The difference between sales price and variable costs. Contribution is used to cover fixed costs and profits.

contribution margin–An amount equal to the difference between sales revenue and variable costs.

contribution margin pricing–A method of setting prices based on the contribution margin. It provides a ceiling and a floor between which the price setter operates. The ceiling is the target selling price–what the seller would like to get–and the floor is the total variable costs of the product using traditional accounting.

control board–A visual means of showing machine loading or project planning, usually a variation of the basic Gantt chart. Syn: dispatch(ing) board, planning board, schedule board. See: schedule chart.

control center–In a centralized dispatching operation, the place at which the dispatching is done.

control chart–A graphic comparison of process performance data with predetermined computed control limits. The process performance data usually consist of groups of measurements selected in regular sequence of production that preserve the order. The primary use of control charts is to detect assignable causes of variation in the process as opposed to random variations. Syn: process control chart.

controlled issue–Syn: planned issue.

control number–Typically, the manufacturing order or schedule number used to identify a specific instance or period of production.

control points–In the theory of constraints, strategic locations in the logical product structure for a product or family that simplify the planning, scheduling, and control functions. Control points include gating operations, convergent points, divergent points, constraints, and shipping points. Detailed scheduling instructions are planned, implemented, and monitored at these locations. Other work centers are instructed to "work if they have work; otherwise, be prepared for work." In this manner, materials flow rapidly through the facility without detailed work center scheduling and control.

control system–A system that has as its primary function the collection and analysis of feedback from a given set of functions for the purpose of controlling the functions. Control may be implemented by monitoring or systematically modifying parameters or policies used in those functions, or by preparing control reports that initiate useful action with respect to significant deviations and exceptions.

convergent point–In theory of constraints, a control point in the logical product structure where nonconstraint parts are assembled with constraint parts. To maintain the flow of parts to products, the schedule of nonconstraint parts must be synchronized with that of constraint parts.

converter–A manufacturer that changes the products of a basic producer into a variety of industrial and consumer products. An example is a firm that changes steel ingot into bar stock, tubing, or plate. Other converter products are paper, soap, and dyes.

cooperative training–An educational process in which students alternate formal studies with actual on-the-job experience. Successful completion of the off-campus experience may be a prerequisite for graduation from the program of study.

co-product–Product that is usually manufactured together or sequentially because of product or process similarities. See: by-product.

core competencies–Bundles of skills or knowledge sets that enable a firm to provide the greatest level of value to its customers in a way that is difficult for competitors to emulate and that provides for future growth. Core competencies are embodied in the skills of the workers and in the organization. They are developed through collective learning, communication, and commitment to work across levels and functions in the organization and with the customers and suppliers. For example, a core competency could be the capability of a firm to coordinate and harmonize diverse production skills and multiple technologies. To illustrate, advanced casting processes for making steel require the integration of machine design with sophisticated sensors to track temperature and speed, and the sensors require mathematical modeling of heat transfer. For rapid and effective development of such a process, materials scientists must work closely with machine designers, software engineers, process specialists, and operating personnel. Core competencies are not directly related to the product or market.

corporate culture–The set of important assumptions that members of the company share. It is a system of shared values about what is important and beliefs about how the company works. These common assumptions influence the ways the company operates.

corrective action–The implementation of solutions resulting in the reduction or elimination of an identified problem.

corrective maintenance–Maintenance required to restore an item to a satisfactory condition.

correlation–The relationship between two sets of data such that when one changes, the other is likely to make a corresponding change. If the changes are in the same direction, there is positive correlation. When changes tend to occur in opposite directions, there is negative correlation. When there is little correspondence or random changes, there is no correlation.

cost–The total acquisition and usage cost of the procurement to the buying firm.

cost allocation–The assignment of costs that cannot be directly related to production activities via more measurable means, e.g., assigning corporate expenses to different products via direct labor costs or hours.

cost analysis–A review and an evaluation of actual or anticipated cost data.

cost center–The smallest segment of an organization for which costs are collected and formally reported, typically a department. The criteria in defining cost centers are that the cost be significant and that the area of responsibility be clearly defined. A cost center is not necessarily identical to a work center; normally, a cost center encompasses more than one work center, but this may not always be the case.

cost control–The application of procedures to monitor expenditures and performance against progress of projects and manufacturing operations with projected completion to measure variances from authorized budgets and allow effective action to be taken to achieve minimal costs.

cost driver–A factor that determines work load and effort required to perform an activity. Also, an event or activity that results in the incurrence of costs.

costed bill of material–A form of bill of material that extends the quantity-per of every component in the bill by the cost of the components.

cost engineer–An engineer whose judgment and experience are used in the application of scientific principles and techniques to problems of cost estimation and cost control in business planning, profitability analysis, project management and production planning, scheduling, and control.

cost, insurance, freight (CIF)–A freight term indicating that the seller is responsible for cost, the marine insurance, and the freight charges on an ocean shipment of goods.

cost of capital–The cost of maintaining a dollar of capital invested for a certain period, normally one year. This cost is normally expressed as a percentage and may be based on factors such as the average expected return on alternative investments and current bank interest rate for borrowing.

cost of goods sold–An accounting classification useful for determining the amount of direct materials, direct labor, and allocated overhead associated with the products sold during a given period of time.

cost of poor quality–The cost associated with providing poor-quality products or services. There are four categories of costs: internal failure costs (costs associated with defects found before the customer receives the product or service), external failure costs (costs associated with defects found after the customer receives the product or service), appraisal costs (costs incurred to determine the degree of conformance to quality requirements), and prevention costs (costs incurred to keep failure and appraisal costs to a minimum).

cost of sales–The total cost attached (allocated) to units of finished product delivered to customers during the period.

cost-plus–A pricing method where the purchaser agrees to pay the supplier an amount determined by the cost incurred by the supplier to produce the goods or services plus a stated percentage or fixed sum.

cost-plus contract–A pricing method where the buyer agrees to pay the seller all the acceptable costs of the product or service up to a maximum cost plus a fixed fee. Syn: cost-type contract.

cost-ratio plan–A variation of the weighted-point plan of supplier evaluation and selection. The cost ratio is obtained by dividing the bid price by the weighted scores determined by the weighted-point plan. This procedure determines the true costs by taking into account compensating factors. Suppliers are selected and/or evaluated based on the lowest cost ratio.

cost reduction–The act of lowering the cost of goods or services by securing a lower price, reducing labor costs, etc. In cost reduction, the item usually is not changed, but the circumstances around which the item is secured are changed, as opposed to value analysis, in which the item itself is actually changed to produce a lower cost.

cost-type contract–Syn: cost-plus contract.

cost variance–The deviation of actual from budgeted cost for a given task.

counseling–The providing of basic, technical, and sometimes professional human assistance to employees to help them with personal and work-related problems.

count chart–Syn: C chart.

counter trade–Any transaction in which partial or full payment is made with goods instead of money.

count-per-unit chart–Syn: U chart.

count point–A point in a flow of material or sequence of operations at which parts, subassemblies, or assemblies are counted as being complete. Count points may be designated at the ends of lines or upon removal from a work center, but most often they are designated as the points at which material transfers from one department to another. Syn: pay point.

count point backflush–A backflush technique using more than one level of the bill of materials and extending back to the previous points where production was counted. Syn: key point backflush.

C$_p$–A widely used process capability index. It is expressed as

$$C_p = \frac{\text{upper control limit} - \text{lower control limit}}{6\sigma}$$

where σ is the standard deviation.

CPI–Abbreviation for *continuous process improvement*.

CPIM–Abbreviation for *Certified in Production and Inventory Management*. This APICS certification is a recognition of a high level of professional knowledge.

C$_{pk}$–A widely used process capability index. It is expressed as

$$C_{pk} = \frac{|\mu - \text{nearer specification}|}{3\sigma}$$

where μ is the mean and σ is the standard deviation.

CPM–Abbreviation for *critical path method*.

CPOF–Abbreviation for *capacity planning using overall factors*.

CPU–Abbreviation for *central processing unit*.

crew size–The number of people required to perform an operation. The associated standard time should represent the total time for all crew members to perform the operation, not the net start to finish time for the crew.

critical characteristics–Attributes of a product that must function properly to avoid the failure of the product. Syn: functional requirements.

critical failure–The malfunction of those parts that are essential for continual operation or the safety of the user.

critical path–Sequence of jobs or activities in a network analysis of a project such that the total duration equals the sum of the durations of the individual jobs in the sequence. There is no time leeway or slack (float) in activities along the critical path (e.g., if the time to complete one or more jobs in the critical path increases, the total production time increases).

critical path lead time–Syn: cumulative lead time.

critical path method (CPM)–A network planning technique for the analysis of a project's completion time, used for planning and controlling the activities in a project. By showing each of these activities and their associated times, the critical path, which identifies those elements that actually constrain the total time for the project, can be determined.

critical process parameters–A variable or a set of variables that dominates the other variables. Focusing on these variables will yield the greatest return in investment in quality control and improvement.

critical ratio–A dispatching rule that calculates a priority index number by dividing the time to due date remaining by the expected elapsed time to finish the job. For example,

$$\frac{\text{time remaining}}{\text{work remaining}} = \frac{30}{40} = .75$$

A ratio less than 1.0 indicates the job is behind schedule, a ratio greater than 1.0 indicates the job is ahead of schedule, and a ratio of 1.0 indicates the job is on schedule.

cross plot–Syn: scatter chart.

cross-shipment–Material flow activity where materials are shipped to customers from a secondary shipping point rather than from a preferred shipping point.

cross-training–The providing of training or experience in several different areas, e.g., training an employee on several machines rather than one. Cross-training provides backup workers in case the primary operator is unavailable.

CRP–Abbreviation for *capacity requirements planning.*

CRT–Abbreviation for *cathode ray tube.*

cubage–Cubic volume of space being used or available for shipping or storage.

cumulative lead time–The longest planned length of time to accomplish the activity in question. For any item planned through MRP, it is found by reviewing the lead time for each bill of material path below the item; whichever path adds up to the greatest number defines cumulative lead time. Syn: aggregate lead time, combined lead time, composite lead time, critical path lead time, stacked lead time. See: planning horizon, planning time fence.

cumulative manufacturing lead time–The cumulative planned lead time when all purchased items are assumed to be in stock. Syn: composite manufacturing lead time.

cumulative MRP–The planning of parts and subassemblies by exploding a master schedule, as in MRP, except that the master-scheduled items and therefore the exploded requirements are time phased in cumulative form. Usually these cumulative figures cover a planning year.

cumulative receipts–A cumulative number, or running total, as a count of parts received in a series or sequence of shipments. The cumulative receipts provide a number that can be compared with the cumulative figures from a plan developed by cumulative MRP.

cumulative sum–The accumulated total of all forecast errors, both positive and negative. This sum will approach zero if the forecast is unbiased. Syn: sum of deviations.

cumulative sum control chart–A control chart on which the plotted value is the cumulative sum of deviations of successive samples from a target value. The ordinate of each plotted point represents the algebraic sum of the previous ordinate and the most recent deviations from the target.

cumulative system–A method for planning and controlling production that makes use of cumulative MRP, cumulative requirements, and cumulative counts.

cumulative trauma disorder–An occupational injury believed to be caused by repetitive motions such as typing or twisting.

cumulative yield–Syn: cascading yield loss.

current cost–The current or replacement cost of labor, material, or overhead. Its computation is based on current performance or measurements, and it is used to address today's costs before production as a revision of annual standard costs.

current price–The price currently being paid as opposed to standard cost.

current reality tree–A logic-based tool for using cause-and-effect relationships to determine root problems that cause the observed undesirable effects of the system.

curve fitting–An approach to forecasting based on a straight line, polynomial, or other curve that describes some historical time series data.

customer–A person or organization who receives a product, or service, or information. See: external customer, internal customer.

customer-defined attributes–Characteristics of a product or service that are viewed as being important in addressing the needs of the customer. See: house of quality.

customer order–An order from a customer for a particular product or a number of products. It is often referred to as an *actual demand* to distinguish it from a forecasted demand.

customer order promising–Syn: order promising.

customer order servicing system–An automated system for order entry, where orders are keyed into a local terminal and a bill-of-material translator converts the catalog ordering numbers into required manufacturing part numbers and due dates for the MRP system. Advanced systems contain customer information, sales history, forecasting information, and product option compatibility checks to facilitate order processing, "cleaning up" orders before placing a demand on the manufacturing system. Syn: configuration system, sales order configuration.

customer-oriented manufacturing management system (COMMS)–Syn: enterprise resources planning system.

customer partner–A customer organization with which a company has formed a customer-supplier partnership. See: outpartnering.

customer partnership–The establishing of working relationships with a customer organization whereby the two organizations (supplier and customer) act as one.

customer satisfaction–The results of delivering a product or service that meets customer requirements.

customer service–1) Ability of a company to address the needs, inquiries, and requests from customers. 2) A measure of the delivery of a product to the customer at the time the customer specified.

customer service ratio–1) A measure of delivery performance of finished goods, usually expressed as a percentage. In a make-to-stock company, this percentage usually represents the number of items or dollars (on one or more customer orders) that were shipped on schedule for a specific time period, compared with the total that were supposed to be shipped in that time period. Syn: fill rate, order-fill ratio, percent of fill. Ant: stockout percentage. 2) In a make-to-order company, it is usually some comparison of the number of jobs or dollars shipped in a given time period (e.g., a week) compared with the number of jobs or dollars that were supposed to be shipped in that time period.

customer-supplier partnership–A long-term relationship between a buyer and a supplier characterized by teamwork and mutual confidence. The supplier is considered an extension of the buyer's organization. The partnership is based on several commitments. The buyer provides long-term contracts and uses fewer suppliers. The supplier implements quality assurance processes so that incoming inspection can be minimized. The supplier also helps the buyer reduce costs and improve product and process designs.

customer tolerance time–Syn: demand lead time.

cut-off control–A procedure for synchronizing cycle counting and transaction processing.

cybernetics–The study of control processes in mechanical, biological, electrical, and information systems.

cybernetic system–The information flow or information system (electronic, mechanical, logical) that controls an industrial process.

cycle–1) The interval of time during which a system or process, such as seasonal demand or a manufacturing operation, periodically returns to similar initial conditions. 2) The interval of time during which an event or set of events is completed.

cycle counter–An individual who is assigned to do cycle counting.

cycle counting–An inventory accuracy audit technique where inventory is counted on a cyclic schedule rather than once a year. A cycle inventory count is usually taken on a regular, defined basis (often more frequently for high-value or fast-moving items and less frequently for low-value or slow-moving items). Most effective cycle counting systems require the counting of a certain number of items every workday with each item counted at a prescribed frequency. The key purpose of cycle counting is to identify items in error, thus triggering research, identification, and elimination of the cause of the errors.

cycle reduction stock–Stock held to reduce delivery time.

cycle stock–One of the two main conceptual components of any item inventory, the cycle stock is the most active component, i.e., that which depletes gradually as customer orders are received and is replenished cyclically when supplier orders are received. The other conceptual component of the item inventory is the safety stock, which is a cushion of protection against uncertainty in the demand or in the replenishment lead time.

cycle time–1) In industrial engineering, the time between completion of two discrete units of production. For example, the cycle time of motors assembled at a rate of 120 per hour would be 30 seconds. 2) In materials management, it refers to the length of time from when material enters a production facility until it exits. Syn: throughput time.

D

dampeners–User-input parameters to suppress the reporting of insignificant or unimportant action messages created during the computer processing of MRP.

dark factory–A completely automated production facility with no labor. Syn: lightless plant.

data–Any representations, such as alphabetic or numeric characters, to which meaning can be assigned.

database–A data processing file-management approach designed to establish the independence of computer programs from data files. Redundancy is minimized, and data elements can be added to, or deleted from, the file designs without necessitating changes to existing computer programs.

database management system (DBMS)–Software designed for organizing data and providing the mechanism for storing, maintaining, and retrieving that data on a physical medium (i.e., a database). A DBMS separates data from the application programs and people who use the data and permits many different views of the data.

data collection–The act of compiling data for recording, analysis, or distribution.

data communications–The transmission of data over a distance.

data dictionary–1) A catalog of requirements and specifications for an information system. 2) A file that stores facts about the files and databases for all systems that are currently being used or for the software involved.

data element–A group of characters that defines an item at a basic level. Syn: data field.

data field–Syn: data element.

data file–A collection of related data records organized in a specific manner (e.g., one record for each inventory item showing product code, unit of measure, production costs, transactions, selling price, production lead time, etc.).

date code–A label on products with the date of production. In food industries, it is often an integral part of the lot number.

date effectivity–A technique used to identify the effective date of a configuration change. A component change is controlled by effective date within the bill of material for the unchanged parent part number.

DBMS–Abbreviation for *database management system*.

D chart–A control chart for evaluating a process in terms of a demerit (or quality score), e.g., a weighted sum of counts of various classified nonconformities. Syn: demerit chart.

deadhead–The return of an empty transportation container to its point of origin. See: backhauling.

deblend–The further processing of product to adjust specific physical and chemical properties to within specification ranges.

debt–An amount owed to creditors. It is generally equal to the total assets in a company less the equity.

decentralized dispatching–The organization of the dispatching function into individual departmental dispatchers.

decentralized inventory control–Inventory decision making exercised at each stocking location for SKUs at that location.

decision matrix–A matrix used by teams to evaluate problems or possible solutions. After a matrix is drawn to evaluate possible solutions, for example, the team lists the solutions in the far left vertical column. Next, the team selects criteria to rate the possible solutions, writing them across the top row. Third, each possible solution is rated on a scale of 1 to 5 for each criterion and the rating recorded in the corresponding grid. Finally, the ratings of all the criteria for each possible solution are added to determine its total score. The total score is then used to help decide which solution deserves the most attention.

decisions under certainty–Simple decisions that assume complete information and no uncertainty connected with the analysis of decisions.

decisions under risks–A decision problem in which the analyst elects to consider several possible futures, the probabilities of which can be estimated.

decisions under uncertainty–Decisions for which the analyst elects to consider several possible futures, the probabilities of which cannot be estimated.

decision support system (DSS)–A computer system designed to assist managers in selecting and evaluating courses of action by providing a logical, usually quantitative, analysis of the relevant factors.

decision table–A means of displaying logical conditions in an array that graphically illustrates actions associated with stated conditions.

decision tree–A method of analysis that evaluates alternative decisions in a tree-like structure to estimate values and/or probabilities. Decision trees take into account the time value of future earnings by using a rollback concept. Calculations are started at the far right-hand side, then traced back through the branches to identify the appropriate decision.

decomposition–A method of forecasting where time series data are separated into up to three components: trend, seasonal, and cyclical; where trend includes the general horizontal upward or downward movement over time; where seasonal includes a recurring demand pattern such as day of the week, weekly, monthly, or quarterly; and cyclical includes any repeating, nonseasonal pattern. A fourth component is random, that is, data with no pattern. The new forecast is made by projecting the patterns individually determined and then combining them.

dedicated capacity–A work center that is designated to produce a single item or a limited number of similar items. Equipment that is dedicated may be special equipment or may be grouped general-purpose equipment committed to a composite part.

dedicated equipment–Equipment whose use is restricted to specific operations on a limited set of components.

dedicated line–A production line permanently configured to run well-defined parts, one piece at a time, from station to station.

de-expedite–The reprioritizing of jobs to a lower level of activity. All extraordinary actions involving these jobs stop.

default–The action that will be taken by a computer program when the user does not specify a variable parameter.

defect–A product's or service's nonfulfillment of an intended requirement or reasonable expectation for use, including safety considerations. There are four classes of defects: Class 1, Very Serious, leads directly to severe injury or catastrophic economic loss; Class 2, Serious, leads directly to significant injury or significant economic loss; Class 3, Major, is related to major problems with respect to intended normal or reasonably foreseeable use; and Class 4, Minor, is related to minor problems with respect to intended normal or reasonably foreseeable use. See: blemish, imperfection, nonconformity.

deficiency–Failure to meet quality standards.

degrees of freedom–A statistical term indicating the number of variables or data points used for testing a relationship. The greater the degrees of freedom, the greater the confidence that can be placed on the statistical significance of the results.

delay report–Syn: anticipated delay report.

delay reporting–Reporting against an operation status of a manufacturing order on an exception basis, when delays are anticipated.

delinquent order–Syn: past due order.

delivery cycle–Syn: delivery lead time.

delivery lead time–The time from the receipt of a customer order to the delivery of the product. Syn: delivery cycle.

delivery policy–The company's goal for the time to ship the product after the receipt of a customer's order. The policy is sometimes stated as "our quoted delivery time."

delivery schedule–The required or agreed time or rate of delivery of goods or services purchased for a future period.

Delphi method–A qualitative forecasting technique where the opinions of experts are combined in a series of iterations. The results of each iteration are used to develop the next, so that convergence of the experts' opinion is obtained. See: management estimation, panel consensus.

demand–A need for a particular product or component. The demand could come from any number of sources, e.g., customer order or forecast, an interplant requirement, or a request from a branch warehouse for a service part or for manufacturing another product. At the finished goods level, demand data are usually different from sales data because demand does not necessarily result in sales; i.e., if there is no stock, there will be no sale.

demand curve–A graphic description of the relationship between price and quantity demanded in a market, assuming that all other factors stay the same. Quantity demanded of a product is measured on the horizontal axis for an array of different prices measured on the vertical axis.

demand during lead time–The quantity of a product expected to be withdrawn for stock or to be consumed during its replenishment lead time when usage is at the forecasted rate. See: expected demand.

demand filter–A standard that is set to monitor sales data for individual items in forecasting models. It is usually set to be tripped when the demand for a period differs from the forecast by more than some number of mean absolute deviations.

demand lead time–The amount of time potential customers are willing to wait for the delivery of a good or a service. Syn: customer tolerance time.

demand management–The function of recognizing all demands for products and services to support the marketplace. It involves doing what is required to help make the demand happen and prioritizing demand when supply is lacking. Proper demand management facilitates the planning and use of resources for profitable business results. It encompasses the activities of forecasting, order entry, order promising, and determining branch warehouse requirements, interplant orders, and service parts requirements.

demand pull–The triggering of material movement to a work center only when that work center is ready to begin the next job. It in effect eliminates the queue from in front of a work center, but it can cause a queue at the end of a previous work center.

demand rate–A statement of requirements in terms of quantity per unit of time (hour, day, week, month, etc.).

demand time fence (DTF)–1) That point in time inside of which the forecast is no longer included in total demand and projected available inventory calculations; inside this point, only customer orders are considered. Beyond this point, total demand is a combination of actual orders and forecasts, depending on the forecast consumption technique chosen. 2) In some contexts, the demand time fence may correspond to that point in the future inside which changes to the master schedule must be approved by an authority higher than the master scheduler. Note, however, that customer orders may still be promised inside the demand time fence without higher authority approval if there are quantities available-to-promise (ATP). Beyond the demand time fence, the master scheduler may change the MPS within the limits of established rescheduling rules, without the approval of higher authority. See: option overplanning, planning time fence, time fence.

demand uncertainty–The uncertainty or variability in demand as measured by the standard deviation, mean absolute deviation (MAD), or variance of forecast errors.

demerit chart–Syn: D chart.

Deming circle–Concept of a continuously rotating wheel of plan-do-check-action (PDCA) used to show the need for interaction among market research, design, production, and sales to improve quality. See: plan-do-check-action.

Deming Prize–Award given annually to organizations that, according to the award guidelines, have successfully applied companywide quality control based on statistical quality control and will keep up with it in the future. Although the award is named in honor of W. Edwards Deming, its criteria are not specifically related to Deming's teachings. There are three separate divisions for the award: the Deming Application Prize, the Deming Prize for Individuals, and the Deming Prize for Overseas Companies. The award process is overseen by the Deming Prize Committee of the Union of Japanese Scientists and Engineers in Tokyo.

Deming's 14 points–Syn: 14 Points.

demonstrated capacity–Proven capacity calculated from actual performance data, usually expressed as the average number of items produced multiplied by the standard hours per item. See: maximum demonstrated capacity.

demurrage–Carrier charges and fees applied when truck trailers are retained beyond a specified loading or unloading time. See: express.

denied party list–A list of organizations that are unauthorized to submit a bid for an activity.

departmental stocks–An informal system of holding some stock in a production department. This action is taken as a protection from stockouts in the stockroom or for convenience; however, it results in increased inventory investment and possible degradation of the accuracy of the inventory records.

department overhead rate–The overhead rate applied to jobs passing through a department.

dependent demand–Demand that is directly related to or derived from the bill of material structure for other items or end products. Such demands are therefore calculated and need not and should not be forecast.

A given inventory item may have both dependent and independent demand at any given time. For example, a part may simultaneously be the component of an assembly and sold as a service part.

depreciation–An allocation of the original value of an asset against current income to represent the declining value of the asset as a cost of that time period. Depreciation does not involve a cash payment. It acts as a tax shield and thereby reduces the tax payment. See: capital recovery.

derived demand–Demand for component products that arises from the demand for final design products. For example, the demand for steel is derived from the demand for automobiles.

design changeover flexibility–The capability of the existing production system to accommodate and introduce a large variety of major design changes quickly.

design engineering–The discipline consisting of process engineering and product engineering.

design for manufacturability–Simplification of parts, products, and processes to improve quality and reduce manufacturing costs.

design for manufacture and assembly–A product development approach that involves the manufacturing function in the initial stages of product design to ensure ease of manufacturing and assembly. Syn: early manufacturing involvement.

design for quality–A product design approach that uses quality measures to capture the extent to which the design meets the needs of the target market (customer attributes), as well as its actual performance, aesthetics, and cost. See: total quality engineering.

designing in quality vs. inspecting in quality–Syn: prevention vs. detection.

design of experiments (DOE)–1) A process for structuring statistically valid studies in any science. 2) A quality management technique used to evaluate the effect of carefully planned and controlled changes to input process variables on the output variable. The objective is to improve production processes.

design review–A technique for evaluating a proposed design to ensure that the design (1) is supported by adequate materials and materials that are available on a timely basis, (2) will perform successfully during use, (3) can be manufactured at low cost, and (4) is suitable for prompt field maintenance.

design-to-order–Syn: engineer-to-order.

detailed scheduling–Syn: operations scheduling.

detail file–A file that contains manufacturing, routing, or specification details. See: master file.

detention–Carrier charges and fees applied when rail freight cars are retained beyond a specified loading or unloading time.

deterioration–Product spoilage, damage to the package, etc. This is one of the considerations in inventory carrying cost.

deterministic models–Models where no uncertainty is included, e.g., inventory models without safety stock considerations.

deviation–The difference, usually the absolute difference, between a number and the mean of a set of numbers, or between a forecast value and the actual value.

diagnostic journey and remedial journey–A two-phase investigation used by teams to solve chronic quality problems. In the first phase–the diagnostic journey–the team journeys from the symptom of a chronic problem to its cause. In the second phase–the remedial journey–the team journeys from the cause to its remedy.

diagnostic study–A brief investigation or cursory methods study of an operation, process, group, or individual to discover causes of operational difficulties or problems for which more detailed remedial studies may be feasible. An appropriate work measurement technique may be used to evaluate alternatives or to locate major areas requiring improvement.

direct costing–Syn: variable costing.

direct costs–Variable costs that can be directly attributed to a particular job or operation.

direct-deduct inventory transaction processing–A method of inventory bookkeeping that decreases the book (computer) inventory of an item as material is issued from stock, and increases the book inventory as material is received into stock by means of individual transactions processed for each item. The key concept here is that the book record is updated coincidentally with the movement of material out of or into stock. As a result, the book record is a representation of what is physically in stock. Syn: discrete issue.

direct delivery–The consignment of goods directly from the supplier to the buyer, frequently used where a third party acts as intermediary between supplier and buyer.

direct labor–Labor that is specifically applied to the product being manufactured or used in the performance of the service. Syn: touch labor.

direct material–Material that becomes a part of the final product in measurable quantities.

direct numerical control (DNC)–A system where sets of numerical control machines are connected to a computer, allowing direct control of machines by the computer without use of tapes.

disbursement–The physical issuance and reporting of the movement of raw material, components, or other items from a stores room or warehouse.

disbursement list–Syn: picking list.

disciplinary action–Action taken to enforce compliance with organizational rules and policies.

discontinuous demand–A demand pattern that is characterized by large demands interrupted by periods with no demand, as opposed to a continuous or steady (e.g., daily) demand. Syn: lumpy demand.

discount–An allowance or deduction granted by the seller to the buyer, usually when the buyer meets certain stipulated conditions that reduce the price of the goods purchased. A quantity discount is an allowance determined by the quantity or value of the purchase. A cash discount is an allowance extended to encourage payment of an invoice on or before a stated date. A trade discount is a deduction from an established price for items or services made by the seller to those engaged in certain businesses. See: price break.

discounted cash flow–A method of investment analysis in which future cash flows are converted, or discounted, to their value at the present time. The rate of return for an investment is that interest rate at which the present value of all related cash flow equals zero.

discrete issue–Syn: direct-deduct inventory transaction processing.

discrete manufacturing–Production of distinct items such as automobiles, appliances, or computers.

discrete order quantity–An order quantity that represents an integer number of periods of demand. Most MRP systems employ discrete order quantities. See: fixed period requirements, least total cost, least unit cost, lot-for-lot, part period balancing, period order quantity, Wagner-Whitin algorithm.

dispatch(ing) board–Syn: control board.

dispatcher–A production control person whose primary function is dispatching.

dispatching–The selecting and sequencing of available jobs to be run at individual workstations and the assignment of those jobs to workers.

dispatching rule–The logic used to assign priorities to jobs at a work center.

dispatch list–A listing of manufacturing orders in priority sequence. The dispatch list, which is usually communicated to the manufacturing floor via hard copy or CRT display, contains detailed information on priority, location, quantity, and the capacity requirements of the manufacturing order by operation. Dispatch lists are normally generated daily and oriented by work center. Syn: work center schedule.

distributed data processing–A data processing organizational concept under which computer resources of a company are installed at more than one location with appropriate communication links. Processing is performed at the user's location generally on a smaller computer and under the user's control and scheduling, as opposed to processing for all users being done on a large, centralized computer system.

distributed numerical control–An approach to automated machining in which each machine tool has its own dedicated microcomputer or computer numerical control (CNC). Each machine tool's CNC is connected via a network with a minicomputer that handles distributed processing between the host mainframe computer and the CNC. This minicomputer handles part program transfers and machine status data collection. This approach is considered more advanced than direct numerical control, in which several machine tools are tied directly to a mainframe computer.

distributed systems–Computer systems in multiple locations throughout an organization, working in a cooperative fashion, with the system at each location primarily serving the needs of that location but also able to receive and supply information from other systems within a network.

distribution–1) The activities associated with the movement of material, usually finished products or service parts, from the manufacturer to the customer. These activities encompass the functions of transportation, warehousing, inventory control, material handling, order administration, site and location analysis, industrial packaging, data processing, and the communications network necessary for effective management. It includes all activities related to physical distribution, as well as the return of goods to the manufacturer. In many cases, this movement is made through one or more levels of field warehouses. Syn: physical distribution. 2) The systematic division of a whole into discrete parts having distinctive characteristics.

distribution by value–Syn: ABC classification.

distribution center–A warehouse with finished goods and/or service items. A company, for example, might have a manufacturing facility in Philadelphia and distribution centers in Atlanta, Dallas, Los Angeles, San Francisco, and Chicago. *Distribution center* is synonymous with the term *branch warehouse,* although the former has become more commonly used recently. When a warehouse serves a group of satellite warehouses, it is usually called a *regional distribution center.* Syn: field warehouse.

distribution cost–Those items of cost related to the activities associated with the movement and storage of finished products. Distribution costs can include inventory costs, transportation costs, and order processing costs.

distribution network structure–The planned channels of inventory disbursement from one or more sources to field warehouses and ultimately to the customer. There may be one or more levels in the disbursement system. Syn: bill of distribution.

distribution of forecast errors–Tabulation of the forecast errors according to the frequency of occurrence of each error value. The errors in forecasting are, in many cases, normally distributed even when the observed data do not come from a normal distribution.

distribution planner–A person who plans inventories and schedules replenishment shipments for the distribution centers.

distribution requirements planning–1) The function of determining the need to replenish inventory at branch warehouses. A time-phased order point approach is used where the planned orders at the branch warehouse level are "exploded" via MRP logic to become gross requirements on the supplying source. In the case of multilevel distribution networks, this explosion process can continue down through the various levels of regional warehouses (master warehouse, factory warehouse, etc.) and become input to the master production schedule. Demand on the supplying sources is recognized as dependent, and standard MRP logic applies. 2) More generally, replenishment inventory calculations, which may be based on other planning approaches such as period order quantities or "replace exactly what was used," rather than being limited to the time-phased order point approach.

distribution resource planning (DRP)–The extension of distribution requirements planning into the planning of the key resources contained in a distribution system: warehouse space, work force, money, trucks, freight cars, etc.

distributor–A business that does not manufacture its own products, but purchases and resells these products. Such a business usually maintains a finished goods inventory.

divergent point–In the theory of constraints, a control point in the logical product structure where a common part or assembly can be directed to two or more different end items. To maintain the flow of parts to products, the schedule of common parts must be synchronized with the constraint schedule and shipping commitments.

diversification strategy–An expansion of the scope of the product line to exploit new markets. A key objective of a diversification strategy is to spread the company's risk over several product lines in case there should be a downturn in any one product's market.

dock receipt–A receipt recorded for a shipment received or delivered at a pier or dock.

DNC–Abbreviation for *direct numerical control.*

documentation–The process of collecting and organizing documents or the information recorded in documents. The term usually refers to the development of material specifying inputs, operations, and outputs of a computer system.

DOE–Abbreviation for *design of experiments.*

double order point system–A distribution inventory management system that has two order points. The smallest equals the original order point, which covers replenishment lead time. The second order point is the sum of the first order point plus normal usage during manufacturing lead time. It enables warehouses to forewarn manufacturing of future replenishment orders.

double smoothing–Syn: second-order smoothing.

downgrade–The substitution of a product of lower quality, value, or status for another either in planning or in fact.

download–Transfer of information from a centralized system such as a mainframe or network server to a personal computer environment.

downstream operation–Tasks subsequent to the task currently being planned or executed.

downtime–Time when a resource is scheduled for operation but is not producing for reasons such as maintenance, repair, or setup.

drawback–A refund of customs duties paid on material imported and later exported.

driver–1) In activity-based accounting, an operation that influences the quantity of work required and cost of an activity. 2) In the theory of constraints, an underlying cause that is responsible for several observed effects.

drop ship–To take the title of the product but not actually handle, stock, or deliver it, e.g., to have one supplier ship directly to another or to have a supplier ship directly to the buyer's customer.

DRP–Abbreviation for *distribution resource planning.*

drum-buffer-rope–The generalized technique used to manage resources to maximize throughput. The drum is the rate or pace of production set by the system's constraint. The buffers establish the protection against uncertainty so that the system can maximize throughput. The rope is a communication process from the constraint to the gating operation that checks or limits material released into the system to support the constraint. See: synchronized production.

DSS–Abbreviation for *decision support system.*

DTF–Abbreviation for *demand time fence.*

due date–The date when purchased material or production material is due to be available for use. Syn: expected receipt date. See: arrival date.

due date rule–A dispatching rule that directs the sequencing of jobs by the earliest due date.

dummy activity–An activity, always of zero duration, used to show logical dependence when an activity cannot start before another is complete, but that does not lie on the same path through the network. Normally, these dummy activities are graphically represented as a dashed line headed by an arrow and inserted between two nodes to indicate a precedence relationship or to maintain the unique numbering of concurrent activities.

dunnage–Packing material used to protect a product from damage during transport.

durable goods–Generally, any producer or consumer goods whose continuous serviceability is likely to exceed three years (e.g., trucks, furniture).

duty–A tax levied by a government on the importation, exportation, or use and consumption of goods.

duty-free zone–An area where merchandise is brought into the country for further work to be done. Duty is paid only on the items brought in, normally at a lower rate than finished goods, and paid only at the time of sale.

dynamic lot sizing–Any lot-sizing technique that creates an order quantity subject to continuous recomputation. See: least total cost, least unit cost, part period balancing, period order quantity, Wagner-Whitin algorithm.

dynamic programming–A method of sequential decision making in which the result of the decision at each stage affords the best possible means to exploit the expected range of likely (yet unpredictable) outcomes in the following decision-making stages.

E

EAP–Abbreviation for *employee assistance program.*

earliest due date (EDD)–A priority rule that sequences the jobs in a queue according to their due dates.

earliest start date–The earliest date an operation or order can start. It may be restricted by the current date, material availability, or management-specified "maximum advance."

earliness–If a job is finished before its due date, the difference between its completion date and the due date. See: lateness, tardiness.

early finish date (EF)–The earliest time an activity may be completed, equal to the early start of the activity plus its remaining duration. See: early start date, late finish date, late start date.

early manufacturing involvement–Syn: design for manufacture and assembly.

early start date (ES)–The earliest time any activity may begin, as logically constrained by the network for a given date. See: early finish date, late finish date, late start date.

early supplier involvement (ESI)–The process of involving suppliers early in the product design activity and drawing on their expertise, insights, and knowledge to generate better designs in less time and designs that are easier to manufacture with high quality.

earmarked material–Reserved material on hand that is physically identified, rather than merely reserved in a balance-of-stores record.

earned hours–A statement of output reflecting the standard hours for actual production reported during the period. Syn: earned volume.

earned value–Syn: budget cost of work performed.

earned volume–Syn: earned hours.

econometric model–A set of equations intended to be used simultaneously to capture the way in which dependent and independent variables are interrelated.

economic indicator–An index of total business activities at the regional, national, and global levels.

economic lot size–Syn: economic order quantity.

economic order quantity (EOQ)–A type of fixed-order-quantity model that determines the amount of an item to be purchased or manufactured at one time. The intent is to minimize the combined costs of acquiring and carrying inventory. The basic formula is

$$\text{Qnty} = \sqrt{\frac{2 \times \text{annual demand} \times \text{avg cost of order preparation}}{\text{annual inventory carrying cost percentage} \times \text{unit cost}}}$$

Syn: economic lot size, minimum cost order quantity.

economy of scale–A phenomenon whereby larger volumes of production reduce unit cost by distributing fixed costs over a larger quantity.

EDD–Abbreviation for *earliest due date.*

EDI–Abbreviation for *electronic data interchange.*

EEO–Abbreviation for *equal employment opportunity.*

EF–Abbreviation for *early finish date.*

effective date–The date on which a component or an operation is to be added or removed from a bill of material or an assembly process. The effective dates are used in the explosion process to create demands for the correct items. Normally, bills of material and routing systems provide for an effectivity start date and stop date, signifying the start or stop of a particular relationship. Effectivity control also may be by serial number rather than date. Syn: effectivity, effectivity date.

effectivity–Syn: effective date.

effectivity date–Syn: effective date.

efficiency–A measure (as a percentage) of the actual output to the standard output expected. Efficiency measures how well something is performing relative to expectations; it does not measure output relative to any input. Efficiency is the ratio of actual units produced to the standard rate of production expected in a time period, or actual hours produced to standard hours, or actual dollar volume to a standard dollar volume in a time period. For example, if there is a standard of 100 pieces per hour and 780 units are produced in one eight-hour shift, the efficiency is 780/800 multiplied by 100%, or 97.5%.

EFT–Abbreviation for *electronic funds transfer.*

EI–Abbreviation for *employee involvement.*

80-20–A term referring to the Pareto principle. The principle suggests that most effects come from relatively few causes; that is, 80% of the effects come from 20% of the possible causes. See: ABC classification.

electronic data interchange (EDI)–The paperless (electronic) exchange of trading documents, such as purchase orders, shipment authorizations, advanced shipment notices, and invoices, using standardized document formats.

electronic funds transfer (EFT)–A computerized system that processes financial transactions and information about these transactions or performs the exchange of value between two parties.

empirical–Pertaining to a statement or formula based upon experience or observation rather than on deduction or theory.

employee assistance program (EAP)–Employer-provided service aimed at helping employees and their families with personal and work-related problems. Examples include financial counseling and chemical-dependency rehabilitation programs.

employee empowerment–The practice of giving nonmanagerial employees the responsibility and the power to make decisions regarding their jobs or tasks. It is associated with the practice of transfer of managerial responsibility to the employee. Empowerment allows the employee to take on responsibility for tasks normally associated with staff specialists. Examples include allowing the employee to make scheduling, quality, process design, or purchasing decisions.

employee involvement (EI)–The concept of using the experience, creative energy, and intelligence of all employees by treating them with respect, keeping them informed, and including them and their ideas in decision-making processes appropriate to their areas of expertise. Employee involvement focuses on quality and productivity improvements.

employee stock ownership plan (ESOP)–A program to encourage workers to purchase stock of the company, generally tied into the compensation/benefits package. The intention is to give workers a feeling of participation in the management and direction of the company.

empowerment–A condition whereby employees have the authority to make decisions and take action in their work areas without prior approval. For example, an operator can stop a production process if a problem is detected, or a customer service representative can send out a replacement product if a customer calls with a problem.

ending inventory–A statement of on-hand quantities or dollar value of an SKU at the end of a period, often determined by a physical inventory.

end item–A product sold as a completed item or repair part; any item subject to a customer order or sales forecast. Syn: end product, finished good, finished product.

endogenous variable–A variable whose value is determined by relationships included within the model.

end product–Syn: end item.

enforced problem solving–The methodology of intentionally restricting a resource (e.g., inventory, storage space, number of workers) to expose a problem that must then be resolved.

engineering change–A revision to a blueprint or design released by engineering to modify or correct a part. The request for the change can be from a customer or from production quality control or another department.

engineering characteristics–The technical features designed into a product.

engineering drawings–A visual representation of the dimensional characteristics of a part or assembly at some stage of manufacture.

engineering order–Syn: experimental order.

engineering standard–Design or test guidelines intended to promote the design, production, and test of a part, component, or product in a manner that promotes standardization, ease of maintenance, consistency, adequacy of test procedures, versatility of design, ease of production and field service, and minimization of the number of different tools and special tools required.

engineer-to-order–Products whose customer specifications require unique engineering design or significant customization. Each customer order results in a unique set of part numbers, bills of material, and routings. Syn: design-to-order.

enterprise resources planning (ERP) system–An accounting-oriented information system for identifying and planning the enterprisewide resources needed to take, make, ship, and account for customer orders. An ERP system differs from the typical MRP II system in technical requirements such as graphical user interface, relational database, use of fourth-generation language, and computer-aided software engineering tools in development, client/server architecture, and open-system portability. Syn: customer-oriented manufacturing management system.

Environmental Protection Agency (EPA)–A federal (U.S.) agency with regulatory authority over matters affecting the environment, including waste generation and habitat destruction.

EOQ–Abbreviation for *economic order quantity*.

EOQ = 1–Reducing setup time and inventory to the point where it is economically sound to produce in batches with a size of one. Often EOQ = 1 is an ideal to strive for, like zero defects.

EOQ tables–Tables listing several ranges of monthly usages in dollars and the appropriate order size in dollars or monthly usage for each usage range.

EPA–Abbreviation for *Environmental Protection Agency*.

equal employment opportunity (EEO)–The laws prohibiting discrimination in employment because of race or color, sex, age, handicap status, religion, and national origin.

equal runout quantities–Order quantities for items in a group that result in a supply that covers an equal time for all items. See: fair-share quantity logic.

equilibrium point–The point in a market where the demand for a product and the supply of that product are exactly equal. If supply were greater, the price would fall. If demand were greater, the price would rise. Free markets tend to move toward their equilibrium point.

equity–The part of a company's total assets not provided by creditors; owner-invested funds.

equivalent days–The standard hour requirements of a job converted to days for scheduling purposes.

equivalent unit cost–A method of costing that uses the total cost incurred for all like units for a period of time divided by the equivalent units completed during the same time period.

equivalent units–A translation of inventories into equivalent finished goods units or of inventories exploded back to raw materials for period end valuation of inventories. An equivalent unit can be the sum of several partially completed units. Two units 50% completed are equivalent to one unit 100% completed.

ergonomics–Approach to job design that focuses on the interactions between the human operator and such traditional environmental elements as atmospheric contaminants, heat, light, sound, and all tools and equipment.

ERP–Abbreviation for *enterprise resources planning*.

ES–Abbreviation for *early start date*.

escalation–An amount or percentage by which a contract price may be adjusted if specified contingencies occur, such as changes in the supplier's raw material or labor costs.

ESI–Abbreviation for *early supplier involvement*.

ESOP–Acronym for *employee stock ownership plan*.

evaporating cloud–In the theory of constraints, a logic-based tool for surfacing assumptions related to a conflict or problem. Once the assumptions are surfaced, actions to break an assumption and hence solve (evaporate) the problem can be determined.

event–An event is an identifiable single point in time among a set of related activities. Graphically, an event can be represented by two approaches: In activity-on-node networks, it is represented by a node; in activity-on-arc networks, the event is represented by the arc.

exception message–Syn: action message.

exception report–A report that lists or flags only those items that deviate from the plan.

excess capacity–A situation where the output capabilities at a nonconstraint resource exceed the amount of productive and protective capacity required to achieve a given level of throughput at the constraint. See: idle capacity, productive capacity, protective capacity.

excess inventory–Any inventory in the system that exceeds the minimum amount necessary to achieve the desired throughput rate at the constraint or that exceeds the minimum amount necessary to achieve the desired due date performance.

excess issue–The removal from stock and assignment to a schedule of a quantity higher than the schedule quantity. Syn: overissue.

exchange unit–The number of units to be produced before changing the bit, tool, or die. See: process batch.

exempt carrier–A for-hire carrier that is free from economic regulation.

exempt positions–Positions that do not require the payment of overtime because they meet the tests of executive, supervisory, or administrative activity, as defined under the Fair Labor Standards Act.

exit interview–An interview given to an employee who is leaving the company. The purpose is to find out why a person is leaving, what was liked and disliked about the job and the company, and what changes would make the department and the company a better place to work.

exogenous variable–A variable whose values are determined by considerations outside the model in question.

expansion–Any increase in the capacity of a plant, facility, or unit, usually by added investment. The scope of this increase extends from the elimination of problem areas to the complete replacement of an existing facility with a larger one.

expected completion quantity–The planned quantity of a manufacturing order after expected scrap.

expected demand–The quantity expected to be consumed during a given time period when usage is at the forecast rate. See: demand during lead time.

expected receipt date–Syn: arrival date, due date.

expected value–The average value that would be observed in taking an action an infinite number of times. The expected value of an action is calculated by multiplying the outcome of the action by the probability of achieving the outcome.

expedite–To rush or chase production or purchase orders that are needed in less than the normal lead time; to take extraordinary action because of an increase in relative priority. Syn: stockchase.

expeditor–A production control person whose primary duty is expediting.

expendables–Syn: consumables.

expense–Expenditures of short-term value, including depreciation, as opposed to land and other fixed capital. See: overhead.

experience curve–Syn: learning curve.

experience curve pricing–The average cost pricing method, but using an estimate of future average costs, based on an experience (learning) curve.

experimental design–A formal plan that details the specifics for conducting an experiment, such as which responses, factors, levels, blocks, treatments, and tools are to be used.

experimental order–An order generated by the laboratory, research and development, or engineering group that must be run through regular production facilities with potential future product or market development as a project or team goal. Syn: engineering order, laboratory order, pilot order, R&D order.

expert system–A type of artificial intelligence computer system that mimics human experts by using rules and heuristics rather than deterministic algorithms.

explode–To perform a bill-of-material explosion.

explode-to-deduct–Syn: post-deduct inventory transaction processing.

explosion–Syn: requirements explosion. Ant: implosion.

explosion level–Syn: low-level code.

exponential distribution–A continuous probability distribution where the probability of occurrence either steadily increases or decreases. The steady increase case (positive exponential distribution) is used to model phenomena such as customer service level versus cost. The steady decrease case (negative exponential distribution) is used to model phenomena such as the weight given to any one time period of demand in exponential smoothing.

exponential smoothing–A type of weighted moving average forecasting technique in which past observations are geometrically discounted according to their age. The heaviest weight is assigned to the most recent data. The smoothing is termed *exponential* because data points are weighted in accordance with an exponential function of their age. The technique makes use of a smoothing constant to apply to the difference between the most recent forecast and the critical sales data, thus avoiding the necessity of carrying historical sales data. The approach can be used for data that exhibit no trend or seasonal patterns. Higher order exponential smoothing models can be used for data with either (or both) trend and seasonality.

exposures–The number of times per year that the system risks a stockout. The number of exposures is arrived at by dividing the lot size into the annual usage.

express–Carrier payment to its customers when ships, rail cars, or trailers are unloaded or loaded in less than the time allowed by contract and returned to the carrier for use. See: demurrage.

express warranty–A positive representation, made by a seller, concerning the nature, character, use, and purpose of goods, that induces the buyer to buy and on which the seller intends the buyer to depend.

external customer–A person or organization that receives a product, a service, or information but is not part of the organization supplying it. See: customer, internal customer.

external factory–A situation where suppliers are viewed as an extension of the firm's manufacturing capabilities and capacities. The same practices and concerns that are commonly applied to the management of the firm's manufacturing system should also be applied to the management of the external factory.

external failures cost–The cost related to problems found after the product reaches the customer. This usually includes such costs as warranty and returns.

external setup time–Time associated with elements of a setup procedure performed while the process or machine is running. Ant: internal setup time.

extrapolation–Estimation of the future value of some data series based on past observations. Statistical forecasting is a common example. Syn: projection.

extrinsic forecast–A forecast based on a correlated leading indicator, such as estimating furniture sales based on housing starts. Extrinsic forecasts tend to be more useful for large aggregations, such as total company sales, than for individual product sales. Ant: intrinsic forecast.

F

fabrication–Manufacturing operations for components, as opposed to assembly operations.

fabrication level–The lowest production level. The only components at this level are parts (as opposed to assemblies or subassemblies). These parts are either procured from outside sources or fabricated within the manufacturing organization.

fabrication order–A manufacturing order to a component-making department authorizing it to produce component parts. See: batch card, manufacturing order.

fabricator–A manufacturer that turns the product of a converter into a larger variety of products. For example, a fabricator may turn steel rods into nuts, bolts, and twist drills, or may turn paper into bags and boxes.

facilities–The physical plant and equipment.

factory within a factory–A technique to improve management focus and overall productivity by creating autonomous business units within a larger physical plant. Syn: plant within a plant.

failsafe techniques–Syn: failsafe work methods, poka-yoke.

failsafe work methods–Methods of performing operations so that actions that are incorrect cannot be completed. For example, a part without holes in the proper place cannot be removed from a jig, or a computer system will reject invalid numbers or require double entry of transaction quantities outside the normal range. Called *poka-yoke* by the Japanese. Syn: failsafe techniques, mistake-proofing, poka-yoke.

failure analysis–The collection, examination, review, and classification of failures to determine trends and to identify poorly performing parts or components.

failure mode analysis (FMA)–A procedure to determine which malfunction symptoms appear immediately before or after a failure of a critical parameter in a system. After all the possible causes are listed for each symptom, the product is designed to eliminate the problems.

failure mode effects analysis (FMEA)–A procedure in which each potential failure mode in every sub-item of an item is analyzed to determine its effect on other sub-items and on the required function of the item.

failure mode effects and criticality analysis (FMECA)–A procedure that is performed after a failure mode effects analysis to classify each potential failure effect according to its severity and probability of occurrence.

Fair Labor Standards Act (FLSA)–Federal law that governs the definitions of management and labor and establishes wage payment and hours worked and other employment practices.

fair-share quantity logic–The process of equitably allocating available stock among field distribution centers. Fair-share quantity logic is normally used when stock available from a central inventory location is less than the cumulative requirements of the field stocking locations. The use of fair-share quantity logic involves procedures that "push" stock out to the field, instead of allowing the field to "pull" in what is needed. The objective is to maximize customer service from the limited available inventory. See: equal runout quantities.

family–A group of end items whose similarity of design and manufacture facilitates being planned in aggregate, whose sales performance is monitored together, and, occasionally, whose cost is aggregated at this level.

family contracts–A purchase order that groups families of similar parts together to obtain pricing advantages and a continuous supply of material.

FAR–Abbreviation for *Federal Acquisition Regulation*.

FAS–1) Abbreviation for *final assembly schedule*. 2) Abbreviation for *free alongside ship*.

fault tolerance–The ability of a system to avoid or minimize the disruptive effects of defects by using some form of redundancy or extra design margins.

fault tree analysis–A logical approach to identify the probabilities and frequencies of events in a system that are most critical to uninterrupted and safe operation. This analysis may include failure mode effects analysis (determining the result of component failure interactions toward system safety) and techniques for human error prediction.

feasibility study–An analysis designed to establish the practicality and cost justification of a given project and, if it appears to be advisable to do so, to determine the direction of subsequent project efforts.

feature–A distinctive characteristic of a product or service. The characteristic is provided by an option, accessory, or attachment. For example, in ordering a new car, the customer must specify an engine type and size (option), but need not necessarily select an air conditioner (attachment). See: accessory, attachment, option.

feature code–An identifying code assigned to a distinct product feature that may contain one or more specific part number configurations.

Federal Acquisition Regulation (FAR)–The primary regulation governing all federal agencies (U.S.) acquiring supplies and services.

fee–The charge for the use of the contractor's organization for the period and to the extent specified in the contract.

feedback–The flow of information back into the control system so that actual performance can be compared with planned performance.

feedback loop–The part of a closed-loop system that allows the comparison of response with command.

feeder workstations–An area of manufacture whose products feed a subsequent work area.

feedstock–The primary raw material in a chemical or refining process normally received by pipeline or large-scale bulk shipments. Feedstock availability is frequently the controlling factor in setting the production schedule and rate for a process.

field–A specified area of a record used for a particular category of data.

field warehouse–Syn: distribution center.

FIFO–Acronym for *first in, first out*.

file–An organized collection of records or the storage device in which these records are kept.

file structure–Manner in which records are stored within a file, e.g., sequential, random, or index-sequential.

fill rate–Syn: customer service ratio.

final assembly–The highest level assembled product, as it is shipped to customers.

final assembly department–The name for the manufacturing department where the product is assembled. See: blending department, pack-out department.

final assembly schedule (FAS)–A schedule of end items to finish the product for specific customers' orders in a make-to-order or assemble-to-order environment. It is also referred to as the *finishing schedule* because it may involve operations other than just the final assembly; also, it may not involve assembly, but simply final mixing, cutting, packaging, etc. The FAS is prepared after receipt of a customer order as constrained by the availability of material and capacity, and it schedules the operations required to complete the product from the level where it is stocked (or master scheduled) to the end-item level.

finished good–Syn: end item.

finished product–Syn: end item.

finished products inventories–Those items on which all manufacturing operations, including final test, have been completed. These products are available for shipment to the customer as either end items or repair parts.

finishing lead time–1) The time that is necessary to finish manufacturing a product after receipt of a customer order. 2) The time allowed for completing the product based on the final assembly schedule.

finish-to-order–Syn: assemble-to-order.

finite forward scheduling–An equipment scheduling technique that builds a schedule by proceeding sequentially from the initial period to the final period while observing capacity limits. A Gantt chart may be used with this technique.

finite loading–Assigning no more work to a work center than the work center can be expected to execute in a given time period. The specific term usually refers to a computer technique that involves calculating shop priority revisions in order to level load operation by operation.

firm planned order (FPO)–A planned order that can be frozen in quantity and time. The computer is not allowed to change it automatically; this is the responsibility of the planner in charge of the item that is being planned. This technique can aid planners working with MRP systems to respond to material and capacity problems by firming up selected planned orders. In addition, firm planned orders are the normal method of stating the master production schedule. See: planning time fence.

first-article inspection–A quality check on the first component run after a new setup has been completed. Syn: first-piece inspection.

first-come-first-served rule–A dispatching rule under which the jobs are sequenced by their arrival times. Syn: first-in, first-out.

first in, first out (FIFO)–1) A method of inventory valuation for accounting purposes. The assumption is that the oldest inventory (first in) is the first to be used (first out), but there is no necessary relationship with the actual physical movement of specific items. 2) Syn: first-come-first-served rule.

first-order smoothing–Single exponential smoothing; a weighted moving average approach that is applied to forecasting problems where the data do not exhibit significant trend or seasonal patterns. Syn: single exponential smoothing, single smoothing.

first-piece inspection–Syn: first-article inspection.

fishbone analysis–A technique to organize the elements of a problem or situation to aid in the determination of the causes of the problem or situation. The analysis relates the effect of the environment to the several possible sources of the problem.

fishbone chart–Syn: cause-and-effect diagram.

fitness for use–A term used to indicate that a product or service fits the customer's defined purpose for that product or service.

five focusing steps–In the theory of constraints, a process to continuously improve organizational profit by evaluating the production system and market mix to determine how to make the most profit using the system constraint. The steps consist of 1) identifying the constraint to the system, 2) deciding how to exploit the constraint to the system, 3) subordinating all nonconstraints to the constraint, 4) elevating the constraint to the system, 5) returning to step 1 if the constraint is broken in any previous step, while not allowing inertia to set in.

five why's–The practice of Japanese managers to ask "why" five times when confronted with a problem. By the time they receive the answer to the fifth "why," they believe they have found the ultimate cause of the problem. Syn: five W's.

five W's–Syn: five why's.

fixed budget–A budget of expected costs based on a specific level of production or other activity.

fixed cost–An expenditure that does not vary with the production volume; for example, rent, property tax, and salaries of certain personnel.

fixed-cost contribution per unit–An allocation process where total fixed cost for a period is divided by total units produced in that given time period.

fixed-interval order system–Syn: fixed reorder cycle inventory model.

fixed-interval review system–A hybrid inventory system in which the inventory analyst reviews the inventory position at fixed time periods. If the inventory level is found to be above a preset reorder point, no action is taken. If the inventory level is below the reorder point, the analyst orders a variable quantity equal to $M - x$ where M is a maximum stock level and x is the current quantity on hand and on order (if any). This hybrid system does not reorder every review interval. It therefore differs from the fixed-interval reorder system, which automatically places an order whenever inventory is reviewed.

fixed-location storage–A method of storage in which a relatively permanent location is assigned for the storage of each item in a storeroom or warehouse. Although more space is needed to store parts than in a random-location storage system, fixed locations become familiar, and therefore a locator file may not be needed. See: random-location storage.

fixed order quantity–A lot-sizing technique in MRP or inventory management that will always cause planned or actual orders to be generated for a predetermined fixed quantity, or multiples thereof, if net requirements for the period exceed the fixed order quantity.

fixed order quantity system–Syn: fixed reorder quantity inventory model.

fixed overhead–Traditionally, all manufacturing costs, other than direct labor and direct materials, that continue even if products are not produced. Although fixed overhead is necessary to produce the product, it cannot be directly traced to the final product.

fixed-period quantity–An MRP lot-sizing technique that sets the lot size equal to the net requirements for a given number of periods.

fixed-period requirements–A lot-sizing technique that sets the order quantity to the demand for a given number of periods. See: discrete order quantity.

fixed-position layout–Layout where resources are portable and come to the job site to perform activities, e.g., bridge or building construction.

fixed-price contract–The buyer agrees to pay a specified price to the seller upon delivery of the product or service. Fixed-price contracts may include clauses that allow price adjustments for unusual changes in material prices, labor costs, and production experience.

fixed property–Property attached to, and not easily removed from, the location.

fixed reorder cycle inventory model–A form of independent demand management model in which an order is placed every *n* time units. The order quantity is variable and essentially replaces the items consumed during the current time period. Let *M* be the maximum inventory desired at any time, and let *x* be the quantity on hand at the time the order is placed. Then, in the simplest model, the order quantity will be *M − x*. The quantity *M* must be large enough to cover the maximum expected demand during the lead time plus a review interval. The order quantity model becomes more complicated whenever the replenishment lead time exceeds the review interval, because outstanding orders then have to be factored into the equation. These reorder systems are sometimes called *fixed-interval order systems, order level systems,* or *periodic review systems.* Syn: fixed-interval order system, order level system, periodic review system. See: fixed reorder quantity inventory model, hybrid inventory system, independent demand item management models, optional replenishment model.

fixed reorder quantity inventory model–A form of independent demand item management model in which an order for a fixed quantity, *Q,* is placed whenever stock on hand plus on order reaches a predetermined reorder level, *R.* The fixed order quantity *Q* may be determined by the economic order quantity, by a fixed order quantity (such as a carton or a truckload), or by another model yielding a fixed result. The reorder point, *R,* may be deterministic or stochastic, and in either instance is large enough to cover the maximum expected demand during the replenishment lead time. Fixed reorder quantity models assume the existence of some form of a perpetual inventory record that is able to determine when the reorder point is reached. These reorder systems are sometimes called *fixed order quantity systems, lot-size systems,* or *order point-order quantity systems.* Syn: fixed order quantity system, lot size system, order point-order quantity system. See: fixed reorder cycle inventory model, hybrid inventory system, independent demand item management models, optional replenishment model, order point,

order point system, statistical inventory control, time-phased order point.

fixture–A device for supporting work during machining. See: jig.

flexibility–The ability of the manufacturing system to respond quickly, in terms of range and time, to external or internal changes. Six different categories of flexibility can be considered: mix flexibility, design changeover flexibility, modification flexibility, volume flexibility, rerouting/program flexibility, and material flexibility (see each term for a more detailed discussion). In addition, flexibility involves concerns of product flexibility. Flexibility can be useful in coping with various types of uncertainty (regarding mix, volume, etc.).

flexibility responsiveness–The ability of the firm and its management to change rapidly in response to changes taking place in the marketplace.

flexible automation–Short setup times and the ability to switch quickly from one product to another.

flexible benefits/cafeteria plans–Plans designed to give employees a core of minimum basic coverage with the option to choose additional coverage or, sometimes, cash. Employees can customize their benefits packages to suit their personal needs.

flexible budget–A budget showing the costs and revenues expected to be incurred or realized over a period of time at different levels of activity, measured in terms of some activity base such as direct labor hours, direct labor costs, or machine hours. A flexible manufacturing overhead budget gives the product costs of various manufacturing overhead items at different levels of activity.

flexible capability–Machinery's ability to be readily adapted to processing different components on an ongoing basis.

flexible capacity–The ability to operate manufacturing equipment at different production rates by varying staffing levels and operating hours or starting and stopping at will.

flexible machine center (FMC)–An automated system, which usually consists of CNC machines with robots loading and unloading parts conveyed into and through the system. Its purpose is to provide quicker throughput, changeovers, setups, etc., to manufacture multiple products.

flexible manufacturing system (FMS)–A group of numerically controlled machine tools interconnected by a central control system. The various machining cells are interconnected via loading and unloading stations by an automated transport system. Operational flexibility is enhanced by the ability to execute all manufacturing tasks on numerous product designs in small quantities and with faster delivery.

flexible work force–A work force whose members are cross-trained and whose work rules permit assignment of individual workers to different tasks.

flextime—An arrangement in which employees are allowed to choose work hours as long as the standard number of work hours is worked.

float—The amount of work-in-process inventory between two manufacturing operations, especially in repetitive manufacturing.

floating order point—An order point that is responsive to changes in demand or to changes in lead time.

floor stocks—Stocks of inexpensive production parts held in the factory from which production workers can draw without requisitions.

flowchart—A chart that shows the operations, transportation, storages, delay, inspections, etc., related to a process. Flowcharts are drawn to better understand processes. The flowchart is one of the seven tools of quality. See: block diagram, flow process chart.

flowcharting—A systems analysis tool that graphically presents a procedure. Symbols are used to represent operations, data, transportations, inspections, storages, delays, and equipment.

flow control—A specific production control system that is based primarily on setting production rates and feeding work into production to meet these planned rates, then monitoring and controlling production.

flow order—An order filled, not by moving material through production as an integral lot, but by production made over time and checked by a cumulative count until the flow order quantity is complete.

flow plant—Syn: flow shop.

flow process chart—A graphic, symbolic representation of the work performed or to be performed on a product as it passes through some or all of the stages of a process. Typically, the information included in the chart is quantity, distance moved, type of work done (by symbol with explanation), and equipment used. Work times may also be included. Flow process chart symbols (ASME Standard Symbol) generally used are as follows:

- ○ *operation:* A subdivision of a process that changes or modifies a part, material, or product, and is done essentially at one workplace location
- ➡ *transportation (move):* Change in location of a person, part, material, or product from one workplace to another
- ☐ *inspection:* Comparison of observed quality or quantity of product with a quality or quantity standard
- ▽ *storage:* Keeping a product, material, or part protected against unauthorized removal
- *D* *delay:* An event that occurs when an object or person waits for the next planned action
- ◉ *combined activity:* Adjustment during testing, e.g., combination of the separate operation and inspection symbols.

See: flowchart.

flow rate—Running rate; the inverse of cycle time; for example, 360 units per shift (or 0.75 units per minute).

flow shop—A form of manufacturing organization in which machines and operators handle a standard, usually uninterrupted, material flow. The operators generally perform the same operations for each production run. A flow shop is often referred to as a mass production shop or is said to have a continuous manufacturing layout. The plant layout (arrangement of machines, benches, assembly lines, etc.) is designed to facilitate a product "flow." Some process industries (chemicals, oil, paint, etc.) are extreme examples of flow shops. Each product, though variable in material specifications, uses the same flow pattern through the shop. Production is set at a given rate, and the products are generally manufactured in bulk. Syn: flow plant.

FLSA—Abbreviation for *Fair Labor Standards Act.*

fluctuation inventory—Inventory that is carried as a cushion to protect against forecast error. See: inventory buffer.

FMA—Abbreviation for *failure mode analysis.*

FMC—Abbreviation for *flexible machine center.*

FMEA—Abbreviation for *failure mode effects analysis.*

FMECA—Abbreviation for *failure mode effects and criticality analysis.*

FMS—Abbreviation for *flexible manufacturing system.*

FOB—Abbreviation for *free on board.*

focused factory—A plant established to focus the entire manufacturing system on a limited, concise, manageable set of products, technologies, volumes, and markets precisely defined by the company's competitive strategy, its technology, and economics.

focus forecasting—A system that allows the user to simulate the effectiveness of numerous forecasting techniques, enabling selection of the most effective one.

follow-up—Monitoring of job progress to see that operations are performed on schedule or that purchased material or products will be received on schedule.

force field analysis—A technique for analyzing the forces that will aid or hinder an organization in reaching an objective. An arrow pointing to an objective is drawn down the middle of a piece of paper. The factors that will aid the objective's achievement (called the driving forces) are listed on the left side of the arrow; the factors that will hinder its achievement (called the restraining forces) are listed on the right side of the arrow.

forecast—An estimate of future demand. A forecast can be determined by mathematical means using historical data, it can be created subjectively by using estimates from informal sources, or it can represent a combination of both techniques.

forecast consumption—Syn: consuming the forecast.

forecast error–The difference between actual demand and forecast demand, stated as an absolute value or as a percentage.

forecast horizon–The period of time into the future for which a forecast is prepared.

forecasting–The business function that attempts to predict sales and use of products so they can be purchased or manufactured in appropriate quantities in advance.

forecast interval–The time unit for which forecasts are prepared, such as week, month, or quarter. Syn: forecast period.

forecast period–Syn: forecast interval.

foreign trade zone (FTZ)–An area within a country that is treated as foreign territory by the U.S. Customs Service. Goods can be landed, stored, and processed within an FTZ without incurring any import duties or domestic taxes.

format–The predetermined arrangement of the characters of data for computer input, storage, or output.

form-fit-function–A term used to describe the process of designing a part or product to meet or exceed the performance requirements expected by customers.

formula–A statement of ingredient requirements. A formula may also include processing instructions and ingredient sequencing directions. Syn: formulation, recipe.

formulation–Syn: formula.

40/30/30 rule–A rule that identifies the sources of scrap, rework, and waste as 40% product design, 30% manufacturing processing, and 30% from suppliers.

forward buying–The practice of buying materials in a quantity exceeding current requirements but not beyond the point that the long-term need exists.

forward flow scheduling–A procedure for building process train schedules that starts with the first stage and proceeds sequentially through the process structure until the last stage is scheduled.

forward integration–Process of buying or owning elements of the production cycle and the channel of distribution forward toward the final customer.

forward pass–1) In construction, network calculations that determine the earliest start/earliest finish time (date) of each activity. 2) In manufacturing, often referred to as forward scheduling. Syn: forward scheduling. Ant: backward pass.

forward scheduling–A scheduling technique where the scheduler proceeds from a known start date and computes the completion date for an order, usually proceeding from the first operation to the last. Dates generated by this technique are generally the earliest start dates for operations. Syn: forward pass. Ant: back scheduling.

4GL–Abbreviation for *fourth-generation language.*

Fourier series–A form of analysis useful for forecasting. The model is based on fitting sine waves with increasing frequencies and phase angles to a time series.

14 Points–W. Edwards Deming's 14 management practices to help companies increase their quality and productivity: (1) create constancy of purpose for improving products and services; (2) adopt the new philosophy; (3) cease dependence on inspection to achieve quality; (4) end the practice of awarding business on price alone; instead, minimize total cost by working with a single supplier; (5) improve constantly and forever every process for planning, production, and service; (6) institute training on the job; (7) adopt and institute leadership; (8) drive out fear; (9) break down barriers between staff areas; (10) eliminate slogans, exhortations, and targets for the work force; (11) eliminate numerical quotas for the work force and numerical goals for management; (12) remove barriers that rob people of pride of workmanship and eliminate the annual rating or merit system; (13) institute a vigorous program of education and self-improvement for everyone; and (14) put everybody in the company to work to accomplish the transformation. Syn: Deming's 14 points.

fourth-generation language (4GL)–A general term for a series of high-level nonprocedural languages that enable users or programmers to prototype and to code new systems. Nonprocedural languages use menus, question-and-answer combinations, and a simpler, English-like wording to design and implement systems, update databases, generate reports, create graphs, and answer inquiries.

four-wall inventory–Syn: wall-to-wall inventory.

FPO–Abbreviation for *firm planned order.*

free alongside ship (FAS)–A term of sale indicating the seller is liable for all changes and risks until the goods sold are delivered to the port on a dock that will be used by the vessel. Title passes to the buyer when the seller has secured a clean dock or ship's receipt of goods.

free on board (FOB)–The terms of sale that identify where title passes to the buyer.

free slack–The amount of time that the completion of an activity in a project network can increase without delaying the start of the next activity.

freight consolidation–The grouping of shipments to obtain reduced costs or improved utilization of the transportation function. Consolidation can occur by market area grouping, grouping according to scheduled deliveries, or using third-party pooling services such as public warehouses and freight forwarders.

freight equalization–The practice of more distant suppliers of absorbing the additional freight charges to match the freight charges of a supplier geographically closer to the customer. This is done to eliminate the competitive advantage of lower freight charges that the nearest supplier has.

frequency distribution–A table that indicates the frequency with which data fall into each of any number of subdivisions of the variable. The subdivisions are usually called *classes*.

fringe benefits–Employer-granted compensations that are not directly tied to salary.

FTZ–Abbreviation for *foreign trade zone.*

full cost pricing–Establishing price at some markup over the full cost (absorption costing). Full costing includes direct manufacturing as well as applied overhead.

full pegging–The ability of a system to automatically trace requirements for a given component all the way up to its ultimate end item, customer, or contract number. Syn: contract pegging.

functional layout–A facility configuration in which operations of a similar nature or function are grouped together; an organizational structure based on departmental specialty (e.g., saw, lathe, mill, heat treat, and press). Syn: job shop layout, process layout.

functional requirements–Syn: critical characteristics.

functional systems design–The development and definition of the business functions to be accomplished by a computer system–i.e., the work of preparing a statement of the data input, data manipulation, and information output of the proposed computer system in common business terms that can be reviewed, understood, and approved by a user organization. This statement, after approval, provides the basis for the computer systems design.

functional test–Measure of a production component's ability to work as designed to meet a level of performance.

funnel experiment–An experiment that demonstrates the effects of tampering. Marbles are dropped through a funnel in an attempt to hit a flat-surfaced target below. The experiment shows that adjusting a stable process to compensate for an undesirable result or an extraordinarily good result will produce output that is worse than if the process had been left alone. See: tampering.

future order–An order entered for shipment at some future date.

future reality tree–In the theory of constraints, a logic-based tool for constructing and testing potential solutions before implementation. The objectives are to (1) develop, expand, and complete the solution and (2) identify and solve or prevent new problems created by implementing the solution.

futures–Contracts for the sale and delivery of commodities at a future time, made with the intention that no commodity be delivered or received immediately.

future worth–1) The equivalent monetary value at a designated future date based on time value of money. 2) The monetary sum, at a given future time, that is equivalent to one or more sums at given earlier times when interest is compounded at a given rate. See: time value of money.

G

GAAP–Acronym for *generally accepted accounting principles.*

gain sharing–A method of incentive compensation where employees share collectively in savings from productivity improvements.

Gantt chart–The earliest and best-known type of planning and control chart, especially designed to show graphically the relationship between planned performance and actual performance over time; named after its originator, Henry L. Gantt. It is used for machine loading, where one horizontal line is used to represent capacity and another to represent load against that capacity, or for following job progress, where one horizontal line represents the production schedule and another parallel line represents the actual progress of the job against the schedule in time. Syn: job progress chart.

gapped schedule–A schedule in which every piece in a lot is finished at one work center before any piece in the lot can be processed at the succeeding work center; the movement of material in complete lots, causing time gaps between the end of one operation and the beginning the next. It is a result of using a batched schedule at each operation (work center), where process batch and transfer batch are assumed to be the same or equal. Syn: gap phasing, straight-line schedule. Ant: overlapped schedule.

gap phasing–Syn: gapped schedule.

gateway work center–A work center that performs the first operation of a particular routing sequence.

gauge–An instrument for measuring or testing.

generally accepted accounting principles (GAAP)–Accounting practices that conform to conventions, rules, and procedures that have general acceptability by the accounting profession.

generally accepted manufacturing practices–A group of practices and principles, independent of any one set of techniques, that defines how a manufacturing company should be managed. Included are such elements as the need for data accuracy, frequent communications between marketing and manufacturing, top management control of the production planning process, systems capable of validly translating high-level plans into detailed schedules, etc.

general stores–Syn: supplies.

generic processing–A means of developing routings or processes for the manufacture of products through a family relationship, usually accomplished by means of tabular data to establish interrelationships. It is especially prevalent in the manufacture of raw material such as steel, aluminum, or chemicals.

global measures–That set of measurements that refers to the overall performance of the firm. Net profit, return on investment, and cash flow are examples of financial measures; and throughput, operating expense, and inventory are examples of operational measures.

go/no-go–State of a unit or product. Two parameters are possible: go (conforms to specification) and no-go (does not conform to specification).

goodwill–An intangible item that is only recorded on a company's books as the result of a purchase. Generally, it is inseparable from the enterprise but makes the company more valuable; for example, a good reputation.

grades–The sublabeling of items to identify their particular makeup and separate one lot from other production lots of the same item.

grievance–A complaint by an employee concerning alleged contract violations handled formally through contractually fixed procedures. If unsettled, a grievance may lead to arbitration.

grievance procedures–Methods identified in a collective bargaining agreement to resolve problems that develop or to determine if a contract has been violated.

gross margin–Sales revenue less all manufacturing costs, both fixed and variable.

gross requirement–The total of independent and dependent demand for a component before the netting of on-hand inventory and scheduled receipts.

gross sales–The total amount charged to all customers during the accounting time period.

group classification code–A part of a material classification technique that provides for designation of characteristics by successively lower order groups of code. Classification may denote function, type of material, size, shape, etc.

grouping–Matching like operations together and running them together sequentially, thereby taking advantage of common setup.

group technology (GT)–An engineering and manufacturing philosophy that identifies the physical similarity of parts (common routing) and establishes their effective production. It provides for rapid retrieval of existing designs and facilitates a cellular layout.

GT–Abbreviation for *group technology.*

guarantee–A contractual obligation by one entity to another that a fact regarding a product is true. See: warranty.

H

handling cost–The cost involved in the movement of material. In some cases, the handling cost depends on the size of the inventory.

hard automation–Use of specialized machines to manufacture and assemble products. Each machine is normally dedicated to one function, such as milling.

hard copy–A printed (computer) report, message, or special listing.

hardware–1) In manufacturing, relatively standard items such as nuts, bolts, washers, or clips. 2) In data processing, the computer and its peripherals.

harmonic smoothing–An approach to forecasting based on fitting some set of sine and cosine functions to the historical pattern of a time series. Syn: seasonal harmonics.

hash total–A control process used to ensure that all documents in a group are present or processed. In practice, the arithmetic sum of data not normally added together is found, the checking (audit) process adds the same data, and a comparison is made. If the sums do not agree, an error exists. Example: the last digit of every part number in an assembly is added and the last digit of the sum becomes the last digit of the assembly. If the last digit of an assembly is not the same as the sum of the last digit of the components' sum, the assembly must be missing a part or must have the wrong combination of parts.

hedge–1) An action taken in an attempt to shield the company from an uncertain event such as a strike, price increase, or currency reevaluation. 2) In master scheduling, a scheduled quantity to protect against uncertainty in demand or supply. The hedge is similar to safety stock, except that a hedge has the dimension of timing as well as amount. A volume hedge or market hedge is carried at the master schedule or production plan level. The master scheduler plans excess quantities over and above the demand quantities in given periods beyond some time fence such that, if the hedge is not needed, it can be rolled forward before major resources must be committed to produce the hedge and put it in inventory. A product mix hedge is an approach where several interrelated optional items are overplanned. Sometimes, using a planning bill, the sum of the percent mix can exceed 100% by a defined amount, thus triggering additional hedge planning. 3) In purchasing, any purchase or sale transaction having as its purpose the elimination of the negative aspects of price fluctuations. See: market hedge, option overplanning, planning bill of material, safety stock, time fence, two-level master production schedule.

hedge inventory–A form of inventory buildup to buffer against some event that may not happen. Hedge inventory planning involves speculation related to potential labor strikes, price increases, unsettled governments, and events that could severely impair a company's strategic initiatives. Risk and consequences are unusually high, and top management approval is often required.

hedging–The practice of entering into contracts on a commodity exchange to protect against future fluctuations in the commodity. This practice allows a company to isolate profits to the value-added process rather than to uncontrolled pricing factors.

heel–In the process industry, an item used in the manufacture of itself. For example, in the manufacture of plastic, the ingredients will include the parent as well as the components.

heuristic–A form of problem solving in which the results or rules have been determined by experience or intuition instead of by optimization.

hierarchical database–A method of constructing a database that requires that related record types be linked in tree-like structures, where no child record can have more than one physical parent record.

high-level language (HLL)–Relatively sophisticated computer language that allows users to employ a notation with which they are already familiar. For example: COBOL (business), ALGOL (mathematical and scientific), FORTRAN, and BASIC.

histogram–A graph of contiguous vertical bars representing a frequency distribution in which the groups or classes of items are marked on the x axis and the number of items in each class is indicated on the y axis. The pictorial nature of the histogram lets people see patterns that are difficult to see in a simple table of numbers. The histogram is one of the seven tools of quality.

historical analogy–A judgmental forecasting technique based on identifying a sales history that is analogous to a present situation, such as the sales history of a similar product, and using that past pattern to predict future sales. See: management estimation.

HLL–Abbreviation for *high-level language.*

hold order–A written order directing that certain operations or work be interrupted or terminated pending a change in design or other disposition of the material. Syn: stop work order.

hold points–Stockpoints for semifinished inventory.

horizontal display–A method of displaying output from a material requirements planning, distribution requirements planning, or other time-phased system in which requirements, scheduled receipts, projected balance, etc., are displayed across the document. Horizontal displays routinely summarize data into time periods or buckets. Ant: vertical display.

HOQ–Abbreviation for *house of quality.*

Hoshin planning–Breakthrough planning. A Japanese strategic planning process in which a company develops up to four vision statements that indicate where the company should be in the next five years. Company goals and work plans are developed based on the vision statements. Periodic audits are then conducted to monitor progress.

housekeeping–The manufacturing activity of identifying and maintaining an orderly environment for preventing errors and contamination in the manufacturing process.

house of quality (HOQ)–A structured process that relates customer-defined attributes to the product's technical features needed to support and generate these attributes. This technique achieves this mapping by means of a six-step process: (1) identification of customer attributes; (2) identification of supporting technical features; (3) correlation of the customer attributes with the supporting technical features; (4) assignment of priorities to the customer requirements and technical features; (5) evaluation of competitive stances and competitive products; and (6) identification of those technical features to be used (deployed) in the final design of the product. HOQ is part of the quality function deployment (QFD) process and forces designers to consider customer needs and the degree to which the proposed designs satisfy these needs. See: customer-defined attributes, quality function deployment.

human factors engineering–A merging of those branches of engineering and the behavioral sciences that concern themselves principally with the human component in the design and operation of human-machine systems. Human factors engineering is based on a fundamental knowledge and study of human physical and mental abilities and emotional characteristics.

hurdle rate–The minimum acceptable rate of return on a project.

hybrid inventory system–An inventory system combining features of the fixed reorder quantity inventory model and the fixed reorder cycle inventory model. Features of the fixed reorder cycle inventory model and the fixed reorder quantity inventory model can be combined in many different ways. For example, in the order point-periodic review combination system, an order is placed if the inventory level drops below a specified level before the review date; if not, the order quantity is determined at the next review date. Another hybrid inventory system is the optional replenishment model. See: fixed reorder cycle inventory model, fixed reorder quantity inventory model, optional replenishment model, order point system.

hypothesis testing–Use of statistical models to test conclusions about a population or universe based on sample information.

I

idle capacity–The capacity generally not used in a system of linked resources. Idle capacity consists of protective capacity and excess capacity. See: excess capacity, productive capacity, protective capacity.

idle time–Time when operators or resources (e.g., machines) are not producing product because of setup, maintenance, lack of material, lack of tooling, or not being scheduled. Syn: wait time.

IFB–Abbreviation for *invitation for bid*.

IIE–Abbreviation for *Institute of Industrial Engineers*.

imperfection–A quality characteristic's departure from its intended level or state without any association to conformance to specification requirements or to the usability of a product or service. See: blemish, defect, nonconformity.

implementation–The act of installing a system into operation. It concludes the system project with the exception of appropriate follow-up or post-installation review.

implode–1) Compression of detailed data in a summary-level record or report. 2) Tracing a usage and/or cost impact from the bottom to the top (end product) of a bill of material using where-used logic.

implosion–The process of determining the where-used relationship for a given component. Implosion can be single-level (showing only the parents on the next higher level) or multilevel (showing the ultimate top-level parent). See: where-used list. Ant: explosion.

import/export license–Official authorization issued by a government allowing the shipping or delivery of a product across national boundaries.

inactive inventory–Stock designated as in excess of consumption within a defined period or stocks of items that have not been used for a defined period.

inbound stockpoint–A defined location next to the place of use on a production floor to which materials are brought as needed and from which material is taken for immediate use. Inbound stockpoints are used with a pull system of material control.

incentive–A reward, financial or otherwise, that compensates a worker for high or continued performance above standard. An incentive is also a motivating influence to induce effort above normal.

incentive contract–A contract where the buyer and seller agree to a target cost and maximum price. Cost savings below the target are shared between buyer and seller. If actual cost exceeds the target cost, the cost overrun is shared between buyer and seller up to the maximum price.

incoming business–The number of orders, the dollar value of orders, or the quantity of units that have been received on orders from customers. This volume is particularly important to the forecaster, who must compare incoming business against the forecast rather than against actual shipments when actual shipments do not reflect true customer demand. This situation may exist because of back-ordered items, bottlenecks in the shipping room, etc.

in-control process–A process in which the statistical measure being evaluated is in a state of statistical control (i.e., the variations among the observed sampling results can be attributed to a constant system of chance causes). Ant: out-of-control process.

incremental analysis–A method of economic analysis in which the cost of a single additional unit is compared to its revenue. When the net contribution of an additional unit is zero, total contribution is maximized.

incremental cost–1) Cost added in the process of finishing an item or assembling a group of items. If the cost of the components of a given assembly equals $5 and the additional cost of assembling the components is $1, the incremental assembly cost is $1, while the total cost of the finished assembly is $6. 2) Additional cost incurred as a result of a decision.

indented bill of material–A form of multilevel bill of material. It exhibits the highest level parents closest to the left margin, and all the components going into these parents are shown indented toward the right. All subsequent levels of components are indented farther to the right. If a component is used in more than one parent within a given product structure, it will appear more than once, under every subassembly in which it is used.

indented tracking–The following of all lot numbers of intermediates and ingredients consumed in the manufacture of a given batch of product down through all levels of the formula.

indented where-used–A listing of every parent item, and the respective quantities required, as well as each of their respective parent items, continuing until the ultimate end item or level-0 item is referenced. Each of these parent items calls for a given component item in a bill-of-material file. The component item is shown closest to the left margin of the listing, with each parent indented to the right, and each of their respective parents indented even further to the right.

independent demand–Demand for an item that is unrelated to the demand for other items. Demand for finished goods, parts required for destructive testing, and service parts requirements are examples of independent demand.

independent demand item management models–Models for the management of items whose demand is not strongly influenced by other items managed by the same company. These models can be characterized as follows: (1) stochastic or deterministic, depending on the variability of demand and other factors; (2) fixed quantity, fixed cycle, or hybrid (optional replenishment). See: fixed reorder cycle inventory model, fixed reorder quantity inventory model, optional replenishment model.

indicator–An index of business activities.

indirect costs–Costs that are not directly incurred by a particular job or operation. Certain utility costs, such as plant heating, are often indirect. An indirect cost is typically distributed to the product through the overhead rates.

indirect labor–Work required to support production in general without being related to a specific product; e.g., floor sweeping.

indirect materials–Syn: supplies.

industrial engineering–The engineering discipline concerned with facilities layout, methods measure and improvement, statistical quality control, job design and evaluation, and the use of management sciences to solve business problems.

industrial facilities management–The installation and maintenance of the physical plant, its surroundings, and the physical assets of an organization.

industry analysis–A major study of an industry; its major competitors, customers, and suppliers; and the focus and driving forces within that industry.

infinite loading–Calculation of the capacity required at work centers in the time periods required regardless of the capacity available to perform this work.

information–Data arranged or presented so that they yield an understanding not available from any single data element.

ingredient–In the process industries, the raw material or component of a mixture. See: component.

in-process inventory–Syn: work in process.

input–Work arriving at a work center or production facility.

input control–Management of the release of work to a work center or production facility.

input/output control–A technique for capacity control where planned and actual inputs and planned and actual outputs of a work center are monitored. Planned inputs and outputs for each work center are developed by capacity requirements planning and approved by manufacturing management. Actual input is compared to planned input to identify when work center output might vary from the plan because work is not available at the work center. Actual output is also compared to planned output to identify problems within the work center. Syn: production monitoring. See: capacity control.

input/output devices–Modems, terminals, or various pieces of equipment whose designed purpose relates to manual, mechanical, electronic, visual, or audio entry to and from the computer's processing unit.

inspection–Measuring, examining, testing, or gauging one or more characteristics of a product or service and comparing the results with specified requirements to determine whether conformity is achieved for each characteristic.

inspection order–An authorization to an inspection department or group to perform an inspection operation.

inspection ticket–Frequently used as a synonym for an inspection order; more properly a reporting of an inspection function performed.

instantaneous receipt–The receipt of an entire lot-size quantity in a very short period of time.

instant pudding–A term used to illustrate an obstacle to achieving quality: the supposition that quality and productivity improvement are achieved quickly through an affirmation of faith rather than through sufficient effort and education.

instruction sheet–Syn: routing.

interactive–A characteristic of those applications where a user communicates with a computer program via a terminal, entering data and receiving responses from the computer.

interactive scheduling–Computer scheduling where the process is either automatic or manually interrupted to allow the scheduler the opportunity to review and change the schedule.

interactive system–A data processing system in which the response to an inquiry is developed within the system within a time period acceptable to the user and regarded as immediate.

interest–1) Financial share in a project or enterprise. 2) Periodic compensation for lending money. 3) In an economy study, synonymous with required return, expected profit, or charge for the use of capital. 4) The cost for the use of capital. Sometimes referred to as the time value of money.

interest rate–The ratio of the interest payment to the principal for a given unit of time. It is usually expressed as a percentage of the principal.

intermediately positioned warehouse–Warehouse located between customers and manufacturing plants to provide increased customer service and reduced distribution cost.

intermediate part–Material processed beyond raw material and used in higher level items. See: component.

intermittent production–A form of manufacturing in which the jobs pass through the functional departments in lots, and each lot may have a different routing. See: job shop.

intermodal transport–1) Shipments moved by different types of equipment combining the best features of each mode. 2) Use of two or more different carrier modes in the through movement of a shipment.

internal controls–The policies and procedures, the documentation, and the plan for an organization that authorize transactions, safeguard assets, and maintain the accuracy of financial records.

internal customer–The recipient (person or department) of another person's or department's output (product, service, or information) within an organization. See: customer, external customer.

internal failure cost–The cost of things that go wrong before the product reaches the customer. Internal failure costs usually include rework, scrap, downgrades, reinspection, retest, and process losses.

internal rate of return–The rate of compound interest at which the company's outstanding investment is repaid by proceeds from the project.

internal setup time–Time associated with elements of a setup procedure performed while the process or machine is not running. Ant: external setup time.

international logistics–All functions concerned with the movement of materials and finished goods on a global scale.

interoperation time–The time between the completion of one operation and the start of the next.

interplant demand–One plant's need for a part or product that is produced by another plant or division within the same organization. Although it is not a customer order, it is usually handled by the master production scheduling system in a similar manner. See: interplant transfer.

interplant transfer–The shipment of a part or product by one plant to another plant or division within the corporation. See: interplant demand, transfer pricing.

interpolation–The process of finding a value of a function between two known values. Interpolation may be performed numerically or graphically.

interrelationship diagram–A technique used to define how factors relate to one another. Complex multivariable problems or desired outcomes can be displayed with their interrelated factors. The logical and often causal relationships between the factors can be illustrated.

interrogate–Retrieve information from computer files by use of predefined inquiries or unstructured queries handled by a high-level retrieval language.

interrupt–A break in the normal flow of a computer routine such that the flow can be resumed from that point at a later time. An interrupt is usually caused by a signal from an external source.

intransit inventory–Material moving between two or more locations, usually separated geographically; for example, finished goods being shipped from a plant to a distribution center.

intransit lead time–The time between the date of shipment (at shipping point) and the date of receipt (at the receiver's dock). Orders normally specify the date by which goods should be at the dock. Consequently, this date should be offset by intransit lead time for establishing a ship date for the supplier.

intrinsic forecast–A forecast based on internal factors, such as an average of past sales. Ant: extrinsic forecast.

inventory–1) Those stocks or items used to support production (raw materials and work-in-process items),

supporting activities (maintenance, repair, and operating supplies), and customer service (finished goods and spare parts). Demand for inventory may be dependent or independent. Inventory functions are anticipation, hedge, cycle (lot size), fluctuation (safety, buffer, or reserve), transportation (pipeline), and service parts. 2) In the theory of constraints, inventory is defined as those items purchased for resale and includes finished goods, work in process, and raw materials. Inventory is always valued at purchase price and includes no value-added costs, as opposed to the traditional cost accounting practice of adding direct labor and allocating overhead as work in process progresses through the production process.

inventory accounting–The branch of accounting dealing with valuing inventory. Inventory may be recorded or valued using either a perpetual or a periodic system. A perpetual inventory record is updated frequently or in real time, while a periodic inventory record is counted or measured at fixed time intervals, e.g., every two weeks or monthly. Inventory valuation methods of LIFO, FIFO, or average costs are used with either recording system.

inventory buffer–Inventory used to protect the throughput of an operation or the schedule against the negative effects caused by statistical fluctuations. Syn: inventory cushion. See: fluctuation inventory, safety stock.

inventory control–The activities and techniques of maintaining the desired levels of items, whether raw materials, work in process, or finished products. Syn: material control.

inventory cushion–Syn: inventory buffer.

inventory cycle–The length of time between two consecutive replenishment shipments.

inventory diversion–The shipment of parts against a project or contract other than the original project or contract for which the items were purchased.

inventory investment–The dollars that are in all levels of inventory.

inventory management–The branch of business management concerned with planning and controlling inventories.

inventory policy–A statement of a company's goals and approach to the management of inventories.

inventory shrinkage–Losses of inventory resulting from scrap, deterioration, pilferage, etc.

inventory tax–Tax based on the value of inventory on hand at a particular time.

inventory turnover–The number of times that an inventory cycles, or "turns over," during the year. A frequently used method to compute inventory turnover is to divide the average inventory level into the annual cost of sales. For example, an average inventory of $3 million divided into an average cost of sales of $21 million means that inventory turned over seven times. Syn: inventory turns, turnover.

inventory turns–Syn: inventory turnover.

inventory usage–The value or the number of units of an inventory item consumed over a period of time.

inventory valuation–The value of the inventory at either its cost or its market value. Because inventory value can change with time, some recognition is taken of the age distribution of inventory. Therefore, the cost value of inventory is usually computed on a first-in-first-out (FIFO) basis, last-in-first-out (LIFO) basis, or a standard cost basis to establish the cost of goods sold.

inventory write-off–A deduction of inventory dollars from the financial statement because the inventory is of less value. An inventory write-off may be necessary because the value of the physical inventory is less than its book value or because the items in inventory are no longer usable.

invitation for bid (IFB)–Syn: request for proposal.

I/O–1) Abbreviation for *input/output control.* 2) Abbreviation for *computer input/output.*

Ishikawa diagram–Syn: cause-and-effect diagram.

islands of automation–Stand-alone pockets of automation (robots, CAD/CAM systems, numerical control machines) that are not connected into a cohesive system.

isolation–The determination of the location of a failure through the use of accessory support and diagnostic equipment.

ISO 9000 Series Standards–A set of five individual but related international standards on quality management and quality assurance developed to help companies effectively document the quality system elements to be implemented to maintain an efficient quality system. The standards, initially published in 1987, are not specific to any particular industry, product, or service. The standards were developed by the International Standards Organization (ISO), a specialized international agency for standardization composed of the national standards bodies of 91 countries.

issue–1) The physical movement of items from a stocking location. 2) Often, the transaction reporting of this activity.

issue cycle–The time required to generate a requisition for material, pull the material from an inventory location, and move it to its destination.

item–Any unique manufactured or purchased part, material, intermediate, subassembly, or product.

item master record–Syn: item record.

item number–A number that serves to uniquely identify an item. Syn: part number, product number, stock code, stock number.

item record–The "master" record for an item. Typically it contains identifying and descriptive data

and control values (lead times, lot sizes, etc.) and may contain data on inventory status, requirements, planned orders, and costs. Item records are linked together by bill of material records (or product structure records), thus defining the bill of material. Syn: item master record, part master record, part record.

J

jidoka–The Japanese term for the practice of stopping the production line when a defect occurs.

jig–A device used to position a piece of work during machining. See: fixture.

JIT–Acronym for *Just-in-Time.*

JIT supplier environment–To effectively participate as a supplier under Just-in-Time (JIT), a company must supply components and subassemblies in exact quantities, delivery time, and quality. Shipments are made within narrow time windows that are rigidly enforced. Virtually every component must be delivered on time and be within specifications.

job analysis–A process of gathering (by observation, interview, or recording systems) significant task-oriented activities and requirements about work required of employees.

job costing–A cost accounting system in which costs are assigned to specific jobs. This system can be used with either actual or standard costs in the manufacturing of distinguishable units or lots of products. Syn: job order costing.

job description–A formal statement of duties, qualifications, and responsibilities associated with a particular job.

job enlargement–An increase in the number of tasks that an employee performs. Job enlargement is associated with the design of jobs, particularly production jobs, and its purpose is to reduce employee dissatisfaction.

job enrichment–An increase in the number of tasks that an employee performs and an increase in the control over those tasks. It is associated with the design of jobs in the firm and especially the production worker's job. Job enrichment is an extension of job enlargement.

job grade–A form of job evaluation that assigns jobs to predetermined job classifications according to the job's relative worth to the organization. Pay scales are usually set for each job grade.

job lot–A specific quantity of a part or product that is produced at one time.

job order–Syn: manufacturing order.

job order costing–Syn: job costing.

job progress chart–Syn: Gantt chart.

job rotation–The practice of an employee periodically changing job responsibilities to provide a broader perspective and a view of the organization as a total system, to enhance motivation, and to provide cross-training.

job shop–An organization in which similar equipment is organized by function. Each job follows a distinct routing through the shop. See: intermittent production.

job shop layout–Syn: functional layout.

job shop scheduling–The production planning and control techniques used to sequence and prioritize production quantities across operations in a job shop.

job status–A periodic report showing the plan for completing a job (usually the requirements and completion date) and the progress of the job against that plan.

job ticket–Syn: time ticket.

joint order–An order on which several items are combined to obtain volume or transportation discounts.

joint replenishment–Coordinating the lot sizing and order release decision for related items and treating them as a family of items. The objective is to achieve lower costs because of ordering, setup, shipping, and quantity discount economies. This term applies equally to joint ordering (family contracts) and to composite part (group technology) fabrication scheduling.

judgment items–Those inventory items that cannot be effectively controlled by algorithms because of age (new or obsolete product) or management decision (promotional product).

Just-in-Time (JIT)–A philosophy of manufacturing based on planned elimination of all waste and continuous improvement of productivity. It encompasses the successful execution of all manufacturing activities required to produce a final product, from design engineering to delivery and including all stages of conversion from raw material onward. The primary elements of Just-in-Time are to have only the required inventory when needed; to improve quality to zero defects; to reduce lead times by reducing setup times, queue lengths, and lot sizes; to incrementally revise the operations themselves; and to accomplish these things at minimum cost. In the broad sense, it applies to all forms of manufacturing, job shop and process, as well as repetitive. Syn: short-cycle manufacturing, stockless production, zero inventories.

K

kaizen–The Japanese term for improvement; continuing improvement involving everyone–managers and workers. In manufacturing, kaizen relates to finding and eliminating waste in machinery, labor, or production methods. See: continuous process improvement.

kanban–A method of Just-in-Time production that uses standard containers or lot sizes with a single card attached to each. It is a pull system in which work centers signal with a card that they wish to withdraw parts from feeding operations or suppliers. The Japanese word *kanban*, loosely translated, means *card, billboard,* or *sign.* The term is often used synonymously for the specific scheduling system developed and used by the Toyota Corporation in Japan. See: move card, production card, synchronized production.

key point backflush–Syn: count point backflush.

kickback–A payment to a firm or its employees from a contractor to get the award of business.

kit–The components of a parent item that have been pulled from stock and readied for movement to a production area. Syn: kitted material, layout, staged material.

kitted material–Syn: kit.

kitting–The process of constructing and staging kits.

knowledge-based system–A computer program that employs knowledge of the structure of relations and reasoning rules to solve problems by generating new knowledge from the relationships about the subject.

knowledge worker–A worker whose job is the accumulation, transfer, validation, analysis, and creation of information.

L

laboratory order–Syn: experimental order.

labor chit–Syn: time ticket.

labor claim–A factory worker's report listing the jobs the employee has worked on, the number of pieces, number of hours, etc., and often the amount of money to which the employee is entitled. A labor claim is usually made on a labor chit or time ticket. Syn: labor ticket, labor voucher.

labor cost–The dollar amount of labor performed during manufacturing. This amount is added to direct material cost and overhead cost to obtain total manufacturing cost.

labor efficiency–1) Syn: worker efficiency. 2) The average of worker efficiency for all direct workers in a department or facility.

labor grade–A classification of workers whose capability indicates their skill level or craft. See: skill-based compensation, skills inventories.

labor productivity–A partial productivity measure, the rate of output of a worker or group of workers per unit of time compared to an established standard or rate of output. Labor productivity can be expressed as output per unit of time or output per labor hour. See: machine productivity.

labor ticket–Syn: labor claim.

labor voucher–Syn: labor claim.

LAN–Acronym for *local area network.*

lap phasing–Syn: overlapped schedule.

last in, first out (LIFO)–Method of inventory valuation for accounting purposes. The assumption is made that the most recently received (last in) is the first to be used or sold (first out), but there is no necessary relationship with the actual physical movement of specific items.

late finish date (LF)–The latest time an activity can be completed without delaying the completion of a project network. This date is determined by back scheduling from the network completion date. See: early finish date, early start date, late start date.

lateness–Delivery date minus due date. Lateness may be positive or, in the case of early jobs, negative. See: earliness, tardiness.

late order–Syn: past due order.

late start date (LS)–The latest time an activity may begin without delaying the project finish date of the network. This date is calculated as the late finish minus the duration of the activity. See: early finish date, early start date, late finish date.

layout–1) Physical arrangement of resources or centers of economic activity (machines, groups of people, workstations, storage areas, aisles, etc.) within a facility. Layouts include product (linear or line), functional (job shop or process), cellular, and fixed position. 2) Syn: kit.

LBO–Abbreviation for *leveraged buyout.*

LCL–1) Abbreviation for *less than carload* (lot shipment). 2) Abbreviation for *lower control limit.*

leading indicator–A specific business activity index that indicates future trends. For example, housing starts is a leading indicator for the industry that supplies builders' hardware.

lead time–1) A span of time required to perform a process (or series of operations). 2) In a logistics context, the time between recognition of the need for an order and the receipt of goods. Individual components of lead time can include order preparation time, queue time, processing time, move or transportation time, and receiving and inspection time. Syn: total lead time. See: manufacturing lead time, purchasing lead time.

lead-time inventory–Inventory that is carried to cover demand during the lead time.

lead-time offset–A technique used in MRP where a planned order receipt in one time period will require the release of that order in an earlier time period based on the lead time for the item. Syn: component lead-time offset, offsetting.

lean manufacturing–Syn: lean production.

lean production–A philosophy of production that emphasizes the minimization of the amount of all the resources (including time) used in the various activities of the enterprise. It involves identifying and eliminating non-value-adding activities in design, production, supply chain management, and dealing with the customers. Lean producers employ teams of multiskilled workers at all levels of the organization and use highly flexible, increasingly automated machines to produce volumes of products in potentially enormous variety. Syn: lean manufacturing.

learning curve–A curve reflecting the rate of improvement in skills as more units of an item are made. This planning technique is particularly useful in project-oriented industries where new products are frequently phased. The basis for the learning curve calculation is that workers will be able to produce the product more quickly after they get used to making it. Syn: experience curve, manufacturing progress curve.

least squares method–A method of curve fitting that selects a line of best fit through a plot of data to minimize the sum of squares of the deviations of the given points from the line. See: regression analysis.

least total cost–A dynamic lot-sizing technique that calculates the order quantity by comparing the setup (or ordering) costs and the carrying cost for various lot sizes and selects the lot size where these costs are most nearly equal. See: discrete order quantity, dynamic lot sizing.

least unit cost–A dynamic lot-sizing technique that adds ordering cost and inventory carrying cost for each trial lot size and divides by the number of units in the lot size, picking the lot size with the lowest unit cost. See: discrete order quantity, dynamic lot sizing.

less than carload (LCL)–Either a small shipment that does not fill the railcar or a shipment of not enough weight to qualify for a carload quantity rate discount.

less than truckload (LTL)–Either a small shipment that does not fill the truck or a shipment of not enough weight to qualify for a truckload quantity (usually set at about 10,000 lbs.) rate discount, offered to a general commodity trucker.

letter of credit–An assurance by a bank that payment will be made as long as the sales terms agreed to by the buyer and seller are met. This method of payment for sales contracts provides a high degree of protection for the seller.

level–Every part or assembly in a product structure is assigned a level code signifying the relative level in which that part or assembly is used within the product structure. Often times the end items are assigned level 0 with the components and subassemblies going into it assigned to level 1 and so on. The MRP explosion process starts from level 0 and proceeds downward one level at a time.

level loading–Syn: load leveling.

level of service–A desired measure (usually expressed as a percentage) of satisfying demand through inventory or by the current production schedule in time to satisfy the customers' requested delivery dates and quantities. In a make-to-stock environment, level of service is sometimes calculated as the percentage of orders picked complete from stock upon receipt of the customer order, the percentage of line items picked complete, or the percentage of total dollar demand picked complete. In make-to-order and design-to-order environments, level of service is the percentage of time that the customer-requested or acknowledged date was met by shipping complete product quantities. Syn: measure of service, service level.

level production method–A production planning method that maintains a stable production rate while varying inventory levels to meet demand.

level schedule–1) In traditional management, a production schedule or master production schedule that generates material and labor requirements that are as evenly spread over time as possible. Finished goods inventories buffer the production system against seasonal demand. See: level production method. 2) In JIT, a level schedule (usually constructed monthly) ideally means scheduling each day's worth of customer demand to be built on the day it will be shipped. A level schedule is the output of the load leveling process. See: load leveling.

leveraged buyout (LBO)–An acquisition of a company using borrowed funds. Generally, the funds are borrowed, and the assets of the firm to be acquired are used as collateral. The funds are to be paid back with cash flows of the acquired firm. A leveraged buyout is more risky than an acquisition through stock issuance, and the acquisition price is usually higher than the stock price value.

LF–Abbreviation for *late finish date*.

life cycle analysis–A quantitative forecasting technique based on applying past patterns of demand data covering introduction, growth, maturity, saturation, and decline of similar products to a new product family.

life cycle costing–The identification, evaluation, tracking, and accumulation of actual costs for each product from its initial research and development through final customer servicing and support in the marketplace.

life testing–The simulation of a product's life under controlled real-world conditions to see if it holds up and performs as required.

LIFO–Acronym for *last in, first out*.

lightless plant–Syn: dark factory.

LIMIT–Acronym for *lot-size inventory management interpolation technique*.

limited life material–Material having a finite shelf life.

limiting operation–The operation with the least capacity in a series of operations with no alternative routings. The capacity of the total system can be no greater than the limiting operation, and as long as this limiting condition exists, the total system can be effectively scheduled by scheduling the limiting operation and providing this operation with proper buffers. See: protective capacity, protective inventory.

line–A specific physical space for the manufacture of a product that in a flow shop layout is represented by a straight line. This may be in actuality a series of pieces of equipment connected by piping or conveyor systems.

linear decision rules–A modeling technique using simultaneous equations, e.g., the establishment of aggregate work force levels, based upon minimizing the total cost of hiring, firing, holding inventory, backorders, payroll, overtime, and undertime.

linearity–1) Production at a constant quantity. 2) Use of resources at a level rate, typically measured daily or more frequently.

linear layout–A layout of various machines in one straight line. This type of layout makes it difficult to reallocate operations among workers and machinery.

linear production–Actual production to a level schedule, so that a plotting of actual output versus planned output forms a straight line, even when plotted for a short segment of time.

linear programming–Mathematical models for solving linear optimization problems through minimization or maximization of a linear function subject to linear constraints. For example, in blending gasoline and other petroleum products, many intermediate distillates may be available. Prices and octane ratings as well as upper limits on capacities of input materials that can be used to produce various grades of fuel are given. The problem is to blend the various inputs in such a way that (1) cost will be minimized (profit will be maximized), (2) specified optimum octane ratings will be met, and (3) the need for additional storage capacity will be avoided.

line balancing–1) The balancing of the assignment of the tasks to workstations in a manner that minimizes the number of workstations and minimizes the total amount of idle time at all stations for a given output level. In balancing these tasks, the specified time requirement per unit of product for each task and its sequential relationship with the other tasks must be considered. 2) A technique for determining the product mix that can be run down an assembly line to provide a fairly consistent flow of work through that assembly line at the planned line rate.

line efficiency–A measure of actual work content versus cycle time of the limiting operation in a production line. Line efficiency (percentage) is equal to the sum of all station task times divided by the longest task time multiplied by the number of stations. In an assembly line layout, the line efficiency is 100% minus the balance delay percentage.

line item–One item on an order, regardless of quantity.

line loading–The loading of a production line by multiplying the total pieces by the rate per piece for each item to come up with a finished schedule for the line.

line of balance planning–A project planning technique using a lead-time offset chart and a chart of required final assembly completions to graph a third bar chart showing the number of each component that should be completed to date. This bar chart forms a descending line, and aggregate component completions are then plotted against this line of balance. This is a crude form of material planning.

live load–Syn: available work.

load–The amount of planned work scheduled for and actual work released to a facility, work center, or operation for a specific span of time. Usually expressed in terms of standard hours of work or, when items consume similar resources at the same rate, units of production.

load center–Syn: work center.

load leveling–Spreading orders out in time or rescheduling operations so that the amount of work to be done in sequential time periods tends to be distributed evenly and is achievable. Although both material and labor are ideally level loaded, specific businesses and industries may load to one or the other exclusively (e.g., service industries). Syn: capacity smoothing, level loading. See: level schedule.

load profile–A display of future capacity requirements based on released and/or planned orders over a given span of time. See: capacity requirements plan, load projection.

load projection–Syn: load profile.

local area network (LAN)–A high-speed data communication system for linking computer terminals, programs, storage, and graphic devices at multiple workstations distributed over a relatively small geographic area such as a building or campus.

local measures–That set of measurements that relates to a resource, operation, process, or part and usually has low correlation to global organization measures. Examples are errors per printed page, departmental efficiency, and volume discounts.

location audit–A methodical verification of the location records for an item or group of items in inventory to ensure that when the record shows an item's location, it is, in fact, in that location.

locator file–A file used in a stockroom (or anywhere) providing information on where each item is located. See: locator system.

locator system–A system for maintaining a record of the storage locations of items in inventory. See: locator file.

logistics–In an industrial context, the art and science of obtaining, producing, and distributing material and product in the proper place and in proper quantities. In a military sense (where it has greater usage), its meaning can also include the movement of personnel.

logistics system–The planning and coordination of the physical movement aspects of a firm's operations such that a flow of raw materials, parts, and finished goods is achieved in a manner that minimizes total costs for the levels of service desired.

log normal distribution–A continuous probability distribution where the logarithms of the variable are normally distributed.

long-range resource planning–Syn: resource planning.

long-term planning–Business planning that addresses the strategic needs of the organization. See: business plan, resource planning.

loose standard–A standard time greater than that required by a qualified worker with normal skill and effort.

loss leader pricing–Pricing some products below cost to attract customers into the store, in the expectation that they will buy other items as well.

lost time factor–The complement of productivity, that is, one minus the productivity factor. It can also be calculated as the planned hours minus standard hours earned, divided by the planned hours.

lot–A quantity produced together and sharing the same production costs and specifications. See: batch.

lot-for-lot–A lot-sizing technique that generates planned orders in quantities equal to the net requirements in each period. See: discrete order quantity.

lot number–A unique identification assigned to a homogeneous quantity of material. Syn: batch number, mix number.

lot number control–Assignment of unique numbers to each instance of receipt and carrying forth that number into subsequent manufacturing processes so that, in review of an end item, each lot consumed from raw materials through end item can be identified as having been used for the manufacture of this specific end item lot.

lot number traceability–Tracking parts by lot numbers to a group of items. This tracking can assist in tracing quality problems to their source. A lot number identifies a designated group of related items manufactured in a single run or received from a vendor in a single shipment.

lot operation cycle time–Length of time required from the start of setup to the end of cleanup for a production lot at a given operation, including setup, production, and cleanup.

lot size–The amount of a particular item that is ordered from the plant or a supplier or issued as a standard quantity to the production process. Syn: order quantity.

lot-size code–A code that indicates the lot-sizing technique selected for a given item. Syn: order policy code.

lot-size inventory–Inventory that results whenever quantity price discounts, shipping costs, setup costs, or similar considerations make it more economical to purchase or produce in larger lots than are needed for immediate purposes.

lot-size inventory management interpolation technique (LIMIT)–A technique for looking at the lot sizes for groups of similar products to determine the effect economic lot sizes will have on the total inventory, total setup costs, and machine availability.

lot-size system–Syn: fixed reorder quantity inventory model.

lot sizing–The process of, or techniques used in, determining lot size. Syn: order policy.

lot splitting–Dividing a lot into two or more sublots and simultaneously processing each sublot on identical (or very similar) facilities as separate lots, usually to compress lead time or to expedite a small quantity. Syn: operation splitting.

lot tolerance percent defective (LTPD)–Expressed in percent defective, the poorest quality in an individual lot that should be accepted. *Note:* The LTPD is used as a basis for some inspection systems, and is commonly associated with a small consumer's risk.

lot traceability–The ability to identify the lot or batch number of product in terms of one or all of the following: its composition, purchased parts, manufacturing date, or shipped items. In certain regulated industries, lot traceability may be a legislative requirement.

lower control limit (LCL)–Control limit for points below the central line in a control chart.

lower specification limit (LSL)–In statistical process control, charting the line that defines the minimum acceptable level of random output.

low-level code–A number that identifies the lowest level in any bill of material at which a particular component appears. Net requirements for a given component are not calculated until all the gross requirements have been calculated down to that level. Low-level codes are normally calculated and maintained automatically by the computer software. Syn: explosion level.

LS–Abbreviation for *late start date*.

LSL–Abbreviation for *lower specification limit*.

LTL–Abbreviation for *less than truckload*.

LTPD–Abbreviation for *lot tolerance percent defective*.

lumpy demand–Syn: discontinuous demand.

M

machine center–A production area consisting of one or more machines (and, if appropriate for capacity planning, the necessary support personnel) that can be considered as one unit for capacity requirements planning and detailed scheduling.

machine hours–The amount of time, in hours, that a machine is actually running. Machine hours, rather than labor hours, may be used for planning capacity and scheduling and for allocating costs.

machine loading–The accumulation by workstations, machine, or machine group of the hours generated from the scheduling of operations for released orders by time period. Machine loading differs from capacity requirements planning in that it does not use the planned orders from MRP but operates solely from released orders. It may be of limited value because of its limited visibility of resources.

machine productivity–A partial productivity measure. The rate of output of a machine per unit of time compared with an established standard or rate of output. Machine productivity can be expressed as output per unit of time or output per machine hour. See: labor productivity.

machine utilization–A measure of how intensively a machine is being used. Machine utilization compares the actual machine time (setup and run time) to available time.

machining center–A machine capable of performing a variety of metal removal operations on a part, usually under numerical control.

MAD–Acronym for *mean absolute deviation*.

maintainability–The characteristic of equipment design and installation that provides the ability for the equipment to be repaired easily and efficiently.

maintenance, repair, and operating supplies (MRO)–Items used in support of general operations and maintenance such as maintenance supplies, spare parts, and consumables used in the manufacturing process and supporting operations.

major setup–The equipment setup and related activities required to manufacture a group of items in sequence, exclusive of the setup required for each item in the group.

make-or-buy decision–The act of deciding whether to produce an item in house or buy it from an outside supplier.

make-to-order–A production environment where a product or service can be made after receipt of a customer's order. The final product is usually a combination of standard items and items custom-designed to meet the special needs of the customer. Where options or accessories are stocked before customer orders arrive, the term *assemble-to-order* is frequently used. See: assemble-to-order, make-to-stock.

make-to-stock–A production environment where products can be and usually are finished before receipt of a customer order. Customer orders are typically filled from existing stocks, and production orders are used to replenish those stocks. See: assemble-to-order, make-to-order.

Malcolm Baldrige National Quality Award–An award established by Congress in 1987 to raise awareness of quality management and to recognize U.S. companies that have implemented successful quality management systems. Two awards may be given annually in each of three categories: manufacturing company, service company, and small business. The award is named after the late Secretary of Commerce Malcolm Baldrige, a proponent of quality management. The U.S. Commerce Department's National Institute of Standards and Technology manages the award, and ASQC administers it.

management by objectives (MBO)–A participative goal-setting process that enables the manager or supervisor to construct and communicate the goals of the department to each subordinate. At the same time, the subordinate is able to formulate personal goals and influence the department's goals.

management estimation–A judgmental forecasting technique whereby responsible executives predict the demand for new products or alter a quantitative forecast for existing products largely based on experience and intuition. Other judgmental forecasting techniques may be used in combination with management estimation to improve the accuracy of the estimate. See: Delphi method, historical analogy, panel consensus, pyramid forecasting.

management information system (MIS)–A manual or computerized system that anticipates the wide use of data for management planning and control purposes. Accordingly, the data are organized in a database and are readily available to a variety of management functions.

management science–Syn: operations research.

man-hour–A unit of measure representing one person working for one hour. The combination of "n" people working for "h" hours produces *nh* man-hours. Frequent qualifications to the definition include (1) designation of work effort as normal effort; (2) designation of time spent as actual hours.

manual rescheduling–The most common method of rescheduling open orders (scheduled receipts). Under this method, the MRP system provides information on the part numbers and order numbers that need to be rescheduled. Due dates and order quantity changes required are then analyzed and changed by material planners or other authorized persons. Syn: planner intervention. Ant: automatic rescheduling.

manufacturability–A measure of the design of a product or process in terms of its ability to be produced easily, consistently, and with high quality.

manufacturing authorization–Syn: manufacturing order.

manufacturing automation protocol (MAP)–An application-specific protocol based on the International Standards Organization's open systems interconnection (OSI) standards. It is designed to allow communication between a company's computers and computers from different vendors in the manufacturing shop floor environment.

manufacturing calendar–A calendar used in inventory and production planning functions that consecutively numbers only the working days so that the component and work order scheduling may be done based on the actual number of workdays available. Syn: M-day calendar, planning calendar, production calendar, shop calendar.

manufacturing cycle–Syn: manufacturing lead time.

manufacturing data sheet–Syn: routing.

manufacturing engineering–The engineering discipline concerned with designing and improving production processes.

manufacturing environment–The framework in which manufacturing strategy is developed and implemented. Elements of the manufacturing environment include external environmental forces, corporate strategy, business unit strategy, other functional strategies (marketing, engineering, finance, etc.), product selection, product/process design, product/process technology, and management competencies. Often refers to whether a company, plant, product or service is make-to-stock, make-to-order, or assemble-to-order.

manufacturing execution system (MES)–A factory floor information and communication system with several functional capabilities. It includes functions such as resource allocation and status, operation/detailed scheduling, dispatching production units, document control, data collection and acquisition, labor management, quality management, process management, maintenance management, product tracking and genealogy, and performance analysis. It can provide feedback from the factory floor on a real-time basis. It interfaces with and complements accounting-oriented, resource planning systems.

manufacturing instruction–A set of detailed instructions for carrying out a manufacturing process. It is usually referenced by the routing and thus can simplify the content of the routing.

manufacturing layout strategies–An element of manufacturing strategy. It is the analysis of physical capacity, geography, functional needs, corporate philosophy, and product-market/process focus to systematically respond to required facility changes driven by organizational, strategic, and environmental considerations.

manufacturing lead time–The total time required to manufacture an item, exclusive of lower level purchasing lead time. For make-to-order products, it is the length of time between the release of an order to production process and shipment to the final customer. For make-to-stock products, it is the length of time between the release of an order to the production process and receipt into finished inventory. Included here are order preparation time, queue time, setup time, run time, move time, inspection time, and put-away time. Syn: manufacturing cycle, production cycle, production lead time. See: lead time.

manufacturing order–A document, group of documents, or schedule conveying authority for the manufacture of specified parts or products in specified quantities. Syn: job order, manufacturing authorization, production order, production release, run order, shop order. See: assembly parts list, batch card, blend order, fabrication order, work order.

manufacturing order reporting–Syn: production reporting and status control.

manufacturing philosophy–The set of guiding principles, driving forces, and ingrained attitudes that helps communicate goals, plans, and policies to all employees and that is reinforced through conscious and subconscious behavior within the manufacturing organization.

manufacturing process–The series of operations performed upon material to convert it from the raw material or a semifinished state to a state of further completion. Manufacturing processes can be arranged in a process layout, product layout, cellular layout, or fixed-position layout. Manufacturing processes can be planned to support make-to-stock, make-to-order, assemble-to-order, etc., based on the strategic use and placement of inventories.

manufacturing process development–The definition and implementation of an execution system for making a part, product, or service that is consistent with the objectives of the firm.

manufacturing progress curve–Syn: learning curve.

manufacturing ramp-up–The final phase of new product and process development, whereby the new product moves from pilot production to full-scale manufacturing.

manufacturing release–The issuance of a manufacturing order into the factory.

manufacturing resource planning (MRP II)–A method for the effective planning of all resources of a manufacturing company. Ideally, it addresses operational planning in units, financial planning in dollars, and has a simulation capability to answer "what if" questions. It is made up of a variety of functions, each linked together: business planning, sales and operations planning, production planning, master production scheduling, material requirements planning, capacity requirements planning, and the execution support systems for capacity and material. Output from these systems is integrated with financial reports such as the business plan, purchase commitment report, shipping budget, and inventory projections in dollars. Manufacturing resource planning is a direct outgrowth and extension of closed-loop MRP.

manufacturing strategy–A collective pattern of decisions that act upon the formulation and deployment of manufacturing resources. To be most effective, the manufacturing strategy should act in support of the overall strategic direction of the business and provide for competitive advantages (edges).

manufacturing volume strategy–An element of manufacturing strategy that includes a series of assumptions and predictions about long-term market, technology, and competitive behavior in the following areas: (1) the predicted growth and variability of demand, (2) the costs of building and operating different sized plants, (3) the rate and direction of technological improvement, (4) the likely behavior of competitors, and (5) the anticipated impact of international competitors, markets, and sources of supply. It is the sequence of specific volume decisions over time that determines an organization's long-term manufacturing volume strategy.

MAP–Acronym for *manufacturing automation protocol*.

MAPI method–1) A procedure for equipment replacement analysis sponsored by the Machinery and Allied Products Institute. 2) A method of capital investment analysis that has been formulated by the Machinery and Allied Products Institute. This method uses a fixed format and provides charts and graphs to facilitate calculations. A prominent feature of this method is that it explicitly includes obsolescence.

marginal cost–The incremental costs incurred when the level of output of some operation or process is increased by one unit.

marginal pricing–Pricing products at a markup over the marginal cost of producing the next item. Marginal costs generally include the variable cost of producing and selling an additional item.

marginal revenue–The incremental sales dollars received when the level of output of some operation is increased by one unit.

market demand–The amount of a product or service that people are ready to buy at a given price.

market driven–Responding to customers' needs.

market hedge–Scheduling or holding an inventory quantity greater than the expected demand because of expected inaccuracy or volatility in the forecasted demand. See: hedge.

marketing cost analysis–The study and evaluation of the relative profitability or costs of different marketing operations in terms of customers, marketing units, commodities, territories, or marketing activities. Cost accounting is typically used.

marketing research–The systematic gathering, recording, and analyzing of data about problems relating to the marketing of goods and services. Such research may be undertaken by impartial agencies or by business firms or their agents. Marketing research includes several types: (1) *Market analysis* (product potential is a type) is the study of the size, location, nature, and characteristics of markets, (2) *Sales analysis* (or research) is the systematic study and comparison of sales (or consumption) data, (3) *Consumer research (*motivation research is a type) is concerned with the discovery and analysis of consumer attitudes, reactions, and preferences.

market penetration–The degree to which a product has been accepted by the marketplace.

market-positioned warehouse–Warehouse positioned to replenish customer inventory assortments and to afford maximum inbound transport consolidation economies from inventory origin points with relatively short-haul local delivery.

market segmentation–A marketing strategy in which the total market is disaggregated into submarkets, or segments, sharing some measurable characteristic based on demographics, psychographics, life style, geography, benefits, etc.

market share–The actual portion of current market demand that a company or product achieves.

mass customization–The ability to mass-produce customized products at a low cost and high volume.

mass production–High-quantity production characterized by specialization of equipment and labor. See: continuous production.

master budget–The document that consolidates all other budgets of an organization into an overall plan, including the projection of a cash flow statement and an operating statement for the budget period as well as a balance sheet for the end of the budget period. Syn: static budget.

master file–A main reference file of information, such as the item master file and work center file. See: detail file.

master planning–A grouping of the business processes that includes the following activities: demand management (which includes forecasting and order servicing); production and resource planning; and master scheduling (which includes the final assembly schedule, the master schedule, and the rough-cut capacity plan).

master production schedule (MPS)–1) The anticipated build schedule for those items assigned to the master scheduler. The master scheduler maintains this schedule, and in turn, it becomes a set of planning numbers that drives material requirements planning. It represents what the company plans to produce expressed in specific configurations, quantities, and dates. The master production schedule is not a sales forecast that represents a statement of demand. The master production schedule must take into account the forecast, the production plan, and other important considerations such as backlog, availability of material, availability of capacity, and management policies and goals. Syn: master schedule. 2) The result of the master scheduling process. The master schedule is a presentation of demand, forecast, backlog, the MPS, the projected on-hand inventory, and the available-to-promise quantity. See: master scheduler, master scheduling.

master route sheet–The authoritative route process sheet from which all other format variations and copies are derived.

master schedule–Syn: master production schedule.

master schedule item–A part number selected to be planned by the master scheduler. The item is deemed critical in its impact on lower level components or resources such as skilled labor, key machines, or dollars. Therefore, the master scheduler, not the computer, maintains the plan for these items. A master schedule item may be an end item, a component, a pseudo number, or a planning bill of material.

master scheduler–Often the job title of the person charged with the responsibility of managing, establishing, reviewing, and maintaining a master schedule for select items. Ideally the person should have substantial product, plant, process, and market knowledge because the consequences of this individual's actions often have a great impact on customer service, material, and capacity planning. See: master production schedule.

master scheduling–That process where the master schedule is reviewed and adjustments are made to the master production schedule to ensure that inventory levels and customer service goals are maintained and proper capacity and material planning occurs. See: master production schedule.

material analyst–Person assigned responsibility for and identification of the planning requirements for specific items and responsibility for each order.

material control–Syn: inventory control.

material-dominated scheduling (MDS)–A technique that schedules materials before processors (equipment or capacity). This process facilitates the efficient use of materials. MDS can be used to schedule each stage in a process flow scheduling system. MRP systems use material-dominated scheduling logic.

material flexibility–The ability of the transformation process to handle unexpected variations in material inputs.

material list–Syn: picking list.

material planner–1) The person normally responsible for managing the inventory levels, schedules, and availability of selected items, either manufactured or purchased. 2) In an MRP system, the person responsible for reviewing and acting on order release, action, and exception messages from the system. Syn: parts planner, planner.

material requirements plan–The result from the process of material requirements planning.

material requirements planning (MRP)–A set of techniques that uses bill of material data, inventory data, and the master production schedule to calculate requirements for materials. It makes recommendations to release replenishment orders for material. Further, because it is time-phased, it makes recommendations to reschedule open orders when due dates and need dates are not in phase. Time-phased MRP begins with the items listed on the MPS and determines (1) the quantity of all components and materials required to fabricate those items and (2) the date that the components and material are required. Time-phased MRP is accomplished by exploding the bill of material, adjusting for inventory quantities on hand or on order, and offsetting the net requirements by the appropriate lead times.

material review board (MRB)–An organization within a company, often a standing committee, that determines the resolution or disposition of items that have questionable quality or other attributes.

materials efficiency–A concept that addresses the efficiency with which materials are obtained, converted, and shipped in the overall purchasing, production, and distribution process. It can be considered as a companion concept to labor efficiency, and it is potentially more significant as the materials portion of cost of goods sold continues to grow.

materials handling time–The time necessary to move material from one work center to the next work center. This time includes waiting for the material handling equipment and actual movement time.

materials management–The grouping of management functions supporting the complete cycle of material flow, from the purchase and internal control of production materials to the planning and control of work in process to the warehousing, shipping, and distribution of the finished product.

materials requisition–1) An authorization that identifies the items and quantities to be withdrawn from inventory. 2) An authorization that identifies the items and quantities to be included in a purchase order. Syn: production materials requisition.

material usage variance–The difference between the planned or standard requirements for materials to produce a given item and the actual quantity used for a particular instance of manufacture.

material yield–The ratio of usable or salable product produced compared with the total quantity input to a production run.

materiel–A term, used more frequently in nonmanufacturing organizations, to refer to the equipment, apparatus, and supplies used by an organization.

mathematical programming–The general problem of optimizing a function of several variables subject to a number of constraints. If the function and constraints are linear in the variables and a subset of the constraints restricts the variables to be nonnegative, we have a linear programming problem.

matrix–A mathematical array having one, two, and sometimes more dimensions, into which collections of data may be stored and processed.

matrix bill of material–A chart made up from the bills of material for a number of products in the same or similar families. It is arranged in a matrix with components in columns and parents in rows (or vice versa) so that requirements for common components can be summarized conveniently.

matrix chart–A graphical technique used to analyze the relationship between two related groups of ideas.

maximum allowable cost–In service organizations, the limit of reimbursement allowed by an agency for the cost of a supply item.

maximum demonstrated capacity–The highest amount of actual output produced in the past when all efforts have been made to "optimize" the resource; for instance, overtime, additional personnel, extra hours, extra shifts, reassignment of personnel, or use of any related equipment. Maximum demonstrated capacity is the most one could ever expect to produce in a short period of time but represents a rate that cannot be maintained over a long period of time. See: demonstrated capacity.

maximum inventory–The planned maximum allowable inventory for an item based on its planned size and target safety stock.

maximum order quantity–An order quantity modifier, applied after the lot size has been calculated, that limits the order quantity to a preestablished maximum.

MBO–Abbreviation for *management by objectives*.

M-day calendar–Syn: manufacturing calendar.

M-days–Available manufacturing days excluding holidays and weekends.

MDS–Abbreviation for *material-dominated scheduling*.

mean–The arithmetic average of a group of values. Syn: arithmetic mean.

mean absolute deviation (MAD)–The average of the absolute values of the deviations of observed values from some expected value. MAD can be calculated based on observations and the arithmetic mean of those observations. An alternative is to calculate absolute deviations of actual sales data minus forecast data. These data can be averaged in the usual arithmetic way or with exponential smoothing.

mean time between failures (MTBF)–The average time interval between failures for repairable product for a defined unit of measure (e.g., operating hours, cycles, miles).

mean time for failures (MTFF)–Average time for failure of a nonrepairable product (expected life) or average time to first failure of a repairable product.

measure of service–Syn: level of service.

median–The middle value in a set of measured values when the items are arranged in order of magnitude. If there is no single middle value, the median is the mean of the two middle values.

mediation–The introduction of a neutral third party who attempts to provide alternatives to issues causing conflict that have not been put forth by either party or to change the way the parties perceive the situation. It is often used in collective bargaining to reach an agreement.

MES–Abbreviation for *manufacturing execution system.*

metered issues–Issues of parts or materials from stores in quantities that correspond to the rate at which materials are used.

methods analysis–That part of methods engineering normally involving an examination and analysis of an operation or a work cycle broken down into its constituent parts to improve the operation, eliminate unnecessary steps, and/or establish and record in detail a proposed method of performance.

methods-time measurement (MTM)–A system of predetermined motion-time standards, a procedure that analyzes and classifies the movements of any operation into certain human motions and assigns to each motion a predetermined time standard selected by the nature of the motion and the conditions under which it was made.

milestone schedule–A schedule consisting of key events or milestones selected as a result of coordination between the client's and the contractor's project management. These events are generally critical accomplishments planned at time intervals throughout the project and used as a basis to monitor overall project performance. The format may be either network or bar chart and may contain minimal detail at a highly summarized level.

military standards–Product standards and specifications for products for the military or defense contractors, units, suppliers, etc. These standards sometimes become de facto standards within the civilian community.

milk run–A regular route for pickup of mixed loads from several suppliers. For example, instead of each of five suppliers sending a truckload per week to meet the weekly needs of the customer, one truck visits each of the suppliers on a daily basis before delivering to the customer's plant. Five truckloads per week are still shipped, but each truckload contains the daily requirement from each supplier. See: consolidation.

minimum cost order quantity–Syn: economic order quantity.

minimum inventory–The planned lowest amount or level of inventory for an item.

minimum order quantity–An order quantity modifier, applied after the lot size has been calculated, that increases the order quantity to a preestablished minimum.

min-max system–A type of order point replenishment system where the "min" (minimum) is the order point, and the "max" (maximum) is the "order up to" inventory level. The order quantity is variable and is the result of the max minus available and on-order inventory. An order is recommended when the sum of the available and on-order inventory is at or below the min.

minor setup–The incremental setup activities required when changing from one item to another within a group of items.

MIS–Abbreviation for *management information system.*

mission statement–The company statement of purpose.

mistake-proofing–Syn: failsafe work methods, poka-yoke.

mix control–The control of the individual items going through the plant.

mixed-flow scheduling–A procedure used in some process industries for building process train schedules that start at an initial stage and work toward the terminal process stages. This procedure is effective for scheduling where several bottleneck stages may exist. Detailed scheduling is done at each bottleneck stage.

mixed-model master schedule–The technique of setting and maintaining the master production schedule to support mixed-model production.

mixed-model production–Making several different parts or products in varying lot sizes so that a factory produces close to the same mix of products that will be sold that day. The mixed-model schedule governs the making and the delivery of component parts, including those provided by outside suppliers. The goal is to build every model every day, according to daily demand.

mix flexibility–The ability to handle a wide range of products or variants by using equipment having short setup times.

mix forecast–Forecast of the proportion of products that will be sold within a given product family, or the proportion of options offered within a product line. Product and option mix must be forecasted as well as aggregate product families. Even though the appropriate level of units is forecasted for a given product line, an inaccurate mix forecast can create material shortages and inventory problems.

mix number–Syn: lot number.

mix ticket–A listing of all the raw materials, ingredients, components, etc., that are required to perform a mixing, blending, or similar operation. This listing is often printed on a paper ticket, which also may be used as a turnaround document to report component quantities actually used, final quantity actually produced, etc. This term is often used in batch process or chemical industries. See: assembly parts list, batch card, blend formula, manufacturing order.

mode–The most common or frequent value in a group of values.

model–A representation of a process or system that attempts to relate the most important variables in the system in such a way that analysis of the model leads to insights into the system. Frequently, the model is used to anticipate the result of a particular strategy in the real system.

modification flexibility–The capability of the transformation process to quickly implement minor product design changes.

modular bill of material–A type of planning bill that is arranged in product modules or options. It is often used in companies where the product has many optional features, e.g., assemble-to-order companies such as automobile manufacturers. See: pseudo bill of material.

modular system–A system-design method that recognizes that different levels of experience exist in organizations and develops the system to provide for segments or modules to be installed at a rate compatible with the user's ability to implement the system.

Monte Carlo simulation–A subset of digital simulation models based on random or stochastic processes.

move–The physical transportation of inventory from one location to another within a facility. Movements are usually made under the direction and control of the inventory system.

move card–In a Just-in-Time context, a card or other signal indicating that a specific number of units of a particular item are to be taken from a source (usually an outbound stockpoint) and taken to a point of use (usually an inbound stockpoint). It authorizes the movement of one part number between a single pair of work centers. The card circulates between the outbound stockpoint of the supplying work center and the inbound stockpoint of the using work center. Syn: move signal. See: kanban.

movement inventory–A type of in-process inventory that arises because of the time required to move goods from one place to another.

move order–The authorization to move a particular item from one location to another.

move signal–Syn: move card.

move ticket–A document used in dispatching to authorize or record movement of a job from one work center to another. It may also be used to report other information, such as the actual quantity or the material storage location.

move time–The time that a job spends in transit from one operation to another in the plant.

moving average–An arithmetic average of a certain number *(n)* of the most recent observations. As each new observation is added, the oldest observation is dropped. The value of *n* (the number of periods to use for the average) reflects responsiveness versus stability in the same way that the choice of smoothing constant does in exponential smoothing.

MPS–Abbreviation for *master production schedule*.

MRB–Abbreviation for *material review board*.

MRO–Abbreviation for *maintenance, repair, and operating supplies*.

MRP–Abbreviation for *material requirements planning*.

MRP II–Abbreviation for *manufacturing resource planning*.

MTBF–Abbreviation for *mean time between failures*.

MTFF–Abbreviation for *mean time for failures*.

MTM–Abbreviation for *methods-time measurement*.

multilevel bill of material–A display of all the components directly or indirectly used in a parent, together with the quantity required of each component. If a component is a subassembly, blend, intermediate, etc., all its components and all their components also will be exhibited, down to purchased parts and materials.

multilevel master production schedule–A master scheduling technique that allows any level in an end item's bill of material to be master scheduled. To accomplish this, MPS items must receive requirements from independent and dependent demand sources. See: two-level master production schedule.

multilevel where-used–A display for a component listing all the parents in which that component is directly used and the next higher level parents into which each of those parents is used, until ultimately all top-level (level 0) parents are listed.

multiple-item lot-sizing models–Processes or systems used to determine the total replenishment order quantity for a group of related items.

multiple regression models–A form of regression analysis where the model involves more than one independent variable, such as developing a forecast of dishwasher sales based upon housing starts, gross national product, and disposable income.

multisourcing–Procurement of a good or service from more than one independent supplier. Ant: single sourcing.

multivariate control chart–A control chart for evaluating the stability of a process in terms of the levels of two or more variables or characteristics.

N

n–Sample size (the number of units in a sample).

NAPM–Abbreviation for *National Association of Purchasing Managers*.

NC–Abbreviation for *numerical control*.

national stock number (NSN)–The individual identification number assigned to an item to permit inventory management in the federal (U.S.) supply system.

need date–The date when an item is required for its intended use. In an MRP system, this date is calculated by a bill-of-material explosion of a schedule and the netting of available inventory against that requirement.

negotiation–The process by which a buyer and a vendor agree upon the conditions surrounding the purchase of an item.

nervousness–The characteristic in a MRP system when minor changes in higher level (e.g., level 0 or 1) records or the master production schedule cause significant timing or quantity changes in lower level (e.g., level 5 or 6) schedules and orders.

net change MRP–An approach in which the material requirements plan is continually retained in the computer. Whenever a change is needed in requirements, open order inventory status, or bill of material, a partial explosion and netting is made for only those parts affected by the change. See: requirements alteration. Ant: regeneration MRP.

net inventory–Syn: available inventory.

net present value–The present value of future earnings (operating expenses have been deducted from net operating revenues) for a given number of time periods.

net requirements–In MRP, the net requirements for a part or an assembly are derived as a result of applying gross requirements and allocations against inventory on hand, scheduled receipts, and safety stock. Net requirements, lot-sized and offset for lead time, become planned orders.

net sales–Sales dollars the company receives; gross sales minus returns and allowances.

netting–The process of calculating net requirements.

net weight–The weight of an article exclusive of the weights of all packing materials and containers.

network–1) The interconnection of computers, terminals, and communications channels to facilitate file and peripheral device sharing as well as effective data communication. 2) A graph consisting of nodes connected by arcs.

network planning–A generic term for techniques that are used to plan complex projects. Two of the best known network planning techniques are the critical path method (CPM) and the program evaluation and review technique (PERT).

node–One of the defining points of a network–a junction point joined to some or all of the others by arcs.

noise–The unpredictable or random difference between the observed data and the "true process."

nominal capacity–Syn: rated capacity.

nominal group technique–A technique, similar to brainstorming, used by teams to generate ideas on a particular subject. Team members are asked to silently come up with as many ideas as possible, writing them down. Each member is then asked to share one idea, which is recorded. After all the ideas are recorded, they are discussed and prioritized by the group.

nomogram–A computational aid consisting of two or more scales drawn and arranged so that the results of calculations may be found by the linear connection of points on them. Historically, it was used for calculating economic lot sizes or sample sizes for work measurement observations. Also called an *alignment chart*.

nonconforming material–Any raw material, part, component, or product with one or more characteristics that depart from the specifications, drawing, or other approved product description.

nonconformity–The nonfulfillment of a specified requirement. See: blemish, defect, imperfection.

nondurable goods–Goods whose serviceability is generally limited to a period of less than three years (such as perishable goods and semidurable goods).

nonexempt positions–Employees not meeting the test of executive, supervisory, or administrative personnel who are paid overtime, as defined by the Fair Labor Standards Act.

nonlinear programming–Programming similar to linear programming but incorporating a nonlinear objective function and linear constraints or a linear objective function and nonlinear constraints or both a nonlinear objective function and nonlinear constraints.

nonproduction material (NPM)–Items (indirect materials supplies) in the manufacturing process or in the maintenance or operation of a facility that do not generally become part of the final product.

nonrecurring material–Tooling, gauges, and facilities necessary in the manufacturing of the final product and not consumed during manufacturing or shipped with the final product.

nonscheduled hours–Hours when a machine is not generally available to be scheduled for operation; e.g., nights, weekends, holidays, lunch breaks, major repair, and rebuilding.

nonsignificant part number–A part number that is assigned to each part but does not convey any information about the part. Nonsignificant part numbers are identifiers, not descriptors. Ant: significant part number.

normal and proper usage–Operation of the equipment with a program of regular maintenance in accordance with generally accepted practices and within the rated capacity and service classification for which it was specified and designed.

normal distribution–A particular statistical distribution where most of the observations fall fairly close to one mean, and a deviation from the mean is as likely to be plus as it is to be minus. When graphed, the normal distribution takes the form of a bell-shaped curve.

normalize–To adjust observed data to a standard base.

no-touch exchange of dies (NTED)–The exchange of dies without human intervention.

np chart–A control chart for evaluating the stability of a process in terms of the total number of units in a sample in which an event of a given classification occurs. Syn: number of affected units chart.

NPM–Abbreviation for *nonproduction material.*

NSN–Abbreviation for *national stock number.*

NTED–Abbreviation for *no-touch exchange of dies.*

number of affected units chart–Syn: np chart.

numerical control (NC)–A means of operating a machine tool automatically by the use of coded numerical instructions.

O

objective function–The goal or function that is to be optimized in a model. Most often it is a cost function that should be minimized subject to some restrictions or a profit function that should be maximized subject to some restrictions.

object-oriented programming (OOP)–The use of coding techniques and tools that reflect the concept of viewing the business environment as a set of elements (or objects) with associated properties, e.g., data, data manipulation/actions, inheritance. The objects encapsulate through data and functions the properties of the business that are of interest.

obligated material–Syn: reserved material.

obsolescence–1) The condition of being out of date. A loss of value occasioned by new developments that place the older property at a competitive disadvantage. A factor in depreciation. 2) A decrease in the value of an asset brought about by the development of new and more economical methods, processes, or machinery. 3) The loss of usefulness or worth of a product or facility as a result of the appearance of better or more economical products, methods, or facilities.

Occupational Safety and Health Act (OSHA)–A federal (U.S.) law that applies to all employers in the United States who are engaged in interstate commerce. Its purpose is to ensure safe and healthful working conditions by authorizing enforcement of the standards provided under the act.

OC curve–Abbreviation for *operating characteristic curve.*

OCR–Abbreviation for *optical character recognition.*

OD–Abbreviation for *organizational development.*

OEM–Abbreviation for *original equipment manufacturer.*

offal material–The by-product or waste of production processes, e.g., chips, shavings, and turnings.

off-grade–A product whose physical or chemical properties fall outside the acceptable ranges.

offload–To reschedule or use alternate routings to reduce the work load on a machine, work center, or facility.

offset quantity–Syn: overlap quantity.

offsetting–Syn: lead-time offset.

OJT–Abbreviation for *on-the-job training.*

one less at a time–A process of gradually reducing the lot size of the number of items in the manufacturing pipeline to expose, prioritize, and eliminate waste.

one-touch exchange of die (OTED)–The ideal of reducing or eliminating the setup effort required between operations on the same equipment.

on-hand balance–The quantity shown in the inventory records as being physically in stock.

on-order stock–The total of all outstanding replenishment orders. The on-order balance increases when a new order is released, and it decreases when material is received against an order or when an order is canceled.

on-the-job training (OJT)–Learning the skills and necessary related knowledge useful for the job at the place of work or possibly while at work.

on-time schedule performance–A measure (percentage) of meeting the customer's originally negotiated delivery request date. Performance can be expressed as a percentage based on number of orders, line items, or dollar value shipped on time.

OOP–Abbreviation for *object-oriented programming.*

open order–1) A released manufacturing order or purchase order. Syn: released order. See: scheduled receipt. 2) An unfilled customer order.

open period–Accounting time period for which the books will still accept adjusting entries and postings. Ant: closed period.

open systems interconnection (OSI)–A communication system where a user can communicate with another user without being constrained by a particular manufacturer's equipment.

open-to-buy–A control technique used in aggregate inventory management in which authorizations to purchase are made without being committed to specific suppliers. These authorizations are often reviewed by management using such measures as commodity in dollars and by time period.

open-to-receive–Authorization to receive goods, such as a blanket release, firm purchase order item, or supplier schedule. Open-to-receive represents near-term impact on inventory, and is often monitored as a control technique in aggregate inventory management. The total of open-to-receive, other longer term purchase commitments, and open-to-buy represents the material and services cash exposure of the company.

operating characteristic curve (OC curve)–A graph used to determine the probability of accepting lots as a function of the quality level of the lots or processes when using various sampling plans. There are three types: *Type A curves,* which give the probability of acceptance for an individual lot coming from finite production (will not continue in the future); *Type B curves,* which give the probability of acceptance for lots coming from a continuous process; and *Type C curves,* which, for a continuous sampling plan, give the long-run percentage of product accepted during the sampling phase.

operating efficiency–A ratio (represented as a percentage) of the actual output of a piece of equipment, department, or plant as compared to the planned or standard output.

operating expense–In theory of constraints, the quantity of money spent by the firm to convert inventory into sales in a specific time period.

operating system–A conglomeration of software that controls a computer's environment; hardware and the application programs that perform the logical processing of the system. It is a system of programs that controls the execution of computer programs and may provide scheduling, accounting, debugging, and input/output control.

operation–1) A job or task, consisting of one or more work elements, usually done essentially in one location. 2) The performance of any planned work or method associated with an individual, machine, process, department, or inspection. 3) One or more elements that involve one of the following: the intentional changing of an object in any of its physical or chemical characteristics; the assembly or disassembly of parts or objects; the preparation of an object for another operation, transportation, inspection, or storage; planning, calculating, or giving or receiving information.

operation chart–Syn: routing.

operation costing–A method of costing used in batch manufacturing environments when products produced have common, as well as distinguishing, characteristics; for example, suits. The products are identified and costed by batches or by production runs, based on the variations.

operation description–The details or description of an activity or operation to be performed. The operation description is normally contained in the routing document and could include setup instructions, operating instructions (feeds, speeds, heats, pressure, etc.), and required product specifications or tolerances.

operation duration–The total time that elapses between the start of the setup of an operation and the completion of the operation.

operation list–Syn: routing.

operation number–A sequential number, usually two, three, or four digits long, such as 010, 020, 030, that indicates the sequence in which operations are to be performed within an item's routing.

operation overlapping–Syn: overlapped schedule.

operation priority–1) The relative importance an operation is given based on its scheduled due date and/or start date, usually as determined by the back-scheduling process. 2) The relative importance a job is given in a queue of jobs by a priority dispatching heuristic such as shortest processing time first or least slack remaining first.

operation/process yield–The ratio of usable output from a process, process stage, or operation to the input quantity, usually expressed as a percentage.

operation reporting–The recording and reporting of every manufacturing (shop order) operation occurrence on an operation-to-operation basis.

operation sheet–Syn: routing.

operations management–1) The planning, scheduling, and control of the activities that transform inputs into finished goods and services. 2) A field of study that focuses on the effective planning, scheduling, use, and control of a manufacturing or service organization through the study of concepts from design engineering, industrial engineering, management information systems, quality management, production management, inventory management, accounting and other functions as they affect the operation.

operation splitting–Syn: lot splitting.

operations research–1) The development and application of quantitative techniques to the solution of problems. More specifically, theory and methodology in mathematics, statistics, and computing are adapted and applied to the identification, formulation, solution, validation, implementation, and control of decision-making problems. 2) An academic field of study concerned with the development and application of quantitative analysis to the solution of problems faced by management in public and private organizations. Syn: management science.

operations scheduling–The actual assignment of starting or completion dates to operations or groups of operations to show when these operations must be done if the manufacturing order is to be completed on time. These dates are used in the dispatching function. Syn: detailed scheduling, order scheduling, shop scheduling.

operations sequence–The sequential steps for an item to follow in its flow through the plant. For instance, operation 1: cut bar stock; operation 2: grind bar stock; operation 3: shape; operation 4: polish; operation 5: inspect and send to stock. This information is normally maintained in the routing file.

operations sequencing–A technique for short-term planning of actual jobs to be run in each work center based upon capacity (i.e., existing work force and machine availability) and priorities. The result is a set of projected completion times for the operations and simulated queue levels for facilities.

operation start date–The date when an operation should be started so that its order due date can be met. It can be calculated based on scheduled quantities and lead times (queue, setup, run, move) or on the work remaining and the time remaining to complete the job.

operation time–Total of setup (including teardown) and run time for a specific task.

opportunity cost–The return on capital that could have resulted had the capital been used for some purpose other than its present use.

optical character–A printed character frequently used in utilities billing and credit applications that can be read by a machine without the aid of magnetic ink.

optical character recognition (OCR)–A mechanized method of collecting data involving the reading of hand-printed material or special character fonts. If handwritten, the information must adhere to predefined rules of size, format, and locations on the form.

optical scanning–A technique for machine recognition of characters by their images.

optimization–Achieving the best possible solution to a problem in terms of a specified objective function.

option–A choice or feature that must be made by the customer or company in customizing the end product. In many companies, the term "option" means a mandatory choice from a limited selection. See: feature.

optional replenishment model–A form of independent demand item management model in which a review of inventory on hand plus on order is made at fixed intervals. If the actual quantity is lower than some predetermined threshold, a reorder is placed for a quantity $M - x$, where M is the maximum allowable inventory and x is the current inventory quantity. The reorder point, R, may be deterministic or stochastic, and in either instance is large enough to cover the maximum expected demand during the review interval plus the replenishment lead time. The optional replenishment model is sometimes called a *hybrid system* because it combines certain aspects of the fixed reorder cycle inventory model and the fixed reorder quantity inventory model. See: fixed reorder cycle inventory model, fixed reorder quantity inventory model, hybrid inventory system, independent demand item management models.

option overplanning–Typically, planning extra schedule quantities of a master schedule option greater than the expected sales for that option to protect against unanticipated demand. This schedule quantity may only be planned in the period where new customer orders are currently being accepted, typically just after the demand time fence. This technique is usually used on the second level of a two-level master scheduling approach to create a situation where more of the individual options are available than of the overall family. See: demand time fence, hedge.

order–A general term that may refer to such diverse items as a purchase order, shop order, customer order, planned order, or schedule.

order backlog–Syn: backlog.

order control–Control of manufacturing activities by individual manufacturing, job, or shop orders, released by planning personnel and authorizing production personnel to complete a given batch or lot size of a particular manufactured item. Information needed to complete the order (components required, work centers and operations required, tooling required, etc.) may be printed on paper or tickets, often called shop orders or work orders, which are distributed to production personnel. This use of order control sometimes implies an environment where all the components for a given order are picked and issued from a stocking location, all at one time, and then moved as a kit to manufacturing before any activity begins. It is most frequently seen in job shop manufacturing.

order dating–Syn: order promising.

order entry–The process of accepting and translating what a customer wants into terms used by the manufacturer or distributor. This can be as simple as creating shipping documents for finished goods in a make-to-stock environment, or it might be a more complicated series of activities, including design efforts for make-to-order products. See: order service.

order-fill ratio–Syn: customer service ratio.

ordering cost–Used in calculating order quantities, the costs that increase as the number of orders placed increases. It includes costs related to the clerical work of preparing, releasing, monitoring, and receiving orders, the physical handling of goods, inspections, and setup costs, as applicable. Syn: acquisition cost.

order interval–The time period between the placement of orders.

order level system–Syn: fixed reorder cycle inventory model.

order multiples–An order quantity modifier applied after the lot size has been calculated that increases the order quantity to a predetermined multiple.

order picking–Syn: order selection.

order placement–The commitment of a customer to buy a product and the subsequent administrative and data processing steps followed by the supplier.

order point–A set inventory level where, if the total stock on hand plus on order falls to or below that point, action is taken to replenish the stock. The order point is normally calculated as forecasted usage during the replenishment lead time plus safety stock. Syn: reorder point, statistical order point, trigger level. See: fixed reorder quantity inventory model.

order point-order quantity system–Syn: fixed reorder quantity inventory model.

order point system–Inventory method that places an order for a lot whenever the quantity on hand is reduced to a predetermined level known as the order point. Syn: statistical order point system. See: fixed reorder quantity inventory model, hybrid system.

order policy–A set of procedures for determining the lot size and other parameters related to an order. See: lot sizing.

order policy code–Syn: lot-size code.

order preparation—All activities relating to the administration, picking, and packaging of individual customer or work orders.

order preparation lead time—The time needed to analyze requirements and open order status and to create the paperwork necessary to release a purchase order or a production order.

order priority—The scheduled due date to complete all the operations required for a specific order.

order processing—The activity required to administratively process a customer's order and make it ready for shipment or production.

order promising—The process of making a delivery commitment, i.e., answering the question, When can you ship? For make-to-order products, this usually involves a check of uncommitted material and availability of capacity, often as represented by the master schedule available-to-promise. Syn: customer order promising, order dating. See: available-to-promise, order service.

order qualifiers—Those competitive characteristics that a firm must exhibit to be a viable competitor in the marketplace. For example, a firm may seek to compete on characteristics other than price, but in order to "qualify" to compete, its costs and the related price must be within a certain range to be considered by its customers.

order quantity—Syn: lot size.

order quantity modifiers—Adjustments made to a calculated order quantity. Order quantities are calculated based upon a given lot-sizing rule, but it may be necessary to adjust the calculated lot size because of special considerations (scrap, testing, etc.).

order reporting—Recording and reporting the start and completion of the manufacturing order (shop order) in its entirety.

order scheduling—Syn: operations scheduling.

order selection—Selecting or "picking" the required quantity of specific products for movement to a packaging area (usually in response to one or more shipping orders) and documenting that the material was moved from one location to shipping. Syn: order picking.

order service—The function that encompasses receiving, entering, and promising orders from customers, distribution centers, and interplant operations. Order service is also typically responsible for responding to customer inquiries and interacting with the master scheduler on availability of products. In some companies, distribution and interplant requirements are handled separately. See: order entry, order promising.

order shipment—Activity that extends from the time the order is placed upon the vehicle for movement until the order is received, verified, and unloaded at the buyer's destination.

order-up-to level—Syn: target inventory level.

order winners—Those competitive characteristics that cause a firm's customers to choose that firm's products and services over those of its competitors. Order winners can be considered to be competitive advantages for the firm. Order winners usually focus on one (rarely more than two) of the following strategic initiatives: price/cost, quality, delivery speed, delivery reliability, product design, flexibility, aftermarket service, and image.

organizational development (OD)—Process of improving the way in which an organization functions and is managed, particularly in response to change. It operates through planned interventions by a change agent in the organization's processes and is managed by upper management in accordance with the organization's overall goals.

original equipment manufacturer (OEM)—A manufacturer that buys and incorporates another supplier's products into its own products. Also, products supplied to the original equipment manufacturer or sold as part of an assembly. For example, an engine may be sold to an OEM for use as that company's power source for its generator units.

OS&D—Abbreviation for *over, short, and damaged merchandise.*

OSHA—Acronym for *Occupational Safety and Health Act.*

OSI—Abbreviation for *open systems interconnection.*

OTED—Abbreviation for *one-touch exchange of die.*

outbound stockpoint—Designated locations near the point of use on a plant floor to which material produced is taken until it is pulled to the next operation.

outlier—A data point that differs significantly from other data for a similar phenomenon. For example, if the average sales for some product were 10 units per month, and one month had sales of 500 units, this sales point might be considered an outlier. See: abnormal demand.

out-of-control process—A process in which the statistical measure being evaluated is not in a state of statistical control (i.e., the variations among the observed sampling results can be attributed to a constant system of chance causes). Ant: in-control process.

out-of-pocket costs—Costs that involve direct payments such as labor, freight, or insurance, as opposed to depreciation, which does not.

out of spec—A term used to indicate that a unit does not meet a given specification.

outpartnering—The process of involving the supplier in a close partnership with the firm and its operations management system. Outpartnering is characterized by close working relationships between buyers and suppliers, high levels of trust, mutual respect, and emphasis on joint problem-solving and cooperation. With outpartnering, the supplier is viewed not as an alternative source of goods and service (as observed under outsourcing) but rather as a source of knowledge, expertise, and complementary core competencies. Outpartnering is typically found during the early stages of the product life cycle when dealing with products that are viewed as critical to the strategic survival of the firm. See: customer partner, supplier partner.

output–The product being completed by a process or facility. Syn: unload.

output control–A technique for controlling output where actual output is compared to planned output to identify problems at the work center.

output standard–The expected number of units from a process against which actual output will be measured.

outside shop–Suppliers. This term is used to convey the idea that suppliers are an extension of the inside shop or the firm's production facilities.

outsourcing–The process of having suppliers provide goods and services that were previously provided internally. Outsourcing involves substitution–the replacement of internal capacity and production by that of the supplier.

overall factors–Syn: capacity planning using overall factors.

overhead–Costs incurred in the operation of a business that cannot be directly related to the individual products or services produced. These costs, such as light, heat, supervision, and maintenance, are grouped in several pools (department overhead, factory overhead, general overhead) and distributed to units of product or service by some standard allocation method such as direct labor hours, direct labor dollars, or direct materials dollars. See: expense.

overhead allocation–In accounting, the process of applying overhead to a product on the basis of a predetermined rate.

overhead base–The denominator used to calculate the predetermined overhead rate used in applying overhead, e.g., estimated direct labor hours or estimated direct labor dollars.

overhead pool–The collection of overhead costs that are to be allocated over a specified group of products.

overissue–Syn: excess issue.

overlapped schedule–A manufacturing schedule that "overlaps" successive operations. Overlapping occurs when the completed portion of an order at one work center is processed at one or more succeeding work centers before the pieces left behind are finished at the preceding work centers. Syn: lap phasing, operation overlapping, telescoping. See: send ahead. Ant: gapped schedule.

overlap quantity–The amount of items that needs to be run and sent ahead to the following operation before the following "overlap" operation can begin. Syn: offset quantity.

overload–A condition when the total hours of work outstanding at a work center exceed that work center's capacity.

overrun–1) The quantity received from manufacturing or a supplier that is in excess of the quantity ordered. 2) The condition resulting when expenditures exceed the budget.

over, short, and damaged (OS&D) report–A report submitted by a freight agent showing discrepancies in billing received and actual merchandise received.

overstated master production schedule–A schedule that includes either past due quantities or quantities that are greater than the ability to produce, given current capacity and material availability. An overstated MPS should be made feasible before MRP is run.

overtime–Work beyond normal established working hours that usually requires that a premium be paid to the workers.

P

PAC–Acronym for *production activity control.*

packing and marking–Packing for safe shipping and unitizing one or more items of an order, placing into an appropriate container, and marking and labeling the container with customer shipping destination data, as well as other information that may be required.

packing slip–A document that itemizes in detail the contents of a particular package, carton, pallet, or container for shipment to a customer. The detail includes a description of the items, the shipper's or customer's part number, the quantity shipped, and the stockkeeping unit (SKU) of items shipped.

pack-out department–Department that performs the final steps (often including packaging and labeling) before shipment to the customer. See: final assembly department.

pallet ticket–A label to track pallet-sized quantities of end items produced in order to identify the specific sublot with specifications determined by periodic sampling and analysis during production.

panel consensus–A judgmental forecasting technique by which a committee, sales force, or group of experts arrives at a sales estimate. See: Delphi method, management estimation.

paperless purchasing–A purchasing operation that does not employ purchase requisitions or hard-copy purchase orders. In actual practice, a small amount of paperwork usually remains, normally in the form of the supplier schedule.

parallel conversion–A method of system implementation in which the operation of the new system overlaps with the operation of the system being replaced. The old system is discontinued only when the new system is shown to be working properly, thus minimizing the risk consequences of a poor system.

parallel engineering–Syn: participative design/ engineering.

parallel schedule–Use of two or more machines or job centers to perform identical operations on a lot of material. Duplicate tooling and setup are required.

parameter–A coefficient appearing in a mathematical expression, each value of which determines the specific form of the expression. Parameters define or determine the characteristics of behavior of something, as when the mean and standard deviation are used to describe a set of data.

parent item–The item produced from one or more components.

Pareto analysis–Syn: ABC classification.

Pareto chart–A graphical tool for ranking causes from most significant to least significant. It is based on the Pareto principle, which was first defined with respect to quality by J.M. Juran in 1950. The principle, named after 19th-century economist Vilfredo Pareto, suggests that most effects come from relatively few causes; that is, 80% of the effects come from 20% of the possible causes. The Pareto chart is one of the seven tools of quality.

Pareto's law–A concept developed by Vilfredo Pareto, an Italian economist, that states that a small percentage of a group accounts for the largest fraction of the impact, value, etc. In an ABC classification, for example, 20% of the inventory items may constitute 80% of the inventory value. See: ABC classification.

par level–In service operations, the maximum supply volume based on established quotas from previous use for a particular supply item, in a particular department, for a specified time period.

part–Generally, a material item that is used as a component and is not an assembly, subassembly, blend, intermediate, etc.

part coding and classification–A method used in group technology to identify the physical similarity of parts.

part family–A collection of parts grouped for some managerial purpose.

partial order–Any shipment received or shipped that is less than the amount ordered.

partial productivity factor–Syn: single-factor productivity.

participative design/engineering–A concept that refers to the participation of all the functional areas of the firm in the product design activity. Suppliers and customers are often also included. The intent is to enhance the design with the inputs of all the key stakeholders. Such a process should ensure that the final design meets all the needs of the stakeholders and should ensure a product that can be quickly brought to the marketplace while maximizing quality and minimizing costs. Syn: co-design, concurrent design, concurrent engineering, parallel engineering, simultaneous design/engineering, simultaneous engineering, team design/engineering.

part master record–Syn: item record.

part number–Syn: item number.

part period balancing (PPB)–A dynamic lot-sizing technique that uses the same logic as the least total cost method, but adds a routine called *look ahead/look back*. When the look ahead/look back feature is used, a lot quantity is calculated, and before it is firmed up, the next or the previous period's demands are evaluated to determine whether it would be economical to include them in the current lot. See: discrete order quantity, dynamic lot sizing.

part record–Syn: item record.

parts bank–1) In the narrow sense, an accumulation of inventory between operations that serves to keep a subsequent operation running although there are interruptions in the preceding operations. 2) In the larger sense, a stockroom or warehouse. The implication is that the contents of these areas should be controlled like the contents of a bank.

parts planner–Syn: material planner.

parts requisition–An authorization that identifies the item and quantity required to be withdrawn from an inventory. Syn: requisition. See: purchase requisition.

part standardization–A program for planned elimination of superficial, accidental, and deliberate differences between similar parts in the interest of reducing part and supplier proliferation.

part type–A code for a component within a bill of material, e.g., regular, phantom, reference.

passwords–Computer terms for the set of characters that identify a user in order to log onto and use the system.

past due order–A line item on an open customer order that has an original scheduled ship date that is earlier than the current date. Syn: delinquent order, late order. See: backlog, order backlog.

path–The physically continuous, linear series of connected activities throughout a network.

payback–A method of evaluating an investment opportunity that provides a measure of the time required to recover the initial amount invested in a project.

pay for knowledge–A pay restructuring scheme by which competent employees are rewarded for the knowledge they acquire before or while working for an organization, regardless of whether such knowledge is actually being used at any given time.

pay point–Syn: count point.

PC–Abbreviation for *personal computer*.

P chart–A control chart for evaluating the stability of a process in terms of the percentage of the total number of units in a sample in which an event of a given classification occurs over time. P charts are used where it is difficult or costly to make numerical measurements or where it is desired to combine multiple types of defects into one measurement. Syn: percent chart.

PDCA–Abbreviation for *plan-do-check-action*.

pegged requirement–A requirement that shows the next-level parent item (or customer order) as the source of the demand.

pegging–In MRP and MPS, the capability to identify for a given item the sources of its gross requirements and/or allocations. Pegging can be thought of as active where-used information. See: requirements traceability.

percent chart–Syn: P chart.

percent completed–A comparison of work completed to the current projection of total work.

percent of fill–Syn: customer service ratio.

performance–The degree with which an employee applied skill and effort to an operation or task as measured against an established standard. Standard time divided by actual time expressed as a percentage.

performance appraisal–Supervisory or peer analysis of work performance. May be made in connection with wage and salary review, promotion, transfer, or employee training.

performance efficiency–A ratio, usually expressed as a percentage, of the actual processing time for a part divided by its standard processing time. Setups are excluded from this calculation to prevent distortion. A traditional definition includes setup time as part of operation time, but significant distortions can occur as a result of dependent setups.

performance rating–Observation of worker performance to rate productivity in terms of standard or normal.

performance standard–A criterion or benchmark against which actual performance is measured.

period capacity–The number of standard hours of work that can be performed at a facility or work center in a given time period.

period costs–All costs related to a period of time rather than a unit of product, e.g., marketing costs, property taxes.

periodic inventory–A physical inventory taken at some recurring interval, e.g., monthly, quarterly, or annual physical inventory.

periodic replenishment–A method of aggregating requirements to place deliveries of varying quantities at evenly spaced time intervals, rather than variably spaced deliveries of equal quantities.

periodic review system–Syn: fixed reorder cycle inventory model.

period order quantity–A lot-sizing technique under which the lot size is equal to the net requirements for a given number of periods, e.g., weeks into the future. The number of periods to order is variable, each order size equalizing the holding costs and the ordering costs for the interval. See: discrete order quantity, dynamic lot sizing.

perpetual inventory–An inventory recordkeeping system where each transaction in and out is recorded and a new balance is computed.

perpetual inventory record–A computer record or manual document on which each inventory transaction is posted so that a current record of the inventory is maintained.

personal computer (PC)–A microcomputer usually consisting of a CPU, primary storage, and input/output circuitry on one or more boards, plus a variety of secondary storage devices.

PERT–Acronym for *program evaluation and review technique*.

phantom bill of material–A bill-of-material coding and structuring technique used primarily for transient (nonstocked) subassemblies. For the transient item, lead time is set to zero and the order quantity to lot-for-lot. A phantom bill of material represents an item that is physically built, but rarely stocked, before being used in the next step or level of manufacturing. This permits MRP logic to drive requirements straight through the phantom item to its components, but the MRP system usually retains its ability to net against any occasional inventories of the item. This technique also facilitates the use of common bills of material for engineering and manufacturing. Syn: blowthrough, transient bill of material. See: pseudo bill of material.

physical distribution–Syn: distribution.

physical inventory–1) The actual inventory itself. 2) The determination of inventory quantity by actual count. Physical inventories can be taken on a continuous, periodic, or annual basis. Syn: annual inventory count.

pick date–The start date of picking components for a production order. On or before this date, the system produces a list of orders due to be picked, pick lists, tags, and turnaround cards.

picking–The process of withdrawing from stock the components to make the products or the finished goods to be shipped to a customer.

picking list–A document that lists the material to be picked for manufacturing or shipping orders. Syn: disbursement list, material list, stores issue order, stores requisition.

piece parts–Individual items in inventory at the simplest level in manufacturing, e.g., bolts and washers.

piece rate–The amount of money paid for a unit of production. It serves as the basis for determining the total pay for an employee working in a piece-work system.

piece work–Work done on a piece rate.

piggyback–Syn: piggyback trailer on flatcar.

piggyback trailer on flatcar–A specialized form of containerization in which rail and motor transport coordinate. Syn: piggyback, trailer on flatcar.

pilot lot–A relatively small preliminary order for a product. The purpose of this small lot is to correlate the product design with the development of an efficient manufacturing process.

pilot order–Syn: experimental order.

pilot plant–Small-scale production facilities used to develop production processes and to manufacture small quantities of new products for field testing, etc. Syn: semiworks.

pilot test–1) In computer systems, a test before final acceptance of a new business system using a subset of data with engineered cases and documented results. 2) Generally, production of a quantity to verify manufacturability, customer acceptance, or other management requirements before implementation of ongoing production. Syn: walkthrough.

pipeline inventory–Syn: pipeline stock.

pipeline stock–Inventory to fill the transportation network and the distribution system including the flow through intermediate stocking points. The flow time through the pipeline has a major effect on the amount of inventory required in the pipeline. Time factors involve order transmission, order processing, shipping, transportation, receiving, stocking, review time, etc. Syn: pipeline inventory. See: transportation inventory.

plan–A predetermined course of action over a specified period of time that represents a projected response to an anticipated environment to accomplish a specific set of adaptive objectives.

plan-do-check-act cycle–Syn: plan-do-check-action.

plan-do-check-action (PDCA)–A four-step process for quality improvement. In the first step (plan), a plan to effect improvement is developed. In the second step (do), the plan is carried out, preferably on a small scale. In the third step (check), the effects of the plan are observed. In the last step (action), the results are studied to determine what was learned and what can be predicted. The plan-do-check-act cycle is sometimes referred to as the Shewhart cycle (because Walter A. Shewhart discussed the concept in his book *Statistical Method from the Viewpoint of Quality Control*) and as the Deming cycle (because W. Edwards Deming introduced the concept in Japan; the Japanese subsequently called it the Deming cycle). Syn: plan-do-check-act cycle, Shewhart cycle. See: Deming circle.

planned issue–A disbursement of an item predicted by MRP through the creation of a gross requirement or allocation. Syn: controlled issue.

planned issue receipt–A transaction that updates the on-hand balance and the related allocation or open order.

planned load–The standard hours of work required by MRP-recommended (planned) production orders.

planned order–A suggested order quantity, release date, and due date created by the planning system's logic when it encounters net requirements in processing MRP. In some cases, it can also be created by a master scheduling module. Planned orders are created by the computer, exist only within the computer, and may be changed or deleted by the computer during subsequent processing if conditions change. Planned orders at one level will be exploded into gross requirements for components at the next level. Planned orders, along with released orders, serve as input to capacity requirements planning to show the total capacity requirements by work center in future time periods. See: planning time fence.

planned order receipt–That quantity planned to be received at a future date as a result of a planned order release. Planned order receipts differ from scheduled receipts in that they have not been released. Syn: planned receipt.

planned receipt–1) An anticipated receipt against an open purchase order or open production order. 2) Syn: planned order receipt.

planner–Syn: material planner.

planner/buyer–Syn: supplier scheduler.

planner intervention–Syn: manual rescheduling.

planning bill of material–An artificial grouping of items or events in bill-of-material format, used to facilitate master scheduling and material planning. See: hedge, production forecast, pseudo bill of material.

planning board–Syn: control board.

planning calendar–Syn: manufacturing calendar.

planning fence–Syn: planning time fence.

planning horizon–The amount of time the master schedule extends into the future. This is normally set to cover a minimum of cumulative lead time plus time for lot sizing low-level components and for capacity changes of primary work centers or of key suppliers. See: cumulative lead time, planning time fence.

planning time fence–A point in time denoted in the planning horizon of the master scheduling process that marks a boundary inside of which changes to the schedule may adversely affect component schedules, capacity plans, customer deliveries, and cost. Planned orders outside the planning time fence can be changed by system planning logic. Changes inside the planning time fence must be manually changed by the master scheduler. Syn: planning fence. See: cumulative lead time, demand time fence, firm planned order, planning horizon, planned order, time fence.

plant layout–Configuration of the plant site with lines, buildings, major facilities, work areas, aisles, and other pertinent data, such as department boundaries.

plant within a plant–Syn: factory within a factory.

PLC–Abbreviation for *programmable logic controller*.

point of sale (POS)–The relief of inventory and computation of sales data at the time and place of sale, generally through the use of bar coding or magnetic media and equipment.

point-of-use storage–Keeping inventory in specified locations on a plant floor near the operation where it is to be used.

point reporting—The recording and reporting of milestone manufacturing order occurrences, typically done at checkpoint locations rather than operations and easily controlled from a reporting standpoint.

poka-yoke (mistake-proof)—Mistake-proofing techniques, such as manufacturing or setup activity designed in a way to prevent an error from resulting in a product defect. For example, in an assembly operation, if each correct part is not used, a sensing device detects a part was unused and shuts down the operation, thereby preventing the assembler from moving the incomplete part on to the next station or beginning another one. Sometimes spelled *poke-yoke*. Syn: failsafe techniques, failsafe work methods, mistake-proofing.

policies—Definitive statements of what should be done in the business.

population—The entire set of items from which a sample is drawn.

POS—Abbreviation for *point of sale*.

post-deduct inventory transaction processing—A method of inventory bookkeeping where the book (computer) inventory of components is automatically reduced by the computer only after completion of activity on the components' upper level parent item, based on what should have been used as specified in the bill of material and allocation records. This approach has the disadvantage of a built-in differential between the book record and what is physically in stock. Syn: explode-to-deduct. See: backflush.

post-release—The period after the product design has been released to manufacturing when the product has ongoing support and product enhancement.

potency—The measurement of active material in a specific lot, normally expressed in terms of an active unit. Typically used for such materials as solutions.

PPB—Abbreviation for *part period balancing*.

predecessor activity—Any activity that exists on a common path with the activity in question and occurs before the activity in question.

pre-deduct inventory transaction processing—A method of inventory bookkeeping where the book (computer) inventory of components is reduced before issue, at the time a scheduled receipt for their parents or assemblies is created via a bill-of-material explosion. This approach has the disadvantage of a built-in differential between the book record and what is physically in stock.

predetermined motion time—An organized body of information, procedures, techniques, and motion times employed in the study and evaluation of manual work elements. It is useful in categorizing and analyzing all motions into elements whose unit times are computed according to such factors as length, degree of muscle control, and precision. The element times provide the basis for calculating a time standard for the operations. Syn: synthetic time standard.

predictable maintenance—Syn: predictive maintenance.

prediction—An intuitive estimate of demand taking into account changes and new factors influencing the market, as opposed to a forecast, which is an objective projection of the past into the future.

predictive maintenance—A type of preventive maintenance based on nondestructive testing and statistical analysis, used to predict when required maintenance should be scheduled. Syn: predictable maintenance.

pre-expediting—The function of following up on open orders before the scheduled delivery date, to ensure the timely delivery of materials in the specified quantity.

prepaid—A term denoting that transportation charges have been or are to be paid at the point of shipment by the sender.

prerelease—The period of product specification, design, and design review.

prerequisite tree—In the theory of constraints, a logic-based tool for determining the obstacles that block implementation of a problem solution or idea. Once obstacles have been identified, objectives for overcoming obstacles can be determined.

present value—The value today of future cash flows. For example, the promise of $10 a year from now is worth something less than $10 in hand today.

prevention costs—The costs caused by improvement activities that focus on the reduction of failure and appraisal costs. Typical costs include education, quality training, and supplier certification. Prevention costs are one of four categories of quality costs.

prevention vs. detection—A term used to contrast two types of quality activities. Prevention refers to those activities designed to prevent nonconformances in products and services. Detection refers to those activities designed to detect nonconformances already in products and services. Syn: designing in quality vs. inspecting in quality.

preventive maintenance—Activities, including adjustments, replacements, and basic cleanliness, that forestall machine breakdowns. The purpose is to ensure that production quality is maintained and that delivery schedules are met. In addition, a machine that is well cared for will last longer and cause fewer problems.

price analysis—The examination of a seller's price proposal or bid by comparison with price benchmarks, without examination and evaluation of all of the separate elements of the cost and profit making up the price in the bid.

price break—A discount given for paying early, buying in quantity, etc. See: discount.

price discrimination—Selling the same products to different buyers at different prices.

price elasticity—The degree of change in buyer demand in response to changes in product price. It is calculated by dividing the percentage of change in quantity bought by the percentage of change of price.

Prices are considered elastic if demand varies with changes in price. If demand changes only slightly when the price changes, demand is said to be inelastic. For example, demand for most medical services is relatively inelastic, but demand for automobiles is generally elastic.

price fixing—Sellers illegally conspiring to raise, lower, or stabilize prices.

price point—The relative price position at which the product will enter the market compared to direct and indirect competitors' prices. It is considered within the context of the price-range options available: high, medium, or low.

price prevailing at date of shipment—An agreement between a purchaser and a supplier that the price of the goods ordered is subject to change at the supplier's discretion between the date the order is placed and the date the supplier makes shipment and that the then-established price is the contract price.

price protection—An agreement by a supplier with a purchaser to grant the purchaser any reduction in price that the supplier may establish on its goods before shipment of the purchaser's order or to grant the purchaser the lower price should the price increase before shipment. Price protection is sometimes extended for an additional period beyond the date of shipment.

price schedule—The list of prices applying to varying quantities or kinds of goods.

primary location—The designation of a certain storage location as the standard, preferred location for an item.

primary operation—A manufacturing step normally performed as part of a manufacturing part's routing. Ant: alternate operation.

primary work center—The work center where an operation on a manufactured part is normally scheduled to be performed. Ant: alternate work center.

prime costs—Direct costs of material and labor. Prime costs do not include general sales and administrative costs.

prime operations—Critical or most significant operations whose production rates must be closely planned.

priority—In a general sense, the relative importance of jobs, i.e., the sequence in which jobs should be worked on. It is a separate concept from capacity.

priority control—The process of communicating start and completion dates to manufacturing departments in order to execute a plan. The dispatch list is the tool normally used to provide these dates and priorities based on the current plan and status of all open orders.

priority planning—The function of determining what material is needed and when. Master production scheduling and material requirements planning are the elements used for the planning and replanning process to maintain proper due dates on required materials.

private carrier—A firm that owns or leases vehicles and sells transportation services exclusively to its customers.

private warehouse—Company-owned warehouse.

probabilistic demand models—Statistical procedures that represent the uncertainty of demand by a set of possible outcomes (i.e., a probability distribution) and that suggest inventory management strategies under probabilistic demands.

probability—Mathematically, a number between 0 and 1 that estimates the number of experiments (if the same experiment were being repeated many times) in which a particular result would occur. This number can be either subjective or based upon the empirical results of experimentation. It can also be derived for a process to give the probable outcome of experimentation.

probability distribution—A table of numbers or a mathematical expression that indicates the frequency with which each of all possible results of an experiment should occur.

probability tree—A graphic display of all possible outcomes of an event based on the possible occurrences and their associated probabilities.

problem-solving storyboard—A technique based on the plan/do/check/action problem-solving process. The steps being taken and the progress toward the resolution of a problem are continuously planned and updated.

procedure manual—A formal organization and indexing of a firm's procedures. Manuals are usually printed and distributed to the appropriate functional areas.

process—1) A planned series of actions or operations (e.g., mechanical, electrical, chemical, inspection, test) that advances a material or procedure from one stage of completion to another. 2) A planned and controlled treatment that subjects materials or procedures to the influence of one or more types of energy (e.g., human, mechanical, electrical, chemical, thermal) for the time required to bring about the desired reactions or results.

process average—Expected value of the percentage defective of a given manufacturing process.

process batch—The number of units made between sequential setups at a work center. See: batch, exchange unit.

process capability—Refers to the ability of the process to produce parts that conform to (engineering) specifications. Process capability relates to the inherent variability of a process that is in a state of statistical control. See: C_p, C_{pk}, process capability analysis.

process capability analysis—A procedure to estimate the parameters defining a process. The mean and standard deviation of the process are estimated and compared to the specifications, if known. This comparison is the basis for calculating capability indexes.

Additionally, the form of the relative frequency distribution of the characteristic of interest may be estimated. Syn: capability study.

process capability index–The value of the tolerance specified for the characteristic divided by the process capability. There are several types of process capability indexes, including the widely used C_{pk} and C_p.

process chart–Chart that represents the sequence of work or the nature of events in process. It serves as a basis for examining and possibly improving the way the work is carried out.

process control–The function of maintaining a process within a given range of capability by feedback, correction, etc.

process control chart–Syn: control chart.

process controllers–Computers designed to monitor the manufacturing cycle during production, often with the capability to modify conditions, to bring the production back to within prescribed ranges.

process costing–A cost accounting system in which the costs are collected by time period and averaged over all the units produced during the period. This system can be used with either actual or standard costs in the manufacture of a large number of identical units.

process decision program chart–A technique used to show alternate paths to achieving given goals. Applications include preparing contingency plans and maintaining project schedules.

process engineering–The discipline of designing and improving the manufacturing equipment and production process to support the manufacture of a product line.

process flexibility–The speed and ease with which the manufacturing transformation tasks can respond to internal or external changes.

process flow production–A production approach with minimal interruptions in the actual processing in any one production run or between production runs of similar products. Queue time is virtually eliminated by integrating the movement of the product into the actual operation of the resource performing the work.

process flow scheduling–A generalized method for planning equipment usage and material requirements that uses the process structure to guide scheduling calculations. It is used in flow environments common in process industries.

process-focused organization–Firm in which individual facilities are dedicated to one or more process stages rather than to individual products.

process hours–The time required at any specific operation or task to process product.

process improvement–Activities designed to identify and eliminate causes of poor quality, process variation, and non-value-added activities.

process layout–Syn: functional layout.

process list–A list of operations and procedures in the manufacture of product. It may also include a statement of material requirements.

process manufacturing–Production that adds value by mixing, separating, forming, and/or performing chemical reactions. It may be done in either batch or continuous mode.

processor-dominated scheduling–A technique that schedules equipment (processor) before materials. This technique facilitates scheduling equipment in economic run lengths and the use of low-cost production sequences. This scheduling method is used in some process industries.

process sheet–Detailed manufacturing instructions issued to the plant. The instructions may include specifications on speeds, feeds, temperatures, tools, fixtures, and machines and sketches of setups and semifinished dimensions.

process steps–The operations or stages within the manufacturing cycle required to transform components into intermediates or finished goods.

process stocks–Raw ingredients or intermediates available for further processing into marketable products.

process time–The time during which the material is being changed, whether it is a machining operation or an assembly. Process time per piece is

$$\frac{\text{setup time}}{\text{lot size}} + \text{run time/piece}$$

Syn: residence time.

process train–A representation of the flow of materials through a process industry manufacturing system that shows equipment and inventories. Equipment that performs a basic manufacturing step, such as mixing or packaging, is called a *process unit*. Process units are combined into stages, and stages are combined into process trains. Inventories decouple the scheduling of sequential stages within a process train.

procurement–The business functions of procurement planning, purchasing, inventory control, traffic, receiving, incoming inspection, and salvage operations.

procurement cycle–Syn: procurement lead time.

procurement lead time–The time required to design a product, modify or design equipment, conduct market research, and obtain all necessary materials. Lead time begins when a decision has been made to accept an order to produce a new product and ends when production commences. Syn: procurement cycle, total procurement lead time.

producer's risk (α)–For a given sampling plan, the probability of not accepting a lot, the quality of which has a designated numerical value representing a level that it is generally desired to accept. Usually the designated value will be the acceptable quality level (AQL). See: type I error.

producibility–The characteristics of a design that enable the item to be produced and inspected in the quantity required at least cost and minimum time.

product–Any commodity produced for sale, barter, or internal use.

product configuration catalog–A listing of all upper level configurations contained in an end-item product family. Its application is most useful when there are multiple end-item configurations in the same product family. It is used to provide a transition linkage between the end-item level and a two-level master production schedule. It also provides a correlation between the various units of upper level product definition.

product cost–Cost allocated by some method to the products being produced. Initially recorded in asset (inventory) accounts, product costs become an expense (cost of sales) when the product is sold.

product differentiation–Unique product attributes that set off one brand from another.

product diversification–A marketing strategy that seeks to develop new products to supply current markets.

product engineering–The discipline of designing a product or product line to take advantage of process technology and improve quality, reliability, etc.

product family–A group of products with similar characteristics, often used in production planning.

product flexibility–The ease with which current designs can be modified in response to changing market demands.

product genealogy–A record, usually on a computer file, of the history of a product from its introduction into the production process through its termination. The record includes lot or batch sizes used, operations performed, inspection history, options, and where-used information.

product grade–The categorization of goods based upon the range of specifications met during the manufacturing process.

product group forecast–A forecast for a number of similar products.

production activity control (PAC)–The function of routing and dispatching the work to be accomplished through the production facility and performing supplier control. PAC encompasses the principles, approaches, and techniques needed to schedule, control, measure, and evaluate the effectiveness of production operations. See: shop floor control.

production and inventory management–General term referring to the body of knowledge and activities concerned with planning and controlling rates of purchasing, production, distribution, and related capacity resources to achieve target levels of customer service, backlogs, operating costs, inventory investment, manufacturing efficiency, and ultimately, profit and return on investment.

production calendar–Syn: manufacturing calendar.

production card–In a Just-in-Time context, a card or other signal for indicating that items should be made for use or to replace some items removed from pipeline stock. See: kanban.

production control–The function of directing or regulating the movement of goods through the entire manufacturing cycle from the requisitioning of raw material to the delivery of the finished products.

production cycle–Syn: manufacturing lead time.

production cycle elements–Elements of manufacturing strategy that define the span of an operation by addressing the following areas: (1) the established boundaries for the firm's activities, (2) the construction of relationships outside the firm's boundaries (i.e., suppliers, distributors, and customers), (3) circumstances under which changes in established boundaries or relationships are necessary, (4) the effect of such boundary or relationship changes on the firm's competitive position. The production cycle elements must explicitly address the strategic implications of vertical integration in regard to (a) the direction of such expansion, (b) the extent of the process span desired, and (c) the balance among the resulting vertically linked activities.

production forecast–A projected level of customer demand for a feature (option, accessory, etc.) of a make-to-order or an assemble-to-order product. Used in two-level master scheduling, it is calculated by netting customer backlog against an overall family or product line master production schedule and then factoring this product's available-to-promise by the option percentage in a planning bill of material. See: assemble-to-order, planning bill of material, two-level master production schedule.

production lead time–Syn: manufacturing lead time.

production level–Syn: production rate.

production line–A series of pieces of equipment dedicated to the manufacture of a specific number of products or families.

production management–1) The planning, scheduling, execution, and control of the process of converting inputs into finished goods. 2) A field of study that focuses on the effective planning, scheduling, use, and control of a manufacturing organization through the study of concepts from design engineering, industrial engineering, management information systems, quality management, inventory management, accounting, and other functions as they affect the conversion process.

production material–Any material used in the manufacturing process.

production materials requisition–Syn: materials requisition.

production monitoring–Syn: input/output control.

production network–The complete set of all work centers, processes, and inventory points, from raw materials sequentially to finished products and product families. It represents the logical system that provides the framework to attain the strategic objectives of the firm based on its resources and the products' volumes and processes. It provides the general sequential flow and capacity requirement relationships among raw materials, parts, resources, and product families.

production order–Syn: manufacturing order.

production plan–The agreed-upon plan that comes from the aggregate (production) planning function, specifically the overall level of manufacturing output planned to be produced, usually stated as a monthly rate for each product family (group of products, items, options, features, etc.). Various units of measure can be used to express the plan: units, tonnage, standard hours, number of workers, etc. The production plan is management's authorization for the master scheduler to convert it into a more detailed plan, that is, the master production schedule. See: sales and operations planning, sales plan.

production planning–The function of setting the overall level of manufacturing output (production plan) and other activities to best satisfy the current planned levels of sales (sales plan or forecasts), while meeting general business objectives of profitability, productivity, competitive customer lead times, etc., as expressed in the overall business plan. The sales and production capabilities are compared, and a business strategy that includes a production plan, budgets, pro forma financial statements, and supporting plans for materials and work force requirements, etc., is developed. One of its primary purposes is to establish production rates that will achieve management's objective of satisfying customer demand, by maintaining, raising, or lowering inventories or backlogs, while usually attempting to keep the work force relatively stable. Because this plan affects many company functions, it is normally prepared with information from marketing and coordinated with the functions of manufacturing, engineering, finance, materials, etc. See: aggregate planning, sales and operations planning, sales plan.

production planning and control strategies–An element of manufacturing strategy that includes the design and development of manufacturing planning and control systems in relation to the following considerations: (1) market-related criteria–the required level of delivery speed and reliability in a given market segment, (2) process requirement criteria–consistency between process type (job shop, repetitive, continuous, etc.) and the production planning and control system, (3) organization control levels–systems capable of providing long-term planning and short-term control capabilities for strategic and operational considerations by management. Production planning and control strategies help firms develop systems that enable them to exploit market opportunities while satisfying manufacturing process requirements.

production rate–The rate of production usually expressed in units, cases, or some other broad measure, expressed by a period of time, e.g., per hour, shift, day, or week. Syn: production level.

production release–Syn: manufacturing order.

production report–A statement of the output of a production facility for a specified period. The information normally includes the type and quantity of output; workers' efficiencies; departmental efficiencies; costs of direct labor, direct material, and the like; overtime worked; and machine downtime.

production reporting and status control–A vehicle to provide feedback to the production schedule and allow for corrective action and maintenance of valid on-hand and on-order balances. Production reporting and status control normally include manufacturing order authorization, release, acceptance, operation start, move reporting, scrap and rework reporting, order close-out, and payroll interface. Syn: manufacturing order reporting, shop order reporting.

production schedule–A plan that authorizes the factory to manufacture a certain quantity of a specific item. It is usually initiated by the production planning department.

production standard–A time standard to produce piece parts and assemblies.

productive capacity–The maximum of the output capabilities of a resource (or series of resources) or the market demand for that output for a given time period. See: excess capacity, idle capacity, protective capacity.

productivity–1) An overall measure of the ability to produce a good or a service. It is the actual output of production compared to the actual input of resources. Productivity is a relative measure across time or against common entities. In the production literature, attempts have been made to define total productivity where the effects of labor and capital are combined and divided into the output. One example is a ratio that is calculated by adding the standard hours of labor actually produced plus the standard machine hours actually produced in a given time period divided by the actual hours available for both labor and machines in the time period. 2) In economics, the ratio of output in terms of dollars of sales to an input such as direct labor in terms of the total wages. This is also called a *partial productivity measure*.

product layout–Layout of resources arranged sequentially based on the product's routing.

product life cycle–1) The stages a new product idea goes through from beginning to end, i.e., the stages that a product passes through from introduction through growth, maturity, and decline. 2) The time from initial research and development to the time at which sales and support of the product to customers are withdrawn. 3) The period of time during which a product can be produced and marketed profitably.

product line–A group of products whose similarity in manufacturing procedures, marketing characteristics, or specifications allows them to be aggregated for planning, marketing, or, occasionally, costing.

product load profile–A listing of the required capacity and key resources needed to manufacture one unit of a selected item or family. The resource requirements are further defined by a lead-time offset to predict the impact of the product on the load of the key resources by specific time period. The product load profile can be used for rough-cut capacity planning to calculate the approximate capacity requirements of the master production schedule. See: bill of resources, resource profile, rough-cut capacity planning.

product-market-focused organization–A firm in which individual plants are dedicated to manufacturing a specific product or product group.

product mix–The proportion of individual products that make up the total production or sales volume. Changes in the product mix can mean drastic changes in the manufacturing requirements for certain types of labor and material.

product-mix flexibility–The ability to quickly change over to other products produced in a facility, as required by demand shifts in mix.

product number–Syn: item number.

product or service liability–The obligation of a company to make restitution for loss related to personal injury, property damage, or other harm caused by its product or service.

product-positioned warehouse–Warehouse located close to the manufacturing plants that acts as a consolidation point for products.

product positioning–The marketing effort involved to place a product in a market to serve a particular niche or function.

product profiling–1) A graphical device used to ascertain the level of fit between a manufacturing process and the order-winning criteria of its products. Product profiling can be used at the process or company level to compare the manufacturing capabilities with the market requirements to determine areas of mismatch and identify steps needed for realignment. 2) Removing material around a predetermined boundary by means of numerically controlled machining. The numerically controlled tool path is automatically generated on the system.

product quality–Attribute that reflects the capability of a product to satisfy customers' needs.

product specification–A statement of acceptable physical, electrical, and/or chemical properties or an acceptable range of properties that distinguish one product or grade from another.

product structure–The sequence of operations that components follow during their manufacture into a product. A typical product structure would show raw material converted into fabricated components, components put together to make subassemblies, subassemblies going into assemblies, etc.

product structure record–A computer record defining the relationship of one component to its immediate parent and containing fields for quantity required, engineering effectivity, scrap factor, application selection switches, etc.

profit–1) Gross profit–earnings from an on-going business after direct costs of goods sold have been deducted from sales revenue for a given period. 2) Net profit–earnings or income after subtracting miscellaneous income and expenses (patent royalties, interest, capital gains) and tax from operating profit. 3) Operating profit–earnings or income after all expenses (selling, administrative, depreciation) have been deducted from gross profit.

profitability–A measure of the excess income over expenditure during a given period of time.

profit center–An assigned responsibility center that has authority to affect both the revenues earned and the costs incurred by and allocated to the center. Operational effectiveness is evaluated in terms of the amount of profit generated.

program–A significant long-term activity, as opposed to a project; usually representing some definable portion of the basic organization mission and defined as a line item in the organization's budget.

program directive–A report by the program manager to inform supporting departments concerning an active or planned program or project.

program evaluation and review technique (PERT)– A network planning technique for the analysis of a project's completion time. It uses an algorithm that permits identification of the critical path, the string of sequential activities that determines the project's completion time. PERT time estimates are probabilistic, based on pessimistic, most likely, and optimistic time estimates for each activity.

programmable logic controller (PLC)–An electronic device that is programmed to test the state of input process data and to set output lines in accordance with the input state, thus providing control instructions or branching to another set of tests. Programmable controllers provide factory floor operations with the ability to monitor and rapidly control hundreds of parameters, such as temperature and pressure.

program manager–An official in the program division who has been assigned responsibility for accomplishing a specific set of program objectives. This responsibility involves planning, directing, and controlling one or more projects of a new or continuing nature, initiating any acquisition processes necessary to get project work under way, monitoring contractor performance, and the like.

progress payments–Payments arranged in connection with purchase transactions requiring periodic payments in advance of delivery for certain amounts or for certain percentages of the purchase price.

project–An endeavor with a specific objective to be met within the prescribed time and dollar limitations and that has been assigned for definition or execution.

project costing–An accounting method of assigning valuations that is generally used in industries where services are performed on a project basis. Each assignment is unique and costed without regard to other assignments. Examples are shipbuilding, construction projects, and public accounting firms. Project costing is opposed to process costing, where products to be valued are homogeneous.

project duration–The elapsed duration from project start date through project finish date.

projected available balance–An inventory balance projected into the future. It is the running sum of on-hand inventory minus requirements plus scheduled receipts and planned orders.

projected finish date–The current estimate of the date when an activity will be completed.

projected on hand–Projected available balance, excluding planned orders.

projected start date–The current estimate of the date when an activity will begin.

projection–Syn: extrapolation.

project management–The use of skills and knowledge in coordinating the organizing, planning, scheduling, directing, controlling, monitoring, and evaluating of prescribed activities to ensure that the stated objectives of a project, manufactured product, or service are achieved.

project model–A time-phased project planning and control tool that itemizes major milestones and points of user approval.

project production–Production in which each unit or small group of units is managed by a project team created especially for that purpose.

promotional product–A product that is subject to wide fluctuations in sales because it is usually sold at a reduced price or with some other sales incentive.

proprietary assembly–An assembly designed by a manufacturer that may be serviced only with component parts supplied by the manufacturer and whose design is owned or licensed by its manufacturer.

proprietary data–Any financial, technical, or other information developed at the expense of the person or

other entity submitting it, deemed to be of strategic or tactical importance to the company. It may be offered to customers on a restricted-use basis.

protection time–Syn: safety lead time.

protective capacity–A given amount of extra capacity at nonconstraints above the system constraint's capacity, used to protect against statistical fluctuation (breakdowns, late receipts of materials, quality problems, etc.). Protective capacity provides nonconstraints with the ability to catch up to "protect" throughput and due date performance. See: excess capacity, idle capacity, limiting operation, productive capacity, safety capacity.

protective inventory–The amount of inventory required relative to the protective capacity in the system to achieve a specific throughput rate at the constraint. See: limiting operation.

prototype–A product model constructed for testing and evaluation to see how the product performs before releasing the product to manufacture.

prototyping–A specialized system development technique for performing a determination where user needs are extracted, presented, and developed by building a working model of the system. Generally, these tools make it possible to create all files and processing programs needed for a business application in a matter of days or hours for evaluation purposes.

provisioning–The process of identifying and purchasing the support items and determining the quantity of each support item necessary to operate and maintain a system.

pseudo bill of material–An artificial grouping of items that facilitates planning. See: modular bill of material, phantom bill of material, planning bill of material, super bill of material.

public warehouse–Warehouse space that is rented or leased by an independent business providing a variety of services for a fee or on a contract basis.

pull (system)–1) In production, the production of items only as demanded for use or to replace those taken for use. 2) In material control, the withdrawal of inventory as demanded by the using operations. Material is not issued until a signal comes from the user. 3) In distribution, a system for replenishing field warehouse inventories where replenishment decisions are made at the field warehouse itself, not at the central warehouse or plant.

purchased part–An item sourced from a supplier.

purchase order–The purchaser's authorization used to formalize a purchase transaction with a supplier. A purchase order, when given to a supplier, should contain statements of the name, part number, quantity, description, and price of the goods or services ordered; agreed-to terms as to payment, discounts, date of performance, and transportation; and all other agreements pertinent to the purchase and its execution by the supplier.

purchase price variance–The difference in price between the amount paid to the supplier and the standard cost of that item.

purchase requisition–An authorization to the purchasing department to purchase specified materials in specified quantities within a specified time. See: parts requisition.

purchasing–The term used in industry and management to denote the function of and the responsibility for procuring materials, supplies, and services.

purchasing agent–A person authorized by the company to purchase goods and services for the company.

purchasing capacity–The act of buying capacity or machine time from a supplier. A company can then schedule and use the capacity of the machine or a part of the capacity of the machine as if it were in its own plant.

purchasing lead time–The total lead time required to obtain a purchased item. Included here are order preparation and release time; supplier lead time; transportation time; and receiving, inspection, and put-away time. See: lead time, supplier lead time.

purchasing unit of measure–Syn: unit of measure (purchasing).

push (system)–1) In production, the production of items at times required by a given schedule planned in advance. 2) In material control, the issuing of material according to a given schedule or issuing material to a job order at its start time. 3) In distribution, a system for replenishing field warehouse inventories where replenishment decision making is centralized, usually at the manufacturing site or central supply facility.

put-away–Removing the material from the dock (or other location of receipt), transporting the material to a storage area, placing that material in a staging area and then moving it to a specific location, and recording the movement and identification of the location where the material has been placed.

pyramid forecasting–A forecasting technique that enables management to review and adjust forecasts made at an aggregate level and to keep lower level forecasts in balance. The aggregate family forecasts are forced onto the lower level forecasts, level by level, by prorating the difference between the aggregate forecasts and the rolled-up sum of the lower level forecasts. The approach combines the stability of aggregate forecasts and the application of management judgment with the need to forecast many end items within the constraints of an aggregate forecast or sales plan. See: management estimation.

Q

Q chart– A control chart for evaluating the stability of a process in terms of a quality score. The quality score is the weighted sum of the count of events of various classifications, where each classification is assigned a weight. Syn: quality chart, quality score chart.

QFD–Abbreviation for *quality function deployment.*

Q90 series–Refers to ANSI/ASQC Q90 series of standards, which is the Americanized version of the ISO 9000 series standards. The United States adopted the ISO 9000 series as the ANSI/ASQC Q90 series in 1987.

QRP–Abbreviation for *quick response program.*

qualifiers–Those competitive characteristics (lead time, quality, etc.) that a firm must exhibit to be a viable competitor in the marketplace. For example, a firm may seek to compete on characteristics other than price, but to "qualify" to compete, it must keep its costs and the related price within a certain range.

quality–Conformance to requirements or fitness for use. Quality can be defined through five principal approaches: (1) Transcendent quality is an ideal, a condition of excellence. (2) Product-based quality is based on a product attribute. (3) User-based quality is fitness for use. (4) Manufacturing-based quality is conformance to requirements. (5) Value-based quality is the degree of excellence at an acceptable price. Also, quality has two major components: (1) quality of conformance–quality is defined by the absence of defects, and (2) quality of design–quality is measured by the degree of customer satisfaction with a product's characteristics and features.

quality assurance/control–Two terms that have many interpretations because of the multiple definitions for the words "assurance" and "control." For example, "assurance" can mean the act of giving confidence, the state of being certain, or the act of making certain; "control" can mean an evaluation to indicate needed corrective responses, the act of guiding, or the state of a process in which the variability is attributable to a constant system of chance causes. One definition of *quality assurance* is *all the planned and systematic activities implemented within the quality system that can be demonstrated to provide confidence that a product or service will fulfill requirements for quality.* One definition for *quality control* is *the operational techniques and activities used to fulfill requirements for quality.* Often, however, quality assurance and quality control are used interchangeably, referring to the actions performed to ensure the quality of a product, service, or process. See: quality control.

quality at the source–A producer's responsibility to provide 100% acceptable quality material to the consumer of the material. The objective is to reduce or eliminate shipping or receiving quality inspections and line stoppages as a result of supplier defects.

quality audit–A systematic, independent examination and review to determine whether quality activities and related results comply with planned arrangements and whether these arrangements are implemented effectively and are suitable to achieve the objectives.

quality chart–Syn: Q chart.

quality circle–A small group of people who normally work as a unit and meet frequently to uncover and solve problems concerning the quality of items produced, process capability, or process control.

quality control–The process of measuring quality conformance by comparing the actual with a standard for the characteristic and acting on the difference. See: quality assurance/control.

quality costs–The overall costs associated with prevention activities and the improvement of quality throughout the firm before, during, and after production of a product. These costs fall into four recognized categories: internal failures, external failures, appraisal costs, and prevention costs. Internal failure costs relate to problems before the product reaches the customer. These usually include rework, scrap, downgrades, reinspection, retest, and process losses. External failure costs relate to problems found after the product reaches the customer. These usually include such costs as warranty and returns. Appraisal costs are associated with the formal evaluation and audit of quality in the firm. Typical costs include inspection, quality audits, testing, calibration, and checking time. Prevention costs are those caused by improvement activities that focus on reducing failure and appraisal costs. Typical costs include education, quality training, and supplier certification.

quality function deployment (QFD)–A methodology designed to ensure that all the major requirements of the customer are identified and subsequently met or exceeded through the resulting product design process and the design and operation of the supporting production management system. QFD can be viewed as a set of communication and translation tools. QFD tries to eliminate the gap between what the customer wants in a new product and what the product is capable of delivering. QFD often leads to a clear identification of the major requirements of the customers. These expectations are referred to as the *voice of the customer* (VOC). See: house of quality.

quality loss function–A parabolic approximation of the quality loss that occurs when a quality characteristic deviates from its target value. The quality loss function is expressed in monetary units: The cost of deviating from the target increases quadratically as the quality characteristic moves farther from the target. The formula used to compute the quality loss function depends on the type of quality characteristic being used. The quality loss function was first introduced in this form by Genichi Taguchi.

quality score chart–Syn: Q chart.

quality trilogy–A three-pronged approach to managing for quality. The three legs are quality planning (developing the products and processes required to meet customer needs), quality control (meeting product and process goals), and quality improvement (achieving unprecedented levels of performance).

quantity discount–A price reduction allowance determined by the quantity or value of a purchase.

quantity per–The quantity of a component to be used in the production of its parent. This value is stored in the bill of material and is used to calculate the gross requirements for components during the explosion process of MRP.

quarantine–The setting aside of items from availability for use or sale until all required quality tests have been performed and conformance certified.

queue–A waiting line. In manufacturing, the jobs at a given work center waiting to be processed. As queues increase, so do average queue time and work-in-process inventory.

queue ratio–The hours of slack within the job by the queue originally scheduled between the start of the operation being considered and the scheduled due date.

queue time–The amount of time a job waits at a work center before setup or work is performed on the job. Queue time is one element of total manufacturing lead time. Increases in queue time result in direct increases to manufacturing lead time and work-in-process inventories.

queuing theory–The collection of models dealing with waiting line problems, e.g., problems for which customers or units arrive at some service facility at which waiting lines or queues may build. Syn: waiting line theory.

quick response program (QRP)–System of linking final retail sales with production and shipping schedules back through the chain of supply; employs point-of-sale scanning and electronic data interchange, and may use direct shipment from a factory.

quotation–A statement of price, terms of sale, and description of goods or services offered by a supplier to a prospective purchaser; a bid. When given in response to an inquiry, it is usually considered an offer to sell.

quotation expiration date–The date on which a quoted price is no longer valid.

R

RAB–Abbreviation for *Registrar Accreditation Board.*

rack–A storage device for handling material in pallets. A rack usually provides storage for pallets arranged in vertical sections with one or more pallets to a tier. Some racks accommodate more than one-pallet-deep storage.

racking–Function performed by a rack-jobber, a full-function intermediary who performs all regular warehousing functions and some retail functions, typically stocking a display rack.

random–Having no predictable pattern. For example, sales data may vary randomly about some forecast value with no specific pattern and no attendant ability to obtain a more accurate sales estimate than the forecast value.

random access–A manner of storing records in a computer file so that an individual record may be accessed without reading other records.

random-location storage–A storage technique in which parts are placed in any space that is empty when they arrive at the storeroom. Although this random method requires the use of a locator file to identify part locations, it often requires less storage space than a fixed-location storage method. See: fixed-location storage.

random numbers–A sequence of integers or group of numbers (often in the form of a table) that show absolutely no relationship to each other anywhere in the sequence. At any point, all values have an equal chance of occurring, and they occur in an unpredictable fashion.

random sample–A selection of observations taken from all the observations of a phenomenon in such a way that each chosen observation has the same possibility of selection.

random variation–A fluctuation in data that is caused by uncertain or random occurrences.

R&D order–Syn: experimental order.

range–In statistics, the spread in a series of observations. For example, the anticipated demand for a particular product might vary from a low of 10 to a high of 500 per week. The range would therefore be 500–10, or 490.

range chart–Syn: R chart.

rapid prototyping–1) Transformation of product designs into physical prototypes. Rapid prototyping relies on techniques such as cross-functional teams, data sharing, and advanced computer and communication technology (e.g., CAD, CAM, stereolithography, data links). Rapid prototyping involves producing the prototype on production equipment as often as possible. It improves product development times and allows for cheaper and faster product testing, assessment of the ease of assembly and costs, and validation before actual production tooling. 2) Transformation of system designs into computer system prototypes with which the users can experiment to determine the adequacy of the design to address their needs.

rate-based scheduling–A method for scheduling and producing based on a periodic rate, e.g., daily, weekly, or monthly. This method has traditionally been applied to high-volume and process industries. The concept has recently been applied within job shops using cellular layouts and mixed-model level schedules where the production rate is matched to the selling rate.

rated capacity–1) The expected output capability of a resource or system. Capacity is traditionally calculated from such data as planned hours, efficiency, and utilization. The rated capacity is equal to hours available × efficiency × utilization. Syn: calculated capacity, nominal capacity. 2) In the theory of constraints, rated capacity = hours available × efficiency × activation, where activation is a function of scheduled production and availability is a function of uptime. Syn: standing capacity.

rate of return on investment–The efficiency ratio relating profit or cash flow incomes to investments. Several different measures of this ratio are in common use.

rate variance–The difference between the actual output rate of product and the planned or standard output.

raw material–Purchased items or extracted materials that are converted via the manufacturing process into components and products.

RCCP–Abbreviation for *rough-cut capacity planning.*

R chart–A control chart in which the subgroup range, R, is used to evaluate the stability of the variability within a process. Syn: range chart.

reactor–A special vessel to contain a chemical reaction.

real property–Land and associated rights improvements, utility systems, buildings, and other structures.

real time–Technique of coordinating data processing with external related physical events as they occur, thereby permitting prompt reporting of conditions.

receipt–1) The physical acceptance of an item into a stocking location. 2) Often, the transaction reporting of this activity.

receiving–The function encompassing the physical receipt of material, the inspection of the shipment for conformance with the purchase order (quantity and damage), the identification and delivery to destination, and the preparation of receiving reports.

receiving point–Location to which material is being shipped. Ant: shipping point.

receiving report–A document used by the receiving function of a company to inform others of the receipt of goods purchased.

recipe–Syn: formula.

reconciling inventory–Comparing the physical inventory figures with the perpetual inventory record and making any necessary corrections.

record–1) A collection of data fields arranged in a predefined format. 2) A set of related data that a computer program treats as a unit.

record accuracy–The conformity of recorded values in a bookkeeping system to the actual values, e.g., the on-hand balance of an item maintained in a computer record relative to the actual on-hand balance of the items in the stockroom.

recycle–1) The reintroduction of partially processed product or carrier solvents from one operation or task into a previous operation. 2) A recirculation process.

red bead experiment–An experiment developed by W. Edwards Deming to illustrate the impossibility of putting employees in rank order of performance for the coming year based on their performance during the past year, because performance differences must be attributed to the system, not to employees. Four thousand red and white beads (20% red) in a jar and six people are needed for the experiment. The participants' goal is to produce white beads, because the customer will not accept red beads. One person begins by stirring the beads and then, blindfolded, selects a sample of 50 beads. That person hands the jar to the next person, who repeats the process, and so on. When everyone has his or her sample, the number of red beads for each is counted. The limits of variation between employees that can be attributed to the system are calculated. Everyone will fall within the calculated limits of variation that could arise from the system. The calculations will show that there is no evidence one person will be a better performer than another in the future. The experiment shows that it would be a waste of management's time to try to find out why one participant produced four red beads and another produced 15; management should instead improve the system, making it possible for everyone to produce more white beads.

redundancy–1) A backup capability, coming either from extra machines or from extra components within a machine, to reduce the effects of breakdowns. 2) The use of one or more extra or duplicating components in a system or equipment (often to increase reliability).

refurbished goods–Syn: remanufactured parts.

refurbished parts–Syn: remanufactured parts.

regen–Slang acronym for *regeneration MRP*. Pronounced "ree-jen."

regeneration MRP–An MRP processing approach where the master production schedule is totally reexploded down through all bills of material, to maintain valid priorities. New requirements and planned orders are completely recalculated or "regenerated" at that time. See: requirements alteration. Ant: net change MRP.

Registrar Accreditation Board (RAB)–A board that evaluates the competency and reliability of registrars (organizations that assess and register companies to the appropriate ISO 9000 series standards). The Registrar Accreditation Board, formed in 1989 by ASQC, is governed by a board of directors from industry, academia, and quality management consulting firms.

registration to standards–A process in which an accredited, independent third-party organization conducts an on-site audit of a company's operations against the requirements of the standard to which the company wants to be registered. Upon successful completion of the audit, the company receives a certificate indicating that it has met the standard requirements.

regression analysis–A statistical technique for determining the best mathematical expression describing the functional relationship between one response and one or more independent variables. See: least squares method.

rejected inventory–Inventory that does not meet quality requirements but has not yet been sent to rework, scrapped, or returned to a supplier.

rejection–The act of identifying an item as not meeting quality specifications.

relational database–A software program that allows users to obtain information drawn from two or more databases that are made up of two-dimensional arrays of data.

release–The authorization to produce or ship material that has already been ordered.

released order–Syn: open order.

reliability–The probability that a product will perform its specified function under prescribed conditions without failure for a specified period of time. It is a design parameter that can be made part of a requirements statement.

reliability engineering–Determination and application of appropriate reliability tasks and criteria during the design, development, manufacture, test, and support of a product that will result in achievement of the specified product reliability.

remanufactured parts–Components or assemblies that are refurbished or rebuilt to perform the original function. Syn: refurbished goods, refurbished parts.

remanufacturing–An industrial process in which worn-out products are restored to like-new condition. In contrast, a repaired or rebuilt product normally retains its identity, and only those parts that have failed or are badly worn are replaced or serviced.

remedial maintenance–Unscheduled maintenance performed to return a product or process to a specified performance level after a failure or malfunction.

reorder cycle–Syn: replenishment lead time.

reorder point–Syn: order point.

reorder quantity–1) In a fixed-reorder quantity system of inventory control, the fixed quantity that should be ordered each time the available stock (on-hand plus on-order) falls below the reorder point. 2) In a variable reorder quantity system, the amount ordered from time period to time period will vary. Syn: replenishment order quantity.

repairables–Items that are technically feasible to repair economically.

repair order–Syn: rework order.

repair parts–Syn: service parts.

repair parts demand–Syn: service parts demand.

repetitive manufacturing–The production of discrete units in a high-volume concentration of available capacity using fixed routings. Products may be standard or made from standard modules. Production management is usually based on the production rate.

replacement cost–A method of setting the value of inventories based upon the cost of the next purchase.

replacement order–An order for the replacement of material that has been scrapped.

replacement parts–Parts that can be used as substitutes that differ from completely interchangeable service parts in that they require some physical modification–e.g., boring, cutting, or drilling–before they can replace the original part.

replenishment–Relocating material from a bulk storage area to an order pick storage area, and documenting this relocation.

replenishment interval–Syn: replenishment period.

replenishment lead time–The total period of time that elapses from the moment it is determined that a product should be reordered until the product is back on the shelf available for use. Syn: reorder cycle.

replenishment order quantity–Syn: reorder quantity.

replenishment period–The time between successive replenishment orders. Syn: replenishment interval.

reprocessed material–Goods that have gone through selective rework or recycle.

request for proposal (RFP)–A document that describes requirements for a system or product and requests proposals from suppliers. Syn: invitation for bid, request for quote.

request for quote (RFQ)–Syn: request for proposal.

requirements alteration–Processing a revised master production schedule through MRP to review the impact of the changes. It is not the same as net change, which, in addition to processing changes to the MPS, also processes changes to inventory balances, bills of material, etc., through MRP. Syn: alteration planning. See: net change MRP, regeneration MRP.

requirements definitions–Specifying the inputs, files, processing, and outputs for a new system, but without expressing computer alternatives and technical details.

requirements explosion–The process of calculating the demand for the components of a parent item by multiplying the parent item requirements by the component usage quantity specified in the bill of material. Syn: explosion.

requirements traceability–The capability to determine the source of demand requirements through record linkages. It is used in analyzing requirements to make adjustments to plans for material or capacity. See: pegging.

requisition–Syn: parts requisition.

rerouting flexibility–Accommodating unavailability of equipment by quickly and easily using alternate machines in the processing sequence.

rescheduling–The process of changing order or operation due dates, usually as a result of their being out of phase with when they are needed.

rescheduling assumption–A fundamental piece of MRP logic that assumes that existing open orders can be rescheduled in nearer time periods far more easily than new orders can be released and received. As a result, planned order receipts are not created until all scheduled receipts have been applied to cover gross requirements.

reservation–The process of designating stock for a specific order or schedule. See: allocation.

reserved material–Material on hand or on order that is assigned to specific future production or customer orders. Syn: allocated material, assigned material, obligated material.

reserve stock–Syn: safety stock.

residence time–Syn: process time.

resource–Anything that adds value to a product or service in its creation, production, or delivery.

resource driver–The objects that are linked to an activity that consumes resources at a specified rate. For example, a resource driver is a purchase order (the object), that when placed (the activity), consumes hours (rate) of purchasing (resource).

resource-limited scheduling–The scheduling of activities so that predetermined resource availability pools are not exceeded. Activities are started as soon as resources are available (with respect to logical constraints), as required by the activity. When not enough of a resource exists to do all tasks on a given day, a priority decision is made. Project finish may be delayed, if necessary, to alter schedules constrained by resource usage.

resource management–1) The effective planning, scheduling, execution, and control of all organizational resources to produce a good or a service that provides customer satisfaction and supports the organization's competitive edge and, ultimately, organizational goals. 2) An emerging field of study emphasizing the systems perspective, encompassing both the product and process life cycles, and focusing on the integration of organizational resources toward the effective realization of organizational goals.

Resources include materials; maintenance, repair, and operating supplies; production and supporting equipment; facilities; direct and indirect employees, staff, administration, and professional employees; and capital.

resource planning–Capacity planning conducted at the business plan level. The process of establishing, measuring, and adjusting limits or levels of long-range capacity. Resource planning is normally based on the production plan but may be driven by higher level plans beyond the time horizon for the production plan, e.g., the business plan. It addresses those resources that take long periods of time to acquire. Resource planning decisions always require top management approval. Syn: long-range resource planning, resource requirements planning. See: capacity planning, long-term planning.

resource profile–The standard hours of load placed on a resource, by time period. See: bill of resources, product load profile.

resource requirements planning–Syn: resource planning.

response time–The elapse of time or average delay between the initiation of a transaction and the results of the transaction.

responsibility–A liability to perform assigned duties and activities for which the assignee is held answerable. It constitutes an obligation or accountability for performance.

retail method–A method of inventory valuation in which the value is determined by applying a predetermined percentage based on retail markup to the retail price, to determine its inventory value based on cost.

retirement of debt–The termination of a debt obligation by appropriate settlement with the lender. Understood to be in full amount unless partial settlement is specified.

retrofit–An item that replaces components originally installed on equipment; a modification to in-service equipment.

return on assets (ROA)–A financial measure of the relative income-producing value of an asset. It is calculated as net income divided by total assets.

return on investment (ROI)–A financial measure of the relative return from an investment, usually expressed as a percentage of earnings produced by an asset to the amount invested in the asset.

return to supplier–Material that has been rejected by the buyer's inspection department and is awaiting shipment back to the supplier for repair or replacement.

reverse engineering–The process of disassembling, evaluating, and redesigning a competitor's product for the purpose of manufacturing a product with similar characteristics without violating any of the competitor's proprietary manufacturing technologies.

reverse flow scheduling–A scheduling procedure used in some process industries for building process train schedules that starts with the last stage and proceeds backward (countercurrent to the process flow) through the process structure.

review period–The time between successive evaluations of inventory status to determine whether to reorder.

revision level–A number or letter representing the number of times a part drawing or specification has been changed.

rework–Reprocessing to salvage a defective item or part.

rework lead time–The time required to rework material in-house or at a supplier.

rework order–A manufacturing order to rework and salvage defective parts or products. Syn: repair order, spoiled work order.

RFP–Abbreviation for *request for proposal*.

RFQ–Abbreviation for *request for quote*.

right the first time–A term used to convey the concept that it is beneficial and more cost-effective to take the necessary steps the first time to ensure that a product or service meets its requirements than to provide a product or service that will need rework or not meet customers' needs. In other words, an organization should engage in defect prevention rather than defect detection.

risk analysis–A review of the uncertainty associated with the research, development, and production of a product.

ROA–Abbreviation for *return on assets*.

robotics–Replacing functions previously performed by humans with mechanical devices or robots that can be either operated by humans or run by computer. Hard-to-do, dangerous, or monotonous tasks are likely candidates for robots to perform.

robustness–The condition of a product or process design that remains relatively stable with a minimum of variation even though factors that influence operations or usage, such as environment and wear, are constantly changing.

ROI–Abbreviation for *return on investment*.

rough-cut capacity planning (RCCP)–The process of converting the master production schedule into requirements for key resources, often including labor, machinery, warehouse space, suppliers' capabilities, and, in some cases, money. Comparison to available or demonstrated capacity is usually done for each key resource. This comparison assists the master scheduler in establishing a feasible master production schedule. Three approaches to performing RCCP are the bill of labor (resources, capacity) approach, the capacity planning using overall factors approach, and the resource profile approach. See: bill of resources, capacity planning, capacity planning using overall factors, product load profile.

route sheet–Syn: routing.

routing–Information detailing the method of manufacture of a particular item. It includes the operations to be performed, their sequence, the various work centers involved, and the standards for setup and run. In some companies, the routing also includes information on tooling, operator skill levels, inspection operations, and testing requirements, etc. Syn: bill of operations, instruction sheet, manufacturing data sheet, operation chart, operation list, operation sheet, route sheet, routing sheet. See: bill of labor, bill of resources.

routing sheet–Syn: routing.

run–A quantity of production being processed.

run chart–A graphical technique that illustrates how a process is performing over time. By statistically analyzing a run chart, a process can be determined to be under or out of control. The most common types of data used to construct the charts are ranges, averages, percentages/counts, and individual process attributes (e.g., temperature).

run order–Syn: manufacturing order.

runout list–1) A list of items to be scheduled into production in sequence by the dates at which the present available stock is expected to be exhausted. 2) A statement of ingredients required to use up an available resource, e.g., how much "a" resource is required to consume 300 pounds of "x."

run sheet–A log-type document used in continuous processes to record raw materials used, quantity produced, in-process testing results, etc. It may serve as an input document for inventory records.

run size–Syn: standard batch quantity.

run standards–Syn: run time.

run time–Time required to process a piece or lot at a specific operation. Run time does not include setup time. Syn: run standards.

rush order–An order that for some reason must be fulfilled in less than normal lead time.

S

safety capacity–The planned amount by which the available capacity exceeds current productive capacity. This capacity provides protection from planned activities, such as resource contention, and preventive maintenance and unplanned activities, such as resource breakdown, poor quality, rework, or lateness. Safety capacity plus productive capacity plus excess capacity is equal to 100% of capacity. See: protective capacity.

safety factor–Ratio of average strength to the worst stress expected. It is essential that the variation, in addition to the average value, be considered in design.

safety lead time–An element of time added to normal lead time to protect against fluctuations in lead time so that an order can be completed before its real need date. When used, the MRP system, in offsetting for lead time, will plan both order release and order completion for earlier dates than it would otherwise. Syn: protection time, safety time.

safety stock–1) In general, a quantity of stock planned to be in inventory to protect against fluctuations in demand or supply. 2) In the context of master production scheduling, the additional inventory and capacity planned as protection against forecast errors and short-term changes in the backlog. Overplanning can be used to create safety stock. Syn: buffer stock, reserve stock. See: hedge, inventory buffer.

safety time–Syn: safety lead time.

salable goods–A part or assembly authorized for sale to final customers through the marketing function.

sales and operations planning–A process that provides management the ability to strategically direct its businesses to achieve competitive advantage on a continuous basis by integrating customer-focused marketing plans for new and existing products with the management of the supply chain. The process brings together all the plans for the business (sales, marketing, development, manufacturing, sourcing, and financial) into one integrated set of plans. It is performed at least once a month and is reviewed by management at an aggregate (product family) level. The process must reconcile all supply, demand, and new-product plans at both the detail and aggregate level and tie to the business plan. It is the definitive statement of the company's plans for the near to intermediate term covering a horizon sufficient to plan for resources and support the annual business planning process. Executed properly, the sales and operation planning process links the strategic plans for the business with its execution and reviews performance measures for continuous improvement. See: aggregate planning, production plan, production planning, sales plan.

sales mix–The proportion of individual product-type sales volumes that make up the total sales volume.

sales order configuration–Syn: customer order servicing system.

sales order number–A unique control number assigned to each new customer order, usually during order entry. It is often used by order promising, master scheduling, cost accounting, invoicing, etc. For some make-to-order products, it can also take the place of an end item part number by becoming the control number that is scheduled through the finishing operations.

sales plan–A time-phased statement of expected customer orders anticipated to be received (incoming sales, not outgoing shipments) for each major product family or item. It represents sales and marketing management's commitment to take all reasonable steps necessary to achieve this level of actual customer orders. The sales plan is a necessary input to the production planning process or sales and operations planning process. It is expressed in units identical to those used for the production plan (as well as in sales dollars). See: aggregate planning, production plan, production planning, sales and operations planning.

sales promotion–1) Sales activities that supplement both personal selling and marketing, coordinate the two, and help to make them effective, e.g., displays. 2) More loosely, the combination of personal selling, advertising, and all supplementary selling activities. 3) Promotion activities–other than advertising, publicity, and personal selling–that stimulate interest, trial, or purchase by final customers or others in the channel.

sales representative–Employee authorized to accept a customer's order for a product. Sales representatives usually go to the customer's location when industrial products are being marketed.

salvage–Property that, because of its worn, damaged, deteriorated, or incomplete condition or specialized nature has no reasonable prospect of sale or use as serviceable property without major repairs or alterations, but that has some value in excess of its scrap value.

salvage value–1) The cost recovered or that could be recovered from used property when removed, sold, or scrapped. A factor in appraisal of property value and in computing depreciation. 2) The market value of a machine or facility at any point in time. Normally, an estimate of an asset's net value at the end of its estimated life.

sample–A portion of a universe of data chosen to estimate some characteristics about the whole universe. The universe of data could consist of sizes of customer orders, number of units of inventory, number of lines on a purchase order, etc.

sample size–The number of elements selected for analysis from the population.

sampling–A statistical process where generalizations regarding an entire body of phenomena are drawn from a relatively small number of observations.

sampling distribution–The distribution of values of a statistic calculated from samples of a given size.

sawtooth diagram–A quantity-versus-time graphic representation of the order point/order quantity inventory system showing inventory being received and then used up and reordered.

SBQ–Abbreviation for *standard batch quantity*.

SBU–Abbreviation for *strategic business unit*.

Scanlon plan–A system of group incentives on a companywide or plantwide basis that sets up one measure that reflects the results of all efforts. The universal standard is the ratio of labor costs to sales value added by production. If there is an increase in production sales value with no change in labor

costs, productivity has increased while unit cost has decreased.

scanner–An electronic device that optically converts coded information into electrical control signals for data collection or system transaction input.

scatter chart–A graphical technique to analyze the relationship between two variables. Two sets of data are plotted on a graph, with the *y* axis used for the variable to be predicted and the *x* axis used for the variable to make the prediction. The graph will show possible relationships (although two variables might appear to be related, they might not be–those who know most about the variables must make that evaluation). The scatter chart is one of the seven tools of quality. Syn: cross plot, scatter diagram.

scatter diagram–Syn: scatter chart.

schedule–A timetable for planned occurrences, e.g., shipping schedule, manufacturing schedule, supplier schedule. Some schedules include the starting and ending time for activities.

schedule board–Syn: control board.

schedule chart–Usually a large piece of graph paper used in the same manner as a control board. Where the control board often uses strings and markers to represent plans and progress, the schedule chart is typically filled in with pencil. See: control board.

schedule control–Control of a plant floor by schedules rather than by job orders (called *order control*). Schedules are derived by taking requirements over a period of time and dividing by the number of workdays allowed to run the parts or assemblies. Production completed is compared with the schedule to provide control. This type of control is most frequently used in repetitive and process manufacturing.

scheduled downtime–Planned shutdown of equipment or plant to perform maintenance or to adjust to softening demand.

scheduled load–The standard hours of work required by scheduled receipts, i.e., open production orders.

scheduled receipt–An open order that has an assigned due date. See: open order.

scheduler–A general term that can refer to a material planner, dispatcher, or a combined function.

scheduling–The act of creating a schedule, such as a master production schedule, shop schedule, maintenance schedule, or supplier schedule.

scheduling rules–Basic rules that can be used consistently in a scheduling system. Scheduling rules usually specify the amount of calendar time to allow for a move, queue, load calculation, etc.

scientific inventory control–Syn: statistical inventory control.

scrap–Material outside of specifications and possessing characteristics that make rework impractical.

scrap factor–A percentage factor in the product structure used to increase gross requirements to account for anticipated loss within the manufacture of a particular product. Syn: scrap rate.

scrap rate–Syn: scrap factor.

SDS–Abbreviation for *single-digit setup*.

search models–Operations research models that attempt to find optimal solutions with adaptive searching approaches.

seasonal harmonics–Syn: harmonic smoothing.

seasonal index–A number used to adjust data to seasonal demand. See: base series.

seasonal inventory–Inventory built up to smooth production in anticipation of a peak seasonal demand.

seasonality–A repetitive pattern of demand from year to year (or other repeating time interval) with some periods considerably higher than others. See: base series.

second-order smoothing–A method of exponential smoothing for trend situations that employs two previously computed averages, the singly and doubly smoothed values, to extrapolate into the future. Syn: double smoothing.

secular trend–The general direction of the long-run change in the value of a particular time series.

self-directed work team–Generally a small, independent, self-organized, and self-controlling group in which members flexibly plan, organize, determine, and manage their duties and actions, as well as perform many other supportive functions. It may work without immediate supervision and can often have authority to select, hire, promote, or discharge its members.

seller's market–A market condition in which goods cannot easily be secured and when the economic forces of business tend to cause goods to be priced at the supplier's estimate of value.

selling expense–An expense or class of expense incurred in selling or marketing, e.g., salespersons' salaries and commissions, advertising, samples, and shipping cost.

semifinished goods–Products that have been stored uncompleted awaiting final operations that adapt them to different uses or customer specifications.

semiprocess flow–A manufacturing configuration where most jobs go through the same sequence of operations even though production is in job lots.

semiworks–Syn: pilot plant.

send ahead–The movement of a portion of a lot of material to a subsequent operation before completion of the current operation for all units of the lot. The purpose of sending material ahead is to reduce the manufacturing lead time. See: overlapped schedule.

sensitivity analysis–A technique for determining how much an expected outcome or result will change in response to a given change in an input variable. For example, given a projected level of resources, what would be the effect on net income if variable costs of production increased 20%?

sensors–Devices that can monitor and adjust differences in conditions to control equipment on a dynamic basis.

sequencing–Determining the order in which a manufacturing facility is to process a number of different jobs in order to achieve certain objectives.

sequential–In numeric sequence, normally in ascending order.

serial number–A unique number assigned for identification to a single piece that will never be repeated for similar pieces. Serial numbers are usually applied by the manufacturer but can be applied at other points, including by the distributor or wholesaler.

serviceability–1) Design characteristic that allows the easy and efficient performance of service activities. Service activities include those activities required to keep equipment in operating condition, such as lubrication, fueling, oiling, and cleaning. 2) A measure of the degree to which servicing of an item will be accomplished within a given time under specified conditions.

service blueprint–A service analysis method that allows service designers to identify processes involved in the service delivery system, isolate potential failure points in the system, establish time frames for the service delivery, and set standards for each step that can be quantified for measurement.

service function–A mathematical relationship of the safety factor to service level, i.e., the fraction of demand that is routinely met from stock.

service level–Syn: level of service.

service parts–Those modules, components, and elements that are planned to be used without modification to replace an original part. Syn: repair parts, spare parts.

service parts demand–The need or requirement for a component to be sold by itself, as opposed to being used in production to make a higher level product. Syn: repair parts demand, spare parts demand.

service time–The time taken to serve a customer, e.g., the time required to fill a sales order or the time required to fill a request at a tool crib.

service vs. investment chart–A curve showing the amount of inventory that will be required to give various levels of customer service.

servo system–A control mechanism linking a system's input and output, designed to feed back data on system output to regulate the operation of the system.

setup–1) The work required to change a specific machine, resource, work center, or line from making the last good piece of unit A to the first good piece of unit B. 2) The refitting of equipment to neutralize the effects of the last lot produced; e.g., teardown of the just-completed production and preparation of the equipment for production of the next scheduled item. Syn: changeover, turnaround, turnaround time.

setup costs–Costs such as scrap costs, calibration costs, downtime costs, and lost sales associated with preparing the resource for the next product. Syn: changeover costs, turnaround cost.

setup lead time–The time needed to prepare a manufacturing process to start. Setup lead time may include run and inspection time for the first piece.

setup time–The time required for a specific machine, resource, work center, or line to convert from the production of the last good piece of lot A to the first good piece of lot B.

seven tools of quality–Tools that help organizations understand their processes in order to improve them. The tools are the cause-and-effect diagram, check sheet, control chart, flowchart, histogram, Pareto chart, and scatter chart.

shelf life–The amount of time an item may be held in inventory before it becomes unusable.

shelf life control–A technique of physical first-in, first-out usage aimed at minimizing stock obsolescence.

Shewhart cycle–Syn: plan-do-check-action.

ship-age limit–The date after which a product cannot be shipped to a customer.

shipping–The function that provides facilities for the outgoing shipment of parts, products, and components. It includes packaging, marking, weighing, and loading for shipment.

shipping lead time–The number of working days in transit normally required for goods to move between a shipping and receiving point, plus acceptance time in days at the receiving point.

shipping manifest–A document that lists the pieces in a shipment. A manifest usually covers an entire load regardless of whether the load is to be delivered to a single destination or to many destinations. Manifests usually list the piece count, total weight, and the destination name and address for each destination in the load.

shipping order debit memo–Document used to authorize the shipment of rejected material back to the supplier and create a debit entry in accounts payable.

shipping point–The location from which material is sent. Ant: receiving point.

shipping tolerance–An allowable deviation that the supplier can ship over or under the contract quantity.

shop calendar–Syn: manufacturing calendar.

shop floor control–A system for using data from the shop floor to maintain and communicate status information on shop orders (manufacturing orders) and on work centers. The major subfunctions of shop floor control are (1) assigning priority of each shop order, (2) maintaining work-in-process quantity information, (3) conveying shop order status information to the office, (4) providing actual output data for capacity control purposes, (5) providing quantity by location by shop order for work-in-process inventory and

accounting purposes, and (6) providing measurement of efficiency, utilization, and productivity of the work force and machines. Shop floor control can use order control or flow control to monitor material movement through the facility. See: production activity control.

shop order–Syn: manufacturing order.

shop order close-out station–A stocking point on the shop floor where completed production of components is transacted (received) into and subsequently transacted (issued) to assembly or other downstream operations. This technique is used to reduce material handling by avoiding the need to move items into and out of stockrooms, while simultaneously enabling a high degree of inventory record accuracy.

shop order reporting–Syn: production reporting and status control.

shop packet–A package of documents used to plan and control the shop floor movement of an order. The packet may include a manufacturing order, operations sheets, engineering blueprints, picking lists, move tickets, inspection tickets, and time tickets.

shop planning–The function of coordinating the availability of material handling, material resources, setup, and tooling so that an operation or job can be done on a particular machine. Shop planning is often part of the dispatching function. The term *shop planning* is sometimes used interchangeably with dispatching, although dispatching does not necessarily include shop planning. For example, the selection of jobs might be handled by the centralized dispatching function, while the actual shop planning might be done by the foreman or a representative.

shop scheduling–Syn: operations scheduling.

shop traveler–Syn: traveler.

shortage cost–The marginal profit that is lost when a customer orders an item that is not immediately available in stock.

short-cycle manufacturing–Syn: Just-in-Time.

shortest processing time rule (SPT)–A dispatching rule that directs the sequencing of jobs in ascending order by processing time. If this rule is followed, the most jobs at a work center per time period will be processed. As a result, the average lateness of jobs at that work center is minimized, but some jobs will be very late. Syn: smallest processing time rule.

short-term planning–The function of adjusting limits or levels of capacity within relatively short periods of time, such as parts of a day, a day, or a week.

shrinkage–Reductions of actual quantities of items in stock, in process, or in transit. The loss may be caused by scrap, theft, deterioration, evaporation, etc.

shrinkage factor–A percentage factor used to compensate for the expected loss during the manufacturing cycle of an item. This factor differs from the scrap factor in that it affects all components of the item, where the scrap factor relates to only one component's usage. Syn: shrinkage rate.

shrinkage rate–Syn: shrinkage factor.

SIC–Abbreviation for *standard industrial classification.*

sigma–A Greek letter (σ) commonly used to designate the standard deviation, which is a measure of the dispersion of data, or the spread of the distribution.

significant part number–A part number that is intended to convey certain information, such as the source of the part, the material in the part, or the shape of the part. These usually make part numbers longer. Ant: nonsignificant part number.

significant variances–Those differences between planned and actual performance that exceed established thresholds and that require further review, analysis, and action.

simple interest–1) Interest that is not compounded; i.e., is not added to the income-producing investment or loan. 2) The interest charged under the condition that interest in any time period is only charged on the principal.

simplex algorithm–A procedure for solving a general linear programming problem.

simulation–1) The technique of using representative or artificial data to reproduce in a model various conditions that are likely to occur in the actual performance of a system. It is frequently used to test the behavior of a system under different operating policies. 2) Within MRP II, using the operational data to perform "what-if" evaluations of alternative plans to answer the question, Can we do it? If yes, the simulation can then be run in the financial mode to help answer the question, Do we really want to? See: what-if analysis.

simultaneous design/engineering–Syn: participative design/engineering.

simultaneous engineering–Syn: participative design/ engineering.

single-digit setup (SDS)–The idea of performing set-ups in less than 10 minutes.

single exponential smoothing–Syn: first-order smoothing.

single-factor productivity–The average amount of a given product (output) attributed to a unit of a given resource (input). Factors include labor and capital. Syn: partial productivity factor.

single-level backflush–A form of backflush that reduces inventory of only the parts used in the next level down in an assembly or subassembly.

single-level bill of material–A display of components that are directly used in a parent item. It shows only the relationships one level down.

single-level where-used–Single-level where-used for a component lists each parent in which that component is directly used and in what quantity. This information is usually made available through the technique known as implosion.

single-minute exchange of die (SMED)–The concept of setup times of less than 10 minutes, developed by Shigeo Shingo in 1970 at Toyota.

single-period inventory models–Inventory models used to define economical or profit maximizing lot-size quantities when an item is ordered or produced only once, e.g., newspapers, calendars, tax guides, greeting cards, or periodicals, while facing uncertain demands. Syn: static inventory models.

single smoothing–Syn: first-order smoothing.

single-source supplier–A company that is selected to have 100% of the business for a part although alternate suppliers are available. See: sole source.

single sourcing–A method whereby a purchased part is supplied by only one supplier. Traditional manufacturers usually have at least two suppliers for each component part they purchase to ensure continuity of supply and (more so) to foster price competition between the suppliers. A JIT manufacturer will frequently have only one supplier for a purchased part so that close relationships can be established with a smaller number of suppliers. These close relationships (and mutual interdependence) foster high quality, reliability, short lead times, and cooperative action. Ant: multisourcing.

six-sigma quality–A term used generally to indicate that a process is well-controlled, i.e., ±6 sigma from the centerline in a control chart. The term is usually associated with Motorola, which named one of its key operational initiatives *Six-Sigma Quality.*

skew–The degree of nonsymmetry shown by a frequency distribution.

skill-based compensation–A method of employee compensation that bases the employee's wage rate on the number of skills the employee is qualified to perform. People who are qualified to do a wider variety of skills are paid more. See: labor grade.

skills inventories–An organized file of information on each employee's skills, abilities, knowledge, and experience, usually maintained by a personnel office. See: labor grade.

SKU–Acronym for *stockkeeping unit.*

slack–Syn: slack time.

slack time–1) The difference in calendar time between the scheduled due date for a job and the estimated completion date. If a job is to be completed ahead of schedule, it is said to have slack time; if it is likely to be completed behind schedule, it is said to have negative slack time. Slack time can be used to calculate job priorities using formulas such as the critical ratio. 2) In the critical path method, total slack is the amount of time an activity or job may be delayed in starting without necessarily delaying the project completion time. Free slack is the amount of time an activity or job may be delayed in starting without delaying the start of any other activity in the project. Syn: slack.

slack time rule–A dispatching rule that directs the sequencing of jobs based on (days left × hrs/day) – standard hours of work left on this specific job = priority, e.g., (5 × 8) – 12 = 28. The lower the amount of slack time, the higher the priority.

slow-moving items–Those inventory items with a low turnover, i.e., items in inventory that have a relatively low rate of usage compared to the normal amount of inventory carried.

smallest processing time rule–Syn: shortest processing time rule.

small group improvement activity–An organizational technique for involving employees in continuous improvement activities.

SMED–Acronym for *single-minute exchange of die*.

smoothing–Averaging data by a mathematical process or by curve fitting, such as the method of least squares or exponential smoothing.

smoothing constant–In exponential smoothing, the weighting factor that is applied to the most recent demand, observation, or error. Syn: alpha factor.

software–The programs and documentation necessary to make use of a computer.

sole source–The situation where the supply of a product is available from only one organization. Usually technical barriers such as patents preclude other suppliers from offering the product. See: single source supplier.

sole-source supplier–The only supplier capable of meeting (usually technical) requirements for an item.

sorting–The function of physically separating a homogeneous subgroup from a heterogeneous population of items.

source document–An original written or printed record of some type that is to be converted into machine-readable form.

source inspection–Inspection at the source of supply, e.g., the supplier or the work center, as opposed to inspection following receipt or production of the items.

space buffer–A physical space allocated for safety stock. For example, a space buffer can exist in a product layout to prevent a bottleneck from stopping production because no more room exists to offload finished material from that operation.

spare parts–Syn: service parts.

spare parts demand–Syn: service parts demand.

SPC–Abbreviation for *statistical process control*.

special–A term describing a part or group of parts that are unique to a particular order.

special cause–Syn: assignable cause.

specification–A clear, complete, and accurate statement of the technical requirements of a material, an item, or a service, and of the procedure to determine if the requirements are met.

split delivery–A method by which a larger quantity is ordered on a purchase order to secure a lower price, but delivery is split into smaller quantities and spread out over several dates to control inventory investment, save storage space, etc.

split lot–A manufacturing order quantity that has been divided into two or more smaller quantities, usually after the order has been released. The quantities of a split lot may be worked on in parallel, or a portion of the original quantity may be sent ahead to a subsequent operation to be worked on while work on the remainder of the quantity is being completed at the current operation. The purpose of splitting a lot is to reduce the lead time of part of the order.

spoiled work order–Syn: rework order.

spot buy–A purchase made for standard off-the-shelf material or equipment, on a one-time basis.

SPT–Abbreviation for *shortest processing time rule*.

SQC–Abbreviation for *statistical quality control*.

SQL–Abbreviation for *structured query language*.

stabilization stock–An inventory that is carried on hand above the base inventory level to provide protection against incurring overtime or downtime.

stacked lead time–Syn: cumulative lead time.

staged material–Syn: kit.

staging–Pulling material for an order from inventory before the material is required. This action is often taken to identify shortages, but it can lead to increased problems in availability and inventory accuracy. See: accumulating.

staging and consolidation–Physically moving material from the packing area to a staging area, based on a prescribed set of instructions related to a particular outbound vehicle or delivery route, often for shipment consolidation purposes.

standard–1) An established norm against which measurements are compared. 2) An established norm of productivity defined in terms of units of output per set time or in standard time. 3) The time allowed to perform a specific job including quantity of work to be produced.

standard allowance–The established or accepted amount by which the normal time for an operation is increased within an area, plant, or industry to compensate for the usual amount of fatigue and personal or unavoidable delays.

standard batch quantity (SBQ)–The quantity of a parent that is used as the basis for specifying the material requirements for production. The quantity per is expressed as the quantity to make the SBQ, not to make only one of the parent. Often used by manufacturers that use some components in very small quantities or by process-related manufacturers. Syn: run size.

standard containers–Predetermined, specifically sized containers used for storing and moving components. These containers protect the components from damage and simplify the task of counting components.

standard costs–The target costs of an operation, process, or product including direct material, direct labor, and overhead charges.

standard cost system–A cost system that uses cost units determined before production. For management control purposes, the standards are compared to actual costs, and variances are computed.

standard deviation–A measure of dispersion of data or of a variable. The standard deviation is computed by finding the difference between the average and actual observations, squaring each difference, summing the squared differences, finding the variance (summing the squared differences and dividing by $n - 1$ for a sample or summing the squared differences and dividing by n for the population), and taking the square root of the variance.

standard error–Applied to statistics such as the mean, to provide a distribution within which samples of the statistics are expected to fall.

standard hours–Syn: standard time.

standard industrial classification (SIC)–Classification codes that are used to categorize companies into industry groupings.

standardization–1) The process of designing and altering products, parts, processes, and procedures to establish and use standard specifications for them and their components. 2) Reduction of total numbers of parts and materials used and products, models, or grades produced. 3) The function of bringing a raw ingredient into standard (acceptable) range per the specification before introduction to the main process.

standardized ingredient–A raw ingredient that has been preprocessed to bring all its specifications within standard ranges before it is introduced to the main process. This preprocessing minimizes variability in the production process.

standard ratio–A relationship based on a sample distribution by value for a particular company. When the standard ratio for a particular company is known, certain aggregate inventory predictions can be made, e.g., the amount of inventory increase that would be required to provide a particular increase in customer service.

standard time–The length of time that should be required to (1) set up a given machine or operation and (2) run one part, assembly, batch, or end product through that operation. This time is used in determining machine requirements and labor requirements. Standard time assumes an average worker following prescribed methods and allows time for rest to overcome fatigue. It is also frequently used as a basis for incentive pay systems and as a basis of allocating overhead in cost accounting systems. Syn: standard hours.

standing capacity–Syn: rated capacity.

standing order–Syn: blanket purchase order.

start date–The date that an order or schedule should be released into the plant based upon some form of scheduling rules. The start date should be early enough to allow time to complete the work, but not so early as to overload the shop.

startup–That period starting with the date of initial operation during which the unit is brought up to acceptable production capacity and quality within estimated production costs. Startup is the activity that commences on the date of initial activity and has significant duration on most projects, but is often confused (used interchangeably) with date of initial operation.

startup costs–Extra operating costs to bring the plant or product on-stream incurred between the completion of construction and the start of normal operations. In addition to the difference between actual operating costs during that period and normal costs, they include employee training, equipment tests, process adjustments, salaries and travel expense of temporary labor staff and consultants, report writing, post-startup monitoring, and associated overhead. Additional capital required to correct plant problems may be included. Startup costs are sometimes capitalized.

static budget–Syn: master budget.

static inventory models–Syn: single-period inventory models.

statistical control–The situation where variations among the observed sampling requests can be attributed to a constant system of chance causes.

statistical inventory control–The use of statistical methods to model the demands and lead times experienced by an inventory item or group of items. Demand during lead time and between reviews can be modeled, and reorder points, safety stocks, and maximum inventory levels can be defined to strive for desired customer service levels, inventory investments, manufacturing and distribution efficiency, and targeted returns on investments. Syn: scientific inventory control. See: fixed reorder quantity inventory model.

statistical order point–Syn: order point.

statistical order point system–Syn: order point system.

statistical process control (SPC)–The application of statistical techniques to monitor and adjust an operation. Often the term *statistical process control* is used interchangeably with *statistical quality control.*

statistical quality control (SQC)–The application of statistical techniques to control quality. Often the term *statistical process control* is used interchangeably with *statistical quality control,* although statistical quality control includes acceptance sampling as well as statistical process control.

statistical safety stock calculations–The mathematical determination of safety stock quantities considering forecast errors, lot size, desired customer service levels, and the ratio of lead time to the length of the forecast period. Safety stock is frequently the product of the appropriate safety factor and the standard deviation or mean absolute deviation of the distribution of demand forecast errors.

step budget–A budget that establishes anticipated targets at which an operation will perform for each step or level of production. A step budget can be likened to several different fixed budgets. This method of budgeting is useful because most of the manufacturing overhead expenditures vary in steps, not as a straight line.

step-function scheduling–Scheduling logic that recognizes run length to be a multiple of the number of batches to be run rather than simply a linear relationship of run time to total production quantity.

stochastic models–Models where uncertainty is explicitly considered in the analysis.

stock–1) Items in inventory. 2) Stored products or service parts ready for sale, as distinguished from stores, which are usually components or raw materials.

stockchase–Syn: expedite.

stock code–Syn: item number.

stockkeeping unit (SKU)–An item at a particular geographic location. For example, one product stocked at the plant and at six different distribution centers would represent seven SKUs.

stockless production–Syn: Just-in-Time.

stockless purchasing–Buying material, parts, supplies, etc., for direct use by the departments involved, as opposed to receiving them into stores and subsequently issuing them to the departments. The intent here is to reduce inventory investment, increase cash flow, reduce material handling and storage, and provide better service.

stock number–Syn: item number.

stock order–An order to replenish stock, as opposed to a production order to make a particular product for a specific customer.

stockout–A lack of materials, components, or finished goods that are needed. See: backorder.

stockout costs–The costs associated with a stockout. Those costs may include lost sales, backorder costs, expediting, and additional manufacturing and purchasing costs.

stockout percentage–A measure of the effectiveness with which a company responds to actual demand or requirements. 1) The stockout percentage can be a measurement of total stockouts to total orders, or of line items incurring stockouts to total line items ordered during a period. The formula is

stockout percentage = (1 − customer service ratio) × 100%

2) The stockout percentage can be a comparison of total stockouts to total demands or of items incurring stockouts to total items required during a period. Ant: customer service ratio.

stockpoint–A designated location in an active area of operation into which material is placed and from which

it is taken. Not necessarily a stockroom isolated from activity, it is a way of tracking and controlling active material.

stock record card–A ledger card that contains inventory status for a given item.

stock status–A periodic report showing the inventory on hand and usually showing the inventory on order and some sales or usage history for the products that are covered in the stock status report.

stop work order–Syn: hold order.

storage–The retention of parts or products for future use or shipment.

storage costs–A subset of inventory carrying costs, including the cost of warehouse utilities, material handling personnel, equipment maintenance, building maintenance, and security personnel.

stores–1) Stored materials used in making a product. 2) The room where stored components, parts, assemblies, tools, fixtures, etc., are kept.

stores issue order–Syn: picking list.

stores ledger card–A card on which records of the items on hand and on order are maintained.

stores requisition–Syn: picking list.

straight-line depreciation–Method of depreciation whereby the amount to be recovered (written off) is spread uniformly over the estimated life of the asset in terms of time periods or units of output.

straight-line schedule–Syn: gapped schedule.

strategic business unit (SBU)–An approach to strategic planning that develops a plan based on products. A company's products are typically grouped into strategic business units (SBUs) with each SBU evaluated in terms of strengths and weaknesses vis-à-vis similar business units made and marketed by competitors. The units are evaluated in terms of their competitive strengths, their relative advantages, life cycles, and cash flow patterns.

strategic drivers–Factors that influence business unit and manufacturing strategies.

strategic mission–Defines the business, including the products or services offered, the scope of coverage (customers and markets), and any geographic scope for the business. The mission is used to define the extent of external and internal analysis (strengths, weaknesses, opportunities, and threats–often called *SWOT analysis)* necessary to determine specific action plans, often called strategies.

strategic plan–The plan for how to marshal and determine the actions to support the mission, goals, and objectives. Generally includes an organization's explicit mission, goals, and objectives, and the specific actions needed to achieve those goals and objectives. See: business plan.

structured query language (SQL)–A computer language that is a relational model database language. Such a language has an English vocabulary and is nonprocedural and provides the ability to define tables, screen layouts, and indexes.

subassembly–An assembly that is used at a higher level to build another assembly.

subcontracting–Sending production work outside to another manufacturer.

suboptimization–A problem solution that is best from a narrow point of view but not from a higher or overall company point of view. For example, a department manager who would not have employees work overtime to minimize the department's operating expense may cause lost sales and a reduction in overall company profitability.

subplant–An organizational structure within a factory, consisting of a compact entrepreneurial unit, either process-oriented or product-oriented and structured to achieve maximum productivity.

substitution–The use of a nonprimary product or component, normally when the primary item is not available.

successor activity–Any activity that exists on a common path with the activity in question and occurs after the activity in question.

summarized bill of material–A form of multilevel bill of material that lists all the parts and their quantities required in a given product structure. Unlike the indented bill of material, it does not list the levels of manufacture and lists a component only once for the total quantity used.

summarized where-used–A form of an indented where-used bill of material that shows all parents in which a given component is used, the required quantities, and all the next-level parents until the end item is reached. Unlike the indented where-used, it does not list the levels of manufacture.

sum of deviations–Syn: cumulative sum.

sunk cost–1) The unrecovered balance of an investment. It is a cost, already paid, that is not relevant to the decision concerning the future that is being made. Capital already invested that for some reason cannot be retrieved. 2) A past cost that has no relevance with respect to future receipts and disbursements of a facility undergoing an economic study. This concept implies that since a past outlay is the same regardless of the alternative selected, it should not influence the choice between alternatives.

super bill of material–A type of planning bill, located at the top level in the structure, that ties together various modular bills (and possibly a common parts bill) to define an entire product or product family. The quantity-per relationship of the super bill to its modules represents the forecasted percentage of demand of each module. The master-scheduled quantities of the super bill explode to create requirements for the modules that also are master scheduled. See: pseudo bill of material.

superflush–A technique to relieve all components down to the lowest level using the complete bill of material, based on the count of finished units produced or transferred to finished goods inventory.

supplier–1) Provider of goods or services. Syn: vendor. 2) Seller with whom the buyer does business, as opposed to vendor, which is a generic term referring to all sellers in the marketplace.

supplier alternate–A seller other than the primary one. The supplier alternate may or may not supply the items purchased, but is usually approved to supply those items.

supplier clustering–Deliberately sole sourcing remote suppliers within a small geographical area to facilitate joint shipments of what would otherwise be less-than-truckload quantities.

supplier lead time–The amount of time that normally elapses between the time an order is received by a supplier and the time the order is shipped. Syn: vendor lead time. See: purchasing lead time.

supplier measurement–The act of measuring the supplier's performance to the contract. Measurements usually cover delivery, quality, and price.

supplier number–A numerical code used to distinguish one supplier from another.

supplier partner–A supplier organization with which a company has formed a customer-supplier partnership. See: outpartnering.

supplier partnership–The establishment of a working relationship with a supplier organization whereby two organizations act as one.

supplier quality assurance–Confidence that a supplier's product or service will fulfill its customers' needs. This confidence is achieved by creating a relationship between the customer and supplier that ensures that the product will be fit for use with minimal corrective action and inspection. According to J.M. Juran, nine primary activities are needed: (1) define product and program quality requirements, (2) evaluate alternative suppliers, (3) select suppliers, (4) conduct joint quality planning, (5) cooperate with the supplier during the execution of the contract, (6) obtain proof of conformance to requirements, (7) certify qualified suppliers, (8) conduct quality improvement programs as required, and (9) create and use supplier quality ratings.

supplier scheduler–A person whose main job is working with suppliers regarding what is needed and when. Supplier schedulers are in direct contact with both MRP and the suppliers. They do the material planning for the items under their control, communicate the resultant schedules to their assigned suppliers, do follow-up, resolve problems, and advise other planners and the master scheduler when purchased items will not arrive on time to support the schedule. The supplier schedulers are normally organized by commodity, as are the buyers. By using the supplier scheduler approach, the buyers are freed from day-to-day order placement and expediting, and therefore have the time to do cost reduction, negotiation, supplier selection, alternate sourcing, etc. Syn: planner/buyer, vendor scheduler.

supplier scheduling–A purchasing approach that provides suppliers with schedules rather than with individual hard-copy purchase orders. Normally, a supplier scheduling system will include a business agreement (contract) for each supplier, a weekly (or more frequent) schedule for each supplier extending for some time into the future, and individuals called supplier schedulers. Also required is a formal priority planning system that works well, because it is essential in this arrangement to provide the supplier with valid due dates. Syn: vendor scheduling.

supplies–Materials used in manufacturing that are not normally charged to finished production, such as cutting and lubricating oils, machine repair parts, glue, or tape. Syn: general stores, indirect materials.

supply–1) The quantity of goods available for use. 2) The actual or planned replenishment of a product or component. The replenishment quantities are created in response to a demand for the product or component or in anticipation of such a demand.

supply chain–1) The processes from the initial raw materials to the ultimate consumption of the finished product linking across supplier-user companies. 2) The functions within and outside a company that enable the value chain to make products and provide services to the customer.

surge tank–A container to hold output from one process and feed it to a subsequent process. It is used when line balancing is not possible or practical or only on a contingency basis when downstream equipment is nonoperational.

SWOT–Acronym for *strengths, weaknesses, opportunities, and threats.*

SWOT analysis–An analysis of the strengths, weaknesses, opportunities, and threats of and to an organization. SWOT analysis is useful in developing strategy.

synchronized production–A manufacturing management philosophy that includes a consistent set of principles, procedures, and techniques where every action is evaluated in terms of the global goal of the system. Both kanban, which is a part of the JIT philosophy, and drum-buffer-rope, which is a part of the theory-of-constraints philosophy, represent synchronized production control approaches. See: drum-buffer-rope, kanban.

synthetic time standard–Syn: predetermined motion time.

system–A regularly interacting or interdependent group of items forming a unified whole toward the achievement of a goal.

systems analysis–The analyzing in detail of the information needed for an organization, the characteristics and components of the current information system, and the requirements of any proposed changes to the information system.

systems network–A group of interconnected nodes. This implies redundancy in connections and some means (e.g., machines) for implementing the connection.

T

tact time–The time required between completion of successive units of end product. Tact time is used to pace lines in the production environments.

Taguchi methodology–A concept of off-line quality control methods conducted at the product and process design stages in the product development cycle. This concept, expressed by Genichi Taguchi, encompasses three phases of product design: system design, parameter design, and tolerance design. The goal is to reduce quality loss by reducing the variability of the product's characteristics during the parameter phase of product development.

tampering–Action taken to compensate for variation within the control limits of a stable system. Tampering increases rather than decreases variation, as evidenced in the funnel experiment. See: funnel experiment.

tangibles–Things that can be quantitatively measured or valued, such as items of cost and physical assets.

tank inventory–Goods stored in tanks. These goods may be raw materials, intermediates, or finished goods. The description of inventory as tank inventory indicates the necessity of calculating the quantity on hand from the levels within the tanks.

tardiness–For jobs that are late, the delivery date minus the due date. See: earliness, lateness.

tare weight–The weight of a substance, obtained by deducting the weight of the empty container from the gross weight of the full container.

target costing–Designing a product to meet a specific objective. Target costing involves setting the planned selling price, subtracting the desired profit as well as marketing and distribution costs, leaving the required manufacturing or target cost.

target inventory level–In a min-max inventory system, the equivalent of the maximum. The target inventory is equal to the order point plus a variable order quantity. It is often called an *order-up-to* inventory level and is used in a periodic review system. Syn: order-up-to level.

target market–1) A fairly homogeneous group of customers to whom a company wishes to appeal. 2) A definable group of buyers to which a marketer has decided to market.

TBC–Abbreviation for *time-based competition*.

team design/engineering–Syn: participative design/engineering.

teardown–All work items required between the end of one operation or job and the start of setup for the next operation or job, both jobs requiring the same machinery or facilities. See: teardown time.

teardown time–The time needed to remove a setup from a machine or facility. Teardown is an element of manufacturing lead time, but it is often allowed for in setup or run time rather than separately. See: teardown.

technical/office protocol (TOP)–An application-specific protocol based on open systems interconnection (OSI) standards. It is designed to allow communication between computers from different suppliers in the office and technical development environment.

TEI–Abbreviation for *total employee involvement*.

telescoping–Syn: overlapped schedule.

terms and conditions–All the provisions and agreements of a contract.

theoretical capacity–The maximum output capability, allowing no adjustments for preventive maintenance, unplanned downtime, shutdown, etc.

theory of constraints (TOC)–A management philosophy developed by Dr. Eliyahu M. Goldratt that can be viewed as three separate but interrelated areas—logistics, performance measurement, and logical thinking. Logistics include drum-buffer-rope scheduling, buffer management, and VAT analysis. Performance measurement includes throughput, inventory and operating expense, and the five focusing steps. Thinking process tools are important in identifying the root problem (current reality tree), identifying and expanding win-win solutions (evaporating cloud and future reality tree), and developing implementation plans (prerequisite tree and transition tree). Syn: constraint theory. See: constraint management.

third-order smoothing–Syn: triple smoothing.

third-party logistics company–A company that manages all or part of another company's product delivery operations.

Thomas Register–A privately produced reference set that includes a listing of part suppliers by product type and geographic area.

throughput–1) The total volume of production through a facility (machine, work center, department, plant, or network of plants). 2) In theory of constraints, the rate at which the system (firm) generates money through sales.

throughput time–Syn: cycle time.

time and attendance–A collection of data relating to an employee's record of absences and hours worked.

time-based competition (TBC)–A corporate strategy that emphasizes time as the vehicle for achieving and maintaining a sustainable competitive edge. Its characteristics are (1) it deals only with those lead times that are important to the customers; (2) lead time reductions must involve decreases in both the mean and the variance; and (3) the lead time reductions must be achieved through system/process analysis (the processes must be changed to reduce lead times). TBC is a broad-based strategy. Reductions in lead times are achieved by changing the processes and the decision structures used to design, produce, and deliver products to the customers. TBC involves design, manufacturing, and logistical processes.

time bucket–A number of days of data summarized into a columnar display. A weekly time bucket would contain all of the relevant data for an entire week. Weekly time buckets are considered to be the largest possible (at least in the near and medium term) to permit effective MRP.

time buffer–The amount of time materials are released to the production process ahead of the scheduled due date. Time buffers protect against uncertainty.

time card–A document recording attendance time, often used for indicating the number of hours for which wages are to be paid. Syn: clock card.

time fence–A policy or guideline established to note where various restrictions or changes in operating procedures take place. For example, changes to the master production schedule can be accomplished easily beyond the cumulative lead time, while changes inside the cumulative lead time become increasingly more difficult to a point where changes should be resisted. Time fences can be used to define these points. See: demand time fence, hedge, planning time fence.

time-phased order point (TPOP)–MRP-like time planning logic for independent demand items, where gross requirements come from a forecast, not via explosion. This technique can be used to plan distribution center inventories as well as to plan for service (repair) parts, since MRP logic can readily handle items with dependent demand, independent demand, or a combination of both. Time-phased order point is an approach that uses time periods, thus allowing for lumpy withdrawals instead of average demand. See: fixed reorder quantity inventory model.

time phasing–The technique of expressing future demand, supply, and inventories by time period. Time phasing is one of the key elements of material requirements planning.

time series–A set of data that is distributed over time, such as demand data in monthly time period occurrences.

time series analysis–Analysis of any variable classified by time in which the values of the variable are functions of the time periods.

time series planning–An obsolete term for material requirements planning.

time stamping–Tracking with each transaction the time of occurrence. It is used in period closings and to tie end items to samples for certification of item properties.

time standard–The predetermined times allowed for the performance of a specific job. The standard will often consist of two parts, that for machine setup and that for actual running. The standard can be developed through observation of the actual work (time study), summation of standard micro-motion times (predetermined or synthetic time standards), or approximation (historical job times).

time ticket–An operator-entered labor claim, frequently in the form of a handwritten report or a punched card. Syn: job ticket, labor chit.

time-to-market–The total time required to design, build, and deliver a product (timed from concept to delivery).

time-to-product–The total time required to receive, fill, and deliver an order for an existing product to a customer, timed from the moment that the customer places the order until the customer receives the product.

time value of money–1) The cumulative effect of elapsed time on the money value of an event, based on the earning power of equivalent invested funds. See: future worth, present value. 2) The interest rate that capital is expected to earn.

TOC–Abbreviation for *theory of constraints*.

TOC performance measures–In the theory of constraints, throughput, inventory, and operating expense are considered performance measures that link operational decisions to organizational profit.

TOFC–Abbreviation for *trailer on flatcar*.

tolerance–Allowable departure from a nominal value established by design engineers that is deemed acceptable for the functioning of the product or service over its life cycle.

tolerance limits–1) The upper and lower extreme values permitted by the tolerance. 2) In work measurement, the limits between which a specified operation time value or other work unit will be expected to vary.

tool calibration frequency–The recommended length of time between tool calibrations. It is normally expressed in days.

tool issue order–Syn: tool order.

tool number–The identification number assigned to reference and control a specific tool.

tool order–A document authorizing issue of specific tools from the tool crib or other storage. Syn: tool issue order.

TOP–Abbreviation for *technical/office protocol*.

top management commitment (quality)–Participation of the highest-level official in the organization's quality improvement efforts. Participation includes establishing and serving on a quality committee, establishing quality policies and goals, deploying those goals to lower levels of the organization, providing the resources and training that the lower levels need to achieve the goals, participating in quality improvement teams, reviewing organizationwide progress, recognizing those who have performed well, and revising the current reward system to reflect the importance of achieving the quality goals.

total cost concept–The idea that all logistical decisions that provide equal service levels should favor the option that minimizes the total of all logistical costs and not be used on cost reductions in one area alone, such as lower transportation charges.

total employee involvement (TEI)–An empowerment program where employees are invited to participate in actions and decision making that were traditionally reserved for management.

total factor productivity–A measure of the productivity of a department, plant, strategic business unit, firm, etc., that combines the individual productivities of all its resources including labor, capital, energy, material, and equipment. These individual factor productivities are often combined by weighting each according to its monetary value and then adding them. For example, if material accounts for 40% of the total cost of sales and labor 10% of the cost of sales, etc., total factor productivity = .4 (material productivity) + .1 (labor productivity) + etc.

total lead time–Syn: lead time.

total procurement lead time–Syn: procurement lead time.

total productive maintenance (TPM)–Preventive maintenance plus continuing efforts to adapt, modify, and refine equipment to increase flexibility, reduce material handling, and promote continuous flows. It is operator-oriented maintenance with the involvement of all qualified employees in all maintenance activities.

total quality control (TQC)–The process of creating and producing the total composite product and service characteristics by marketing, engineering, manufacturing, purchasing, etc., through which the product and service will meet the expectations of customers.

total quality engineering (TQE)–The discipline of designing quality into the product and manufacturing processes by understanding the needs of the customer and performance capabilities of the equipment. See: design for quality.

total quality management (TQM)–A term coined to describe Japanese-style management approaches to quality improvement. Since then, total quality management (TQM) has taken on many meanings. Simply put, TQM is a management approach to long-term success through customer satisfaction. TQM is based on the participation of all members of an organization in improving processes, products, services, and the culture they work in. The methods for implementing this approach are found in teachings of such quality leaders as Philip B. Crosby, W. Edwards Deming, Armand V. Feigenbaum, Kaoru Ishikawa, and J.M. Juran.

total value analysis–A method of economic analysis in which a model expresses the dependent variable of interest as a function of independent variables, some of which are controllable.

touch labor–Syn: direct labor.

TPM–Abbreviation for *total productive maintenance.*

TPOP–Acronym for *time-phased order point.*

TQC–Abbreviation for *total quality control.*

TQE–Abbreviation for *total quality engineering.*

TQM–Abbreviation for *total quality management.*

traceability–1) Attribute allowing the ongoing location of a shipment to be determined. 2) The registering and tracking of parts, processes, and materials used in production, by lot or serial number.

tracer–A request to a transportation line to trace a shipment to expedite its movement or to verify delivery.

tracking signal–The ratio of the cumulative algebraic sum of the deviations between the forecasts and the actual values to the mean absolute deviation. Used to signal when the validity of the forecasting model might be in doubt.

traffic–A department or function charged with responsibility for arranging the most economic classification and method of shipment for both incoming and outgoing materials and products.

trailer on flatcar (TOFC)–Syn: piggyback trailer on flatcar.

training aid–An item to enhance training, usually minor in nature. Training aids may include charts, graphs, slides, and schematics.

transactions–Individual events reported to the computer system, e.g., issues, receipts, transfers, adjustments.

transfer batch–The quantity of an item moved between sequential work centers during production. See: batch.

transfer price–Price that one segment (subunit, department, division, etc.) of an organization charges for a product or service supplied to another segment of the same organization.

transfer pricing–The pricing of goods or services transferred from one segment of a business to another. See: interplant transfer.

transient bill of material–Syn: phantom bill of material.

transition tree–In the theory of constraints, a logic-based tool for identifying and sequencing actions in accomplishing an objective. The transitions represent the states or stages in moving from the present situation to the desired objective.

transit time–A standard allowance that is assumed on any given order for the movement of items from one operation to the next. Syn: travel time.

transportation inventory–Inventory that is in transit between locations. See: pipeline stock.

transportation method–A linear programming model concerned with minimizing the costs involved in supplying requirements at several locations from several sources with different costs related to the various combinations of source and requirement locations.

transport stocks–A carrier material to move solids in solution or slurry or to dilute ingredients to safe levels for reaction.

traveler–A copy of the manufacturing order that actually moves with the work through the shop. Syn: shop traveler.

traveling purchase requisition–A purchase requisition designed for repetitive use. After a purchase order has been prepared for the goods requisitioned, the form is returned to the originator, who holds it until a repurchase of the goods is required. The name is derived from the repetitive travel between the originating and purchasing departments. Syn: traveling requisition.

traveling requisition–Syn: traveling purchase requisition.

travel time–Syn: transit time.

tree diagram–1) A management technique used to analyze a situation in increasing detail. The full range of tasks to be accomplished to achieve a primary goal and supporting subgoal may be illustrated. 2) In theory of constraints, a diagram relating observed effects to underlying causes.

trend–General upward or downward movement of a variable over time, e.g., demand, process attribute.

trend control chart–A control chart in which the deviation of the subgroup average, X-bar, from an expected trend in the process level is used to evaluate the stability of a process.

trend forecasting models–Methods for forecasting sales data when a definite upward or downward pattern exists. Models include double exponential smoothing, regression, and triple smoothing.

trigger level–Syn: order point.

triple smoothing–A method of exponential smoothing that accounts for accelerating or decelerating trend, such as would be experienced in a fad cycle. Syn: third-order smoothing.

truckload lot–A truck shipment that qualifies for a lower freight rate because it meets a minimum weight and/or volume.

turnaround–Syn: setup.

turnaround costs–Syn: setup costs.

turnaround time–Syn: setup.

turnkey system–Computer packages that are already prepared by a hardware manufacturer or software house and are ready to run.

turnover–1) Syn: inventory turnover. 2) In the United Kingdom and certain other countries, annual sales volume.

two-bin system–A type of fixed-order system in which inventory is carried in two bins. A replenishment quantity is ordered when the first bin is empty. During the replenishment lead time, material is used from the second bin. When the material is received, the second bin (which contains a quantity to cover demand during lead time plus some safety stock) is refilled and the excess is put into the working bin. At this time, stock is drawn from the first bin until it is again exhausted. This term is also used loosely to describe any fixed-order system even when physical "bins" do not exist. Syn: bin reserve system. See: visual review system.

two-level master production schedule–A master scheduling approach where a planning bill of material is used to master schedule an end product or family, along with selected key features (options and accessories). See: hedge, multilevel master production schedule, production forecast.

type I error–An incorrect decision to reject something (such as a statistical hypothesis or a lot of products) when it is acceptable. See: producer's risk.

type II error–An incorrect decision to accept something when it is unacceptable. See: consumer's risk.

U

U chart–A control chart for evaluating the stability of a process in terms of the average count of events of a given classification per unit occurring in a sample. Syn: count-per-unit chart.

UCL–Abbreviation for *upper control limit.*

U-lines–Production lines shaped like the letter "U." The shape allows workers to easily perform several nonsequential tasks without much walk time. The number of workstations in a U-line is usually determined by line balancing. U-lines promote communication.

uncertainty–Unknown future events that cannot be predicted quantitatively within useful limits; e.g., an accident that destroys facilities, a major strike, or an innovation that makes existing products obsolete.

undertime–A condition occurring when there are more personnel on the payroll than are required to produce the planned output.

uniform-delivered pricing–A type of geographic pricing policy where all customers pay the same delivered price regardless of their location. A company allocates the total transportation cost among all customers.

uniform hazardous waste manifest–A U.S. government-required document, which is provided by the applicable state, authorizing the transport of hazardous waste material over public roads, rail, etc.

unit cost–Total labor, material, and overhead cost for one unit of production, e.g., one part, one gallon, one pound.

unit of issue–The standard issue quantity of an item from stores, e.g., pounds, each, box of 12, package of 20, or case of 144.

unit of measure–The unit in which the quantity of an item is managed, e.g., pounds, each, box of 12, package of 10, case of 144.

unit of measure (purchasing)–The unit used to purchase an item. This may or may not be the same unit of measure used in the internal systems. For example, purchasing buys steel by the ton, but it may be issued and used in square inches. Syn: purchasing unit of measure.

universe–The population, or large set of data, from which samples are drawn. Usually assumed to be infinitely large or at least very large relative to the sample.

unload–Syn: output.

unplanned issue–An issue transaction that updates the quantity on hand but for which no allocation exists.

unplanned receipt–A receipt transaction that updates the quantity on hand but for which no order exists.

upgrade–Improvement in operating characteristics.

upper control limit (UCL)–Control limit for points above the central line in a control chart.

upper specification limit (USL)–In statistical process control, the line that defines the maximum acceptable level of random output.

usage–The number of units or dollars of an inventory item consumed over a period of time.

usage variance–Deviation of the actual consumption of materials as compared to the standard.

use as is–Classification for material that has been dispositioned as unacceptable per the specifications, yet can be used.

user-friendly–Characteristic of computer software or hardware that makes it easy for the user or operator to use the programs or equipment with a minimum of specialized knowledge or recourse to operating manuals.

utilization–1) A measure of how intensively a resource is being used to produce a good or a service. Utilization compares actual time used to available time. Traditionally, utilization is the ratio of direct time charged (run time plus setup time) to the clock time scheduled for the resource. This measure led to distortions in some cases. 2) In the theory of constraints, utilization is the ratio of actual time the resource is producing (run time only) to the clock time the resource is scheduled to produce.

valuation–The technique of determining worth, typically of inventory. Valuation of inventories may be expressed in standard dollars, replacement dollars, current average dollars, or last-purchase-price dollars.

value added–1) In accounting, the addition of direct labor, direct material, and allocated overhead assigned at an operation. It is the cost roll-up as a part goes through a manufacturing process to finished inventory. 2) In current manufacturing terms, the actual increase of utility from the viewpoint of the customer as a part is transformed from raw material to finished inventory. It is the contribution made by an operation or a plant to the final usefulness and value of a product, as seen by the customer. The objective is to eliminate all non-value-added activities in producing and providing a good or service.

value analysis–The systematic use of techniques that identify a required function, establish a value for that function, and finally provide that function at the lowest overall cost. This approach focuses on the functions of an item rather than the methods of producing the present product design.

value chain–The functions within a company that add value to the products or services that the organization sells to customers and for which it receives payment.

value engineering and/or analysis–A disciplined approach to the elimination of waste from products or processes through an investigative process that focuses on the functions to be performed and whether such functions add value.

valve inventory–In a Just-in-Time context, inventory at a stockpoint that is too large to be located next to the point of use of the material, and from which material is drawn by a pull system. The valve inventory is often located at a stockpoint in the plant's receiving area.

variable–A quantity that can assume any of a given set of values. Ant: constant.

variable cost–An operating cost that varies directly with a change of one unit in the production volume, e.g., direct materials consumed, sales commissions.

variable costing–An inventory valuation method in which only variable production costs are applied to the product; fixed factory overhead is not assigned to the product. Traditionally, variable production costs are direct labor, direct material, and variable overhead costs. Variable costing can be helpful for internal management analysis but is not widely accepted for external financial reporting. For inventory order quantity purposes, however, the unit costs must include both the variable and allocated fixed costs to be compatible with the other terms in the order quantity formula. For

make/buy decisions, variable costing should be used rather than full absorption costing. Syn: direct costing.

variable overhead–All manufacturing costs, other than direct labor and direct materials, that vary directly with production volume. Variable overhead is necessary to produce the product, but cannot be directly assigned to a specific product.

variables data–Measurement information. Control charts based on variables data include average (X-bar) charts, range (R) charts, and sample standard deviations charts.

variable yield–The condition that occurs when the output of a process is not consistently repeatable either in quantity, quality, or combinations of these.

variance–1) The difference between the expected (budgeted or planned) value and the actual. 2) In statistics, a measure of dispersion of data.

variation–A change in data, a characteristic, or a function that is caused by one of four factors: special causes, common causes, tampering, or structural variation.

VAT analysis–A constraint management procedure for determining the general flow of parts and products from raw materials to finished products (logical product structure). A *V logical structure* starts with one or a few raw materials, and the product expands into a number of different products as it flows through its routings. The shape of an *A logical structure* is dominated by converging points. Many raw materials are fabricated and assembled into a few finished projects. A *T logical structure* consists of numerous similar finished products assembled from common assemblies and subassemblies. Once the general parts flow is determined, the system control points (gating operations, convergent points, divergent points, constraints, and shipping points) can be identified and managed.

VDT–Abbreviation for *video display terminal.*

VDU–Abbreviation for *video display unit.*

vendor–All sellers of an item in the marketplace. Syn: supplier.

vendor lead time–Syn: supplier lead time.

vendor measurement–The act of measuring the vendor's performance to a contract. Measurements usually cover delivery, lead time, quality, and price.

vendor scheduler–Syn: supplier scheduler.

vendor scheduling– Syn: supplier scheduling.

vertical display–A method of displaying or printing output from an MRP system where requirements, scheduled receipts, projected balance, etc., are displayed vertically. Vertical displays are often used in conjunction with bucketless systems. Ant: horizontal display.

vertical integration–The degree to which a firm has decided to directly produce multiple value-adding stages from raw material to the sale of the product to

APICS Dictionary, Eighth Edition

89

the ultimate consumer. The more steps in the sequence, the greater the vertical integration. A manufacturer that decides to begin producing parts, components, and materials that it normally purchases is said to be backward integrated. Likewise, a manufacturer that decides to take over distribution and perhaps sale to the ultimate consumer is said to be forward integrated.

vertical marketing system–A marketing system that focuses on the means to reduce the traditional independence of indirect channels. The system strategically seeks to increase the integration and interdependence of channels by uniting them with common objectives and team management, e.g., franchising, cooperatives, and vertical integration.

vestibule training–A variant of job rotation in which a separate work area is set up for a trainee so that the actual work situation does not pressure the trainee. Examples are cockpit simulators and other machine simulators.

video display terminal (VDT)–Syn: cathode ray tube.

video display unit (VDU)–Syn: cathode ray tube.

virtual corporation–The logical extension of outpartnering. With the virtual corporation, the capabilities and systems of the firm are merged with those of the suppliers, resulting in a new type of corporation where the boundaries between the suppliers' systems and those of the firm seem to disappear. The virtual corporation is dynamic in that the relationships and structures formed change according to the new needs of the customer.

virtual factory–A changed transformation process most frequently found under the virtual corporation. It is a transformation process that involves merging the capabilities and capacities of the firm with those of its suppliers. Typically, the components provided by the supplier are those that are not related to a core competency of the firm, while the components managed by the firm are related to core competencies. One ability found in the virtual factory is that it can be restructured quickly in response to changing customer demands and needs.

visual control–The control of authorized levels of inventory in a way that is instantly and visibly obvious. This type of inventory control is used in a workplace organization where everything has a place and is in its place.

visual inspection–Inspection performed without test instruments.

visual review system–A simple inventory control system where the inventory reordering is based on actually looking at the amount of inventory on hand. Usually used for low-value items, such as nuts and bolts. See: two-bin system.

vital few, useful many–A term used by J.M. Juran to describe his use of the Pareto principle, which he first described in 1950. (The principle was used much earlier in economics and inventory control methodologies.) The principle suggests that most effects come from relatively few causes; that is, 80% of the effects come from 20% of the possible causes. The 20% of the possible causes are referred to as the "vital few"; the remaining causes are referred to as the "useful many." When Juran first defined this principle, he referred to the remaining causes as the "trivial many," but since no problems are trivial in quality assurance, he changed it to "useful many."

VOC–Abbreviation for *voice of the customer*.

voice of the customer (VOC)–Actual customer descriptions in words for the functions and features customers desire for products and services. In the strict definition, as relates to quality function deployment (QFD), the term *customer* indicates the external customer of the supplying entity.

volume flexibility–The ability of the transformation process to quickly accommodate large variations in production levels.

voucher–A written document that bears witness to, or "vouches" for, something. A voucher generally is an instrument showing services performed or goods purchased and authorizing payment to the supplier.

W

Wagner-Whitin algorithm–A mathematically complex, dynamic lot-sizing technique that evaluates all possible ways of ordering to cover net requirements in each period of the planning horizon to arrive at the theoretically optimum ordering strategy for the entire net requirements schedule. See: discrete order quantity, dynamic lot sizing.

waiting line theory–Syn: queuing theory.

wait time–1) Syn: idle time. 2) The time a job remains at a work center after an operation is completed until it is moved to the next operation. It is often expressed as a part of move time.

waiver–Authorization to accept an item that, during production or after inspection, is found to depart from specified requirements, but nevertheless is considered suitable for use as is or after rework.

walkthrough–Syn: pilot test.

wall-to-wall inventory–An inventory management technique in which material enters a plant and is processed through the plant into finished product without ever having entered a formal stock area. Syn: four-wall inventory.

WAN–Acronym for *wide area network*.

wand–A device connected to a bar-code reader to identify a bar code.

warehouse demand–The need for an item to replenish stock at a branch warehouse. Syn: branch warehouse demand.

warranty–A commitment, either expressed or implied, that a certain fact regarding the subject matter of a contract is presently true or will be true. The word should be distinguished from guarantee, which means a contract or promise by an entity to answer for the performance of a product or person. See: guarantee.

waste–1) In Just-in-Time, any activity that does not add value to the product or service in the eyes of the consumer. 2) Hazardous waste, the disposal of which is controlled. 3) A by-product of a process or task with unique characteristics requiring special management control. Waste production can usually be planned and somewhat controlled. Scrap is typically not planned and may result from the same production run as waste.

wave picking–A method of selecting and sequencing picking lists to minimize the waiting time of the delivered material. Shipping orders may be picked in waves combined by common carrier or destination, and manufacturing orders in waves related to work centers.

waybill–A document containing a list of goods with shipping instructions related to a shipment.

weighted moving average–An averaging technique in which the data to be averaged are not uniformly weighted but are given values according to their importance.

weighted-point plan–A supplier selection and rating approach that uses the input gathered in the categorical plan approach and assigns weights to each evaluation category. A weighted sum for each supplier is obtained and a comparison made. The weights used should sum to 100% for all categories.

what-if analysis–The process of evaluating alternate strategies by answering the consequences of changes to forecasts, manufacturing plans, inventory levels, etc. See: simulation.

where-used list–A listing of every parent item that calls for a given component, and the respective quantity required, from a bill-of-material file. See: implosion.

wide area network (WAN)–A public or private data communication system for linking computers distributed over a large geographic area.

WIP–Acronym for *work in process*.

withdrawal–1) Removal of material from stores. 2) A transaction issuing material to a specific location, run, or schedule.

work cell–Dissimilar machines grouped together into a production unit to produce a family of parts having similar routings.

work center–A specific production area, consisting of one or more people and/or machines with identical capabilities, that can be considered as one unit for purposes of capacity requirements planning and detailed scheduling. Syn: load center.

work center schedule–Syn: dispatch list.

work center where-used–A listing (constructed from a routing file) of every manufactured item that is routed (primary or secondary) to a given work center.

worker efficiency–A measure (usually computed as a percentage) of worker performance that compares the standard time allowed to complete a task to the actual worker time to complete it. Syn: labor efficiency.

workers' compensation–The replacement of an employee's loss of earnings capacity caused by an occupational injury or disease. Formerly known as workmen's compensation.

work in process (WIP)–A product or products in various stages of completion throughout the plant, including all material from raw material that has been released for initial processing up to completely processed material awaiting final inspection and acceptance as finished product. Many accounting systems also include the value of semifinished stock and components in this category. Syn: in-process inventory.

work order–1) An order to the machine shop for tool manufacture or equipment maintenance; not to be confused with a manufacturing order. Syn: work ticket. 2) An authorization to start work on an activity (e.g., maintenance) or product. See: manufacturing order.

workplace organization–The arrangement of tools, equipment, materials, and supplies according to their frequency of use. Those items that are never used are removed from the workplace, and those items that are used frequently are located for fast, easy access and replacement. This concept extends the idea of "a place for everything and everything in its place."

work rules–1) Compensation rules concerning such issues as overtime, vacation, and shift premiums. 2) Employee and employer job rights and obligation rules, such as performance standards, promotion procedures, job descriptions, and layoff rules. Work rules are usually a part of a union contract and may include a code of conduct for workers and language to ensure decent conditions and health standards.

work sampling–The use of a number of random samples to determine the frequency with which certain activities are performed.

workstation–The assigned location where a worker performs the job; it could be a machine or a workbench.

work ticket–Syn: work order.

world-class quality–A term used to indicate a standard of excellence: the best of the best.

X-bar chart–Syn: average chart.

yield–The ratio of usable output from a process to its input.

zero-based budgeting–A budget procedure used primarily by governmental agencies, in which managers are required to justify each budgetary expenditure anew, as if the budget were being initiated for the first time rather than being based on an adjustment of prior-year data.

zero defects–A performance standard developed by Philip B. Crosby to address a dual attitude in the workplace: people are willing to accept imperfection in some areas; while in other areas, they expect the number of defects to be zero. This dual attitude has developed as a result of the conditioning that people are human and humans make mistakes. However, the zero-defects methodology states that if people commit themselves to watching details and avoiding errors, they can move closer to the goal of zero defects. The performance standard that must be set is "zero defects," not "close enough."

zero inventories–Syn: Just-in-Time.

zone picking–A method of subdividing a picking list by areas within a storeroom for more efficient and rapid order picking. A zone-picked order must be grouped to a single location before delivery or be delivered to different locations, such as work centers.

About APICS

APICS, the educational society for resource management, is a 70,000-member, international not-for-profit organization. For its programs and materials on the latest business management concepts and techniques, APICS is recognized as the leading organization of education for manufacturing and service industry professionals. More than 25,000 professionals actively participate in APICS educational and certification programs annually.

In addition to an international conference and exhibition, APICS offers symposia, workshops, publications, courseware, and two comprehensive certification programs: Certified in Production and Inventory Management (CPIM) and Certified in Integrated Resource Management (CIRM). All APICS programs and products are designed to help manufacturing professionals expand their knowledge and skills to meet the changing needs of the global marketplace.

The APICS Educational and Research Foundation

The APICS Educational and Research (E&R) Foundation is a 501 (c) (3) nonprofit organization eligible to receive tax-deductible contributions from individual and corporate donors. Through these partnerships between the Foundation and individual and chapter or corporate funders, the Foundation bridges the gap between what is needed and what is known, applying resources to advance learning opportunities for integrated resource managers.

The E&R Foundation invests in educational opportunities by making grants to faculty for applied research to benefit the production and operations manager. Recently, grants have been awarded for studies on harmonizing relations between manufacturing and marketing, supply chain management and performance measurements, and "Goal-Based Workflows for Productivity and Inventory Management." The Foundation has made available Spanish translations of a number of training aids and the *Principles of Materials Management* course. The E&R Foundation manages the Donald W. Fogarty International Student Paper Competition, making awards to regional and society-level winners at both the graduate and undergraduate levels.

The Foundation endowment welcomes support for its George and Marion Plossl Research Fellowship Fund, which supports a Ph.D. candidate in the production and operations management field on an annual basis.

The APICS E&R Foundation also sponsors a number of academic workshops to assist both the professor and the practitioner in mutual learning opportunites to develop faculty and curriculum and to improve the workforce of the future.

For information on grants, fellowships, and programs, please contact the Director of the E&R Foundation at (703) 237-8344 or (800) 444-2742, ext. 202.

© *APICS 1995*

The APICS Educational and Research Foundation gratefully acknowledges the following sponsors:

APICS-Chicago

517 Zenith Drive, Suite A
Glenview, Illinois 60025

(800) 982-7427

APICS Greater Fort Worth Area Chapter

P.O. Box 40424
Fort Worth, TX 76140

(817) 877-4170

APICS Orange County Chapter 70

P.O. Box 15045
Santa Ana, CA 92705

(714) 863-7625

Eagle Enterprises

"Education and Consulting for Manufacturing Excellence"

Carol A. Ptak, CFPIM, CIRM
President

(206) 631-3260
Fax (206) 630-3694

The APICS Educational and Research Foundation gratefully acknowledges the following sponsors:

Middle Tennessee Chapter

Nashville - TN - Shelbyville

Bowling Green - KY - Hopkinsville

PROgressive TECHnologies of America Inc.

Patrick J. Delaney
Michael D. Sheahan

Professional Educators
& Implementers

(708) 415-1635
Fax (708) 993-2984

San Diego Century Chapter APICS

P.O. Box 23695
San Diego, CA 92193

(619) 449-1100, ext. 251
Internet: AKENNEDY@GI.COM

If your organization would like to help sponsor future printings of this dictionary,
contact the APICS E&R Foundation at (800) 444-2742, ext. 202,
or
(703) 237-8344, ext. 202.

Additional sponsors appear on the inside front cover and inside back cover.

Notes

Notes

Feedback Form

The compilation of the eighth edition of the *APICS Dictionary* was a difficult task that involved many activities. Terms were selected for review, references were obtained from the published literature, the internal dictionary committee developed the definitions, the APICS Curricula and Certification Council's subcommittees reviewed the definitions, and the dictionary editors then approved the final definitions. The editors remain responsible for any errors and omissions that have occurred. Great care has been taken in developing this edition of the dictionary, but the field of resource management is undergoing continuous change, and a dictionary can only take a snapshot of the current body of knowledge at any point in time. Therefore, the editors welcome any comments and suggestions on current definitions and recommendations for additions or deletions. Please use this form to make suggestions; send it to the address below.

Terms to be added or changed:

Recommended definitions:

References or sources (Please list two for each term.):
1.

2.

Delete the following terms:

Reasons:

Your name and address:

Send to
APICS Dictionary Editors
Department of Management
Terry College of Business
Brooks Hall, Room 419
University of Georgia
Athens, GA 30602
(706) 542-1294
(706) 542-3743 (Fax)

For further information on ordering additional copies of the *APICS Dictionary*, please contact APICS Customer Service at (800) 444-2742 or (703) 237-8344.